POSTCARD HISTORY SERIES

Bangor

IN VINTAGE POSTCARDS

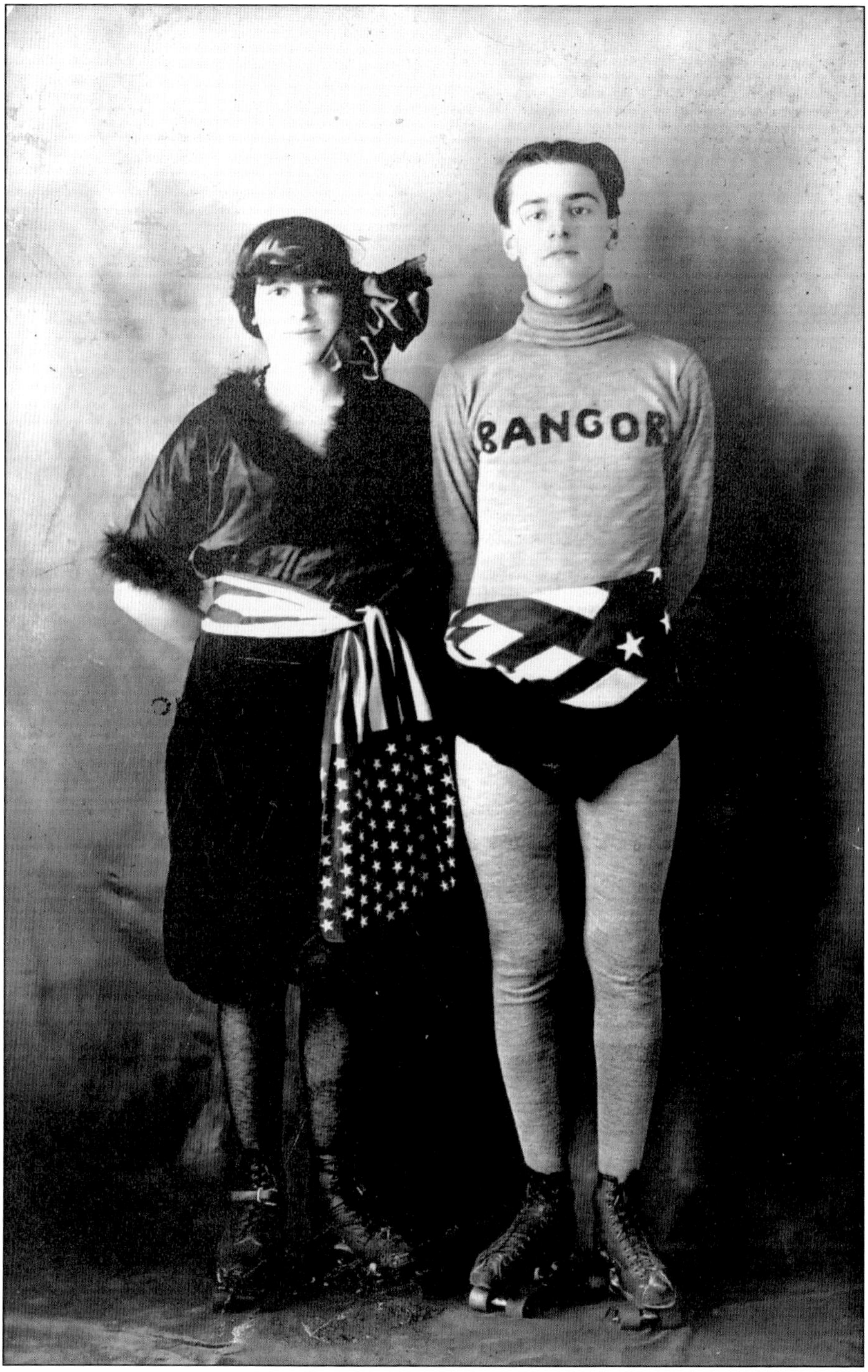

A young roller-skating couple made a dual statement in this postcard photograph; they hailed from Bangor, and they were posing during World War I, as their patriotic colors show. Roller-skating gained popularity in the 1880s at Norumbega Hall and later at the old auditorium building on Main Street and the Chateau Ballroom on Harlow Street. Strong skaters won competitions throughout Maine and New England.

POSTCARD HISTORY SERIES

Bangor IN VINTAGE POSTCARDS

Richard R. Shaw

ARCADIA PUBLISHING

ISBN 978-0-7385-3604-0

Published by Arcadia Publishing
Charleston, South Carolina

Printed in the United States of America

Library of Congress Catalog Card Number: 2004103408

For all general information, contact Arcadia Publishing:
Telephone 843-853-2070
Fax 843-853-0044
E-mail sales@arcadiapublishing.com
For customer service and orders:
Toll-Free 1-888-313-2665

Visit us on the Internet at www.arcadiapublishing.com

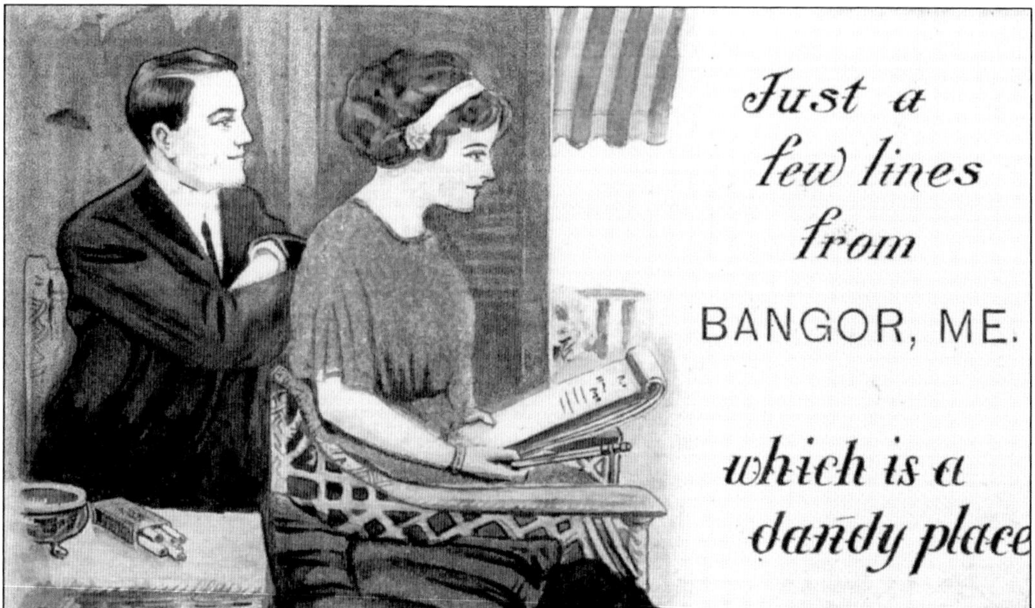

A 1912 novelty card showing formally dressed young people seems innocent by today's standards. Few lifelong residents would deny that Bangor is "a dandy place."

Contents

ACKNOWLEDGMENTS

This book represents six months of my life during which I pored over boxes of vintage postcards and logged countless hours at home writing the photograph captions on my personal computer. Occasionally, I sought help from trusted people in the community and beyond.

Thanks go to the following: Bill Cook, Sue Wennrich, and Barbara McDade of the Bangor Public Library, who made available the James B. Vickery collection numbering more than 100 Bangor postcards; Earle G. Shettleworth Jr., executive director of the Maine Historic Preservation Commission, who shared postcards and his extensive knowledge of Maine people and places; and Linda Jaffe, executive director of the Bangor Museum and Center for History, who along with Dana Lippitt and Jonathan Bagley of the museum staff, shared the museum's postcard collection. My cousin Mary Duran Cronkhite provided the postcard view of her father and my mother reproduced on page 8. Charles Campo and Jill Marston, *Bangor Daily News* colleagues, retrieved news photographs and information from library files. Phil Joyce of the newspaper's computer services department also assisted. Mildred N. Thayer loaned her father's photograph of the 1914 opera house fire ruins (seen on page 94). Betty Shibles let me reproduce her father's picture of the Pekin Restaurant (seen on page 87). Last, but not least, Paul E. Tower commented on the 1911 fire. His patience and generosity are appreciated.

Most of this book's more than 200 postcards and other pictures were chosen from my private collection, but additional images came from other sources. Unless otherwise indicated, the pictures are from my collection.

The following is a key to images not from my collection, noted in parentheses at the end of the captions: *Bangor Daily News* (BDN), Bangor Museum and Center for History (BMCH), Bangor Public Library (BPL), and Maine Historic Preservation Commission (MHPC).

Introduction

I will never forget the first vintage postcard I ever bought. It was at a Bangor-area flea market and showed the old Bangor City Hall, one of many landmarks from my hometown that are not with us anymore. The date was 1972, I was a 20-year-old college student, and my newfound hobby of deltiology was born. The card, by the way, cost the princely sum of 25¢.

Now, in middle age, I am still fascinated with the allure of old penny postcards. I am also still living in Bangor and continue to look backward at all the people and places that came before me. Not surprisingly, a good vintage postcard no longer costs 25¢. A real-photo postcard auctioned on eBay, for example, can run anywhere from $10 to $35 or more. My collection has grown over the years, and I continue to meet people like myself with a penchant for the past. I have found a home for many of my treasures in these Images of America series books.

The history you are holding in your hand is my sixth title for Arcadia Publishing. My first, titled simply *Bangor,* was published in 1994, followed by a second, *Bangor: The Twentieth Century,* and others on the Ellsworth-Blue region of Maine, the towns lining the Lower Penobscot River region, and Bangor's twin city across the Penobscot River, Brewer. Perhaps others will follow. Visual history is a fountain of delights that, like fine wine, can improve with age.

Some of the postcards in this history first appeared in my earlier Arcadia publications, but many more are published here for the first time in more than a half-century. In fact, many have not been seen widely since shoppers pulled them off store shelves, licked a 1¢ stamp, scribbled a brief message, and sent them on their way. So, with this book, I am making history in a small way.

A brief word about Bangor and the pictures in this book. Settled in 1769, Bangor blossomed in the 1800s as the lumbering capital of the world. By 1893, when picture postcards were first seen at the World's Columbian Exposition in Chicago, its boomtown days were over. But another life as eastern Maine's retail and manufacturing hub was just beginning. It continues now, into the 21st century, and it still prospers.

Most of this book's pictures are old postcard views, but a few, such as the ones showing congregations of Beth Israel and Beth Abraham synagogues (see pages 102 to 103), are photographs from the files of the *Bangor Daily News,* where I have been the editorial page assistant, occasional feature writer, and resident historian since 1976. No postcards were available of these places, so I used photographs instead. I trust that readers will understand my quandary.

The same goes for the restaurant advertisements and the other nonpostcard items. The view on page 31 of the old Baldacci family eatery, the Baltimore, was taken from an old city directory, as was the one from Tom Mourkas's Main Street restaurant, the New Atlantic (see page 83). Although not postcards, they add visual appeal.

I hope readers will agree that this book, although only a sampling of Bangor's 20th-century heritage, captures the spirit of the "queen city of the East," from the Penobscot River ferry boats and log drivers to the old theaters of Main and Exchange Streets to the fine residences along Broadway and West Broadway.

Bangor has changed a lot in the 100 years since the first picture postcards began appearing. Much was lost in the 1911 fire and to demolition. At the same time, the city has preserved many treasures that enrich our lives today.

Enjoy this book and take a moment to imagine a time when a postcard, and the postage, each cost 1¢. Those were the days.

—Richard R. Shaw
Bangor, Maine
June 2004

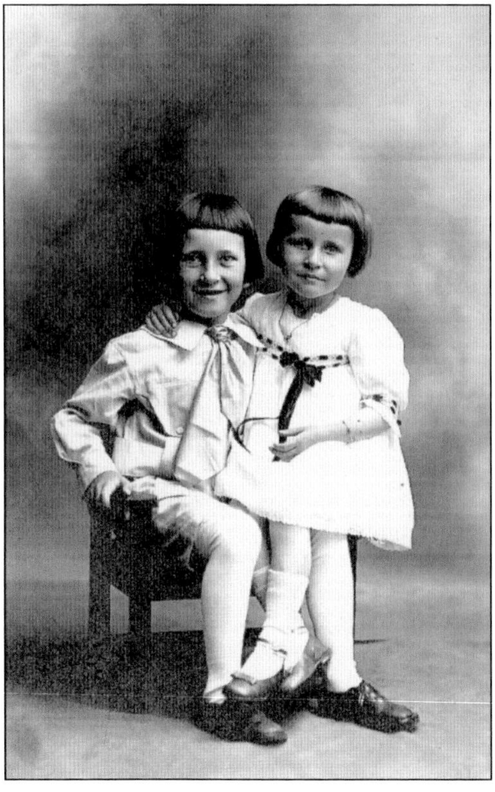

A postcard study in sibling affection pictures my mother, Frances Duran, sitting on the lap of her brother, Eugene Duran, *c.* 1920. Both were born in East Corinth, Maine, and grew up in Bangor, where they attended public schools. Uncle Gene later became East Corinth's postmaster, and Frances was a stay-at-home Bangor mom and wife raising three children. This book is dedicated to the Duran side of my family, who instilled in me a love of antiquity and the simple pleasures of life.

One

Queen City Landmarks

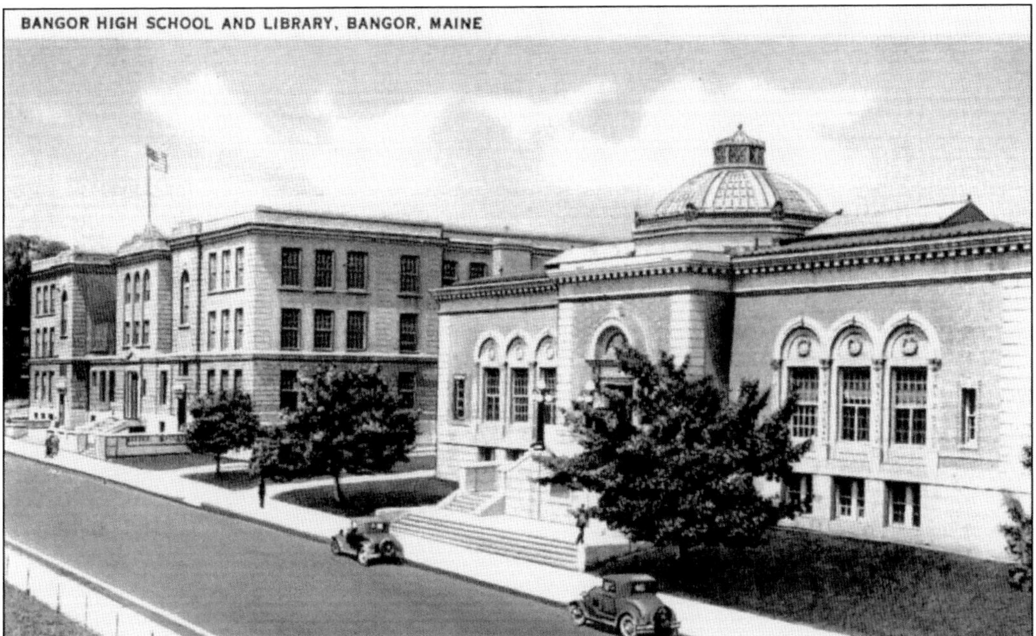

Two of Bangor's best-known landmarks have graced Harlow Street since 1913, when the symmetrically designed high school and library buildings were built on the ashes of the great 1911 fire. The high school (left) replaced the old school in Abbott Square that was claimed by the fire. The library replaced the former institution on State Street. Today, the high school is the Schoolhouse Apartments, and the library is still one of America's best. A gift from the Stephen and Tabitha King Foundation helped finance a wing onto the library's right side in 1998.

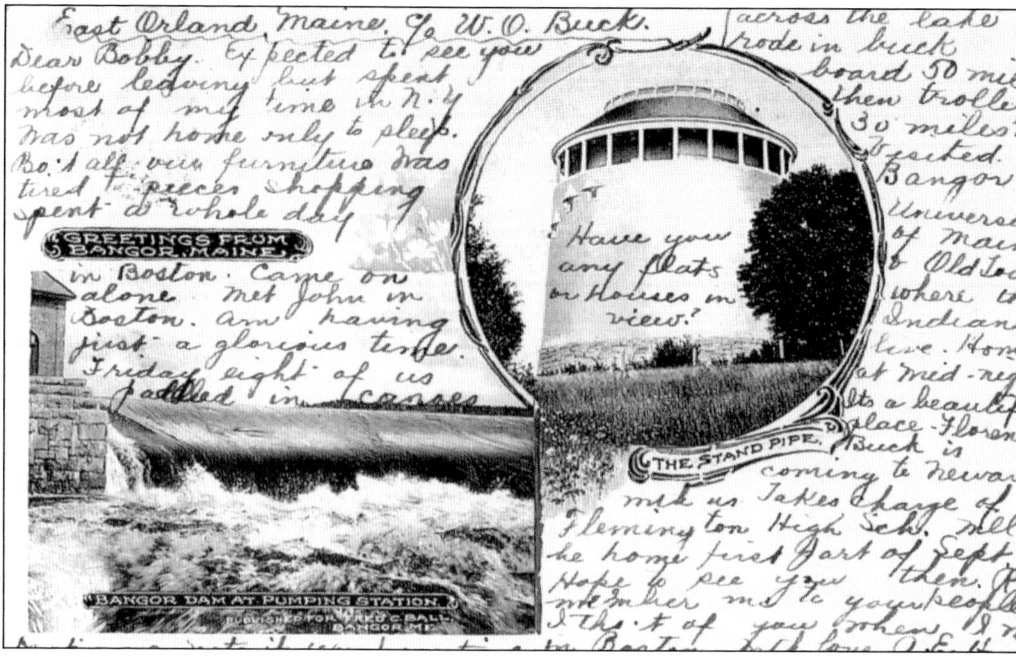

A prolific correspondent scribbled on nearly every inch of this 1905 postcard picturing the Bangor Dam and the water tower known as the Bangor standpipe. Postal regulations later permitted the use of the card's backside for chit-chat. The sender wrote of taking a 30-mile trolley trip to Bangor, Orono, and Old Town. The Penobscot River dam (see page 28) has been removed, but the standpipe still stands atop Thomas Hill.

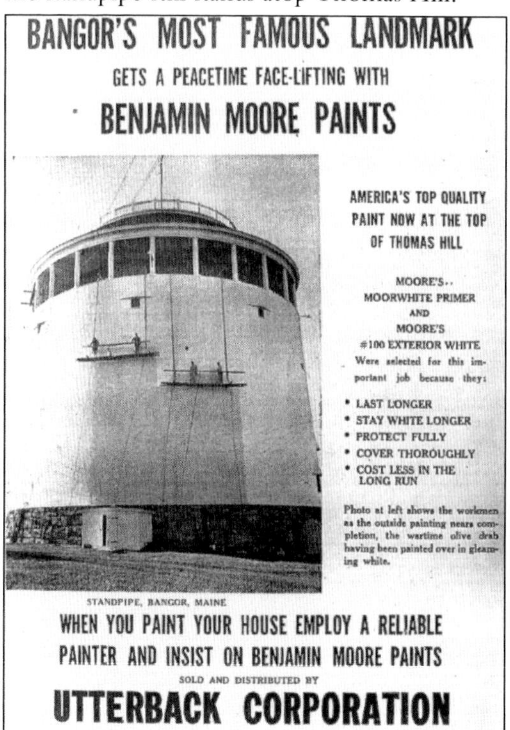

Benjamin Moore Paints capitalized on the city landmark for a clever advertisement appearing in the October 22, 1949, edition of the *Bangor Daily News*. One can only guess how many buckets of white paint were needed to cover the olive drab that camouflaged the water tower during World War II. The water reservoir was located near the military base, making it a potential enemy target. (BDN.)

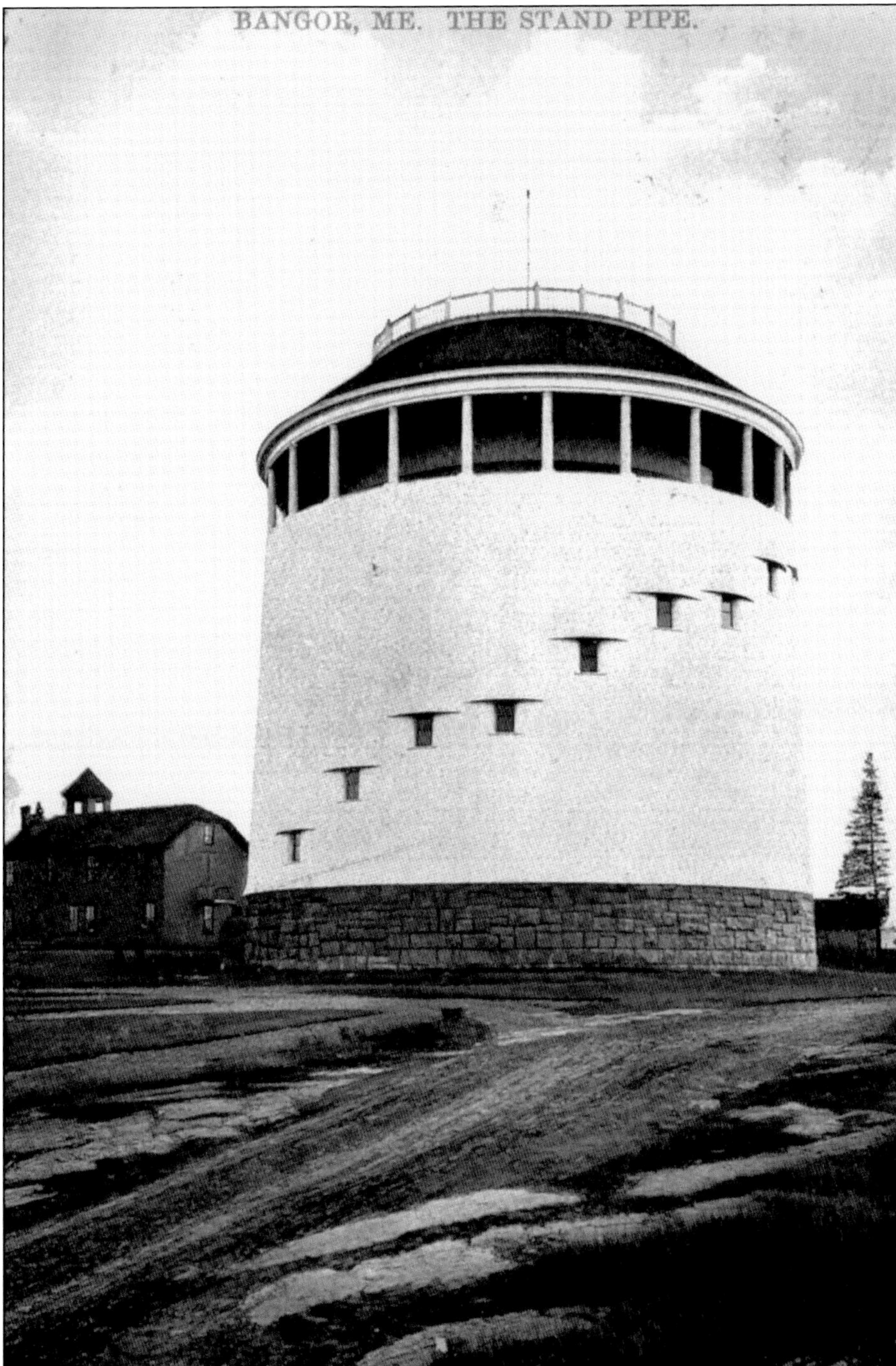

Since its completion in 1898, the Bangor standpipe has stood like a sentinel on Thomas Hill, a high point on the city's west side. The wooden tower encircles a steel tank containing 1.75 million gallons of potable water. Several times a year the Bangor Water District opens the landmark to visitors, who ascend its 100 steps to an observation deck from which Mount Katahdin and other peaks can be viewed.

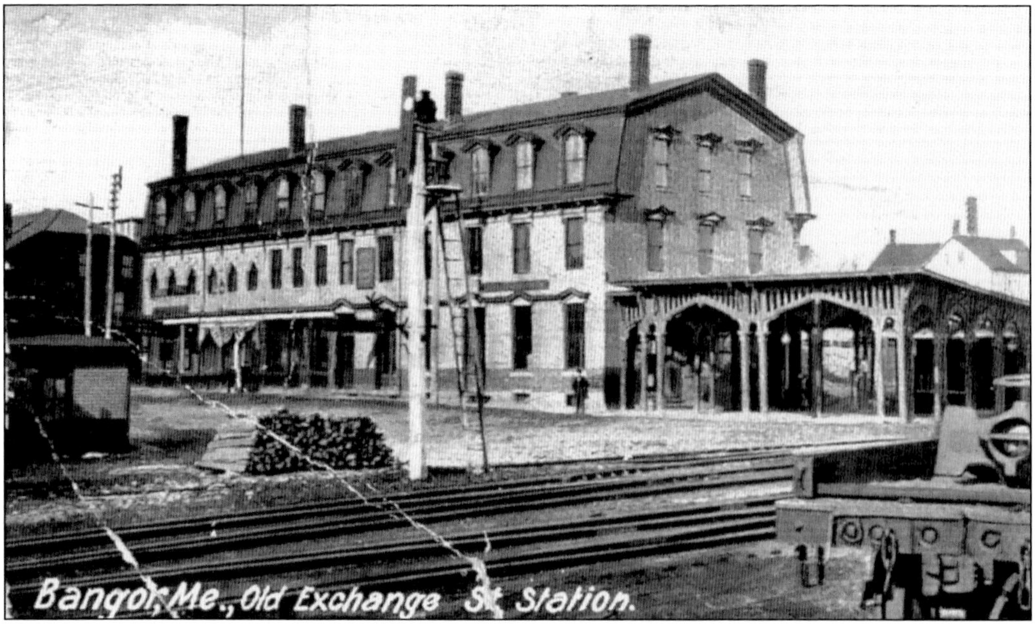

This three-story 19th-century railroad terminal stood on the site of the later Union Station on Washington Street. Renovated in 1874 by the European and North American Railroad, it was a landmark at the end of Exchange Street for more than 30 years before railroad and city planners razed it in favor of a larger, more substantial modern terminal.

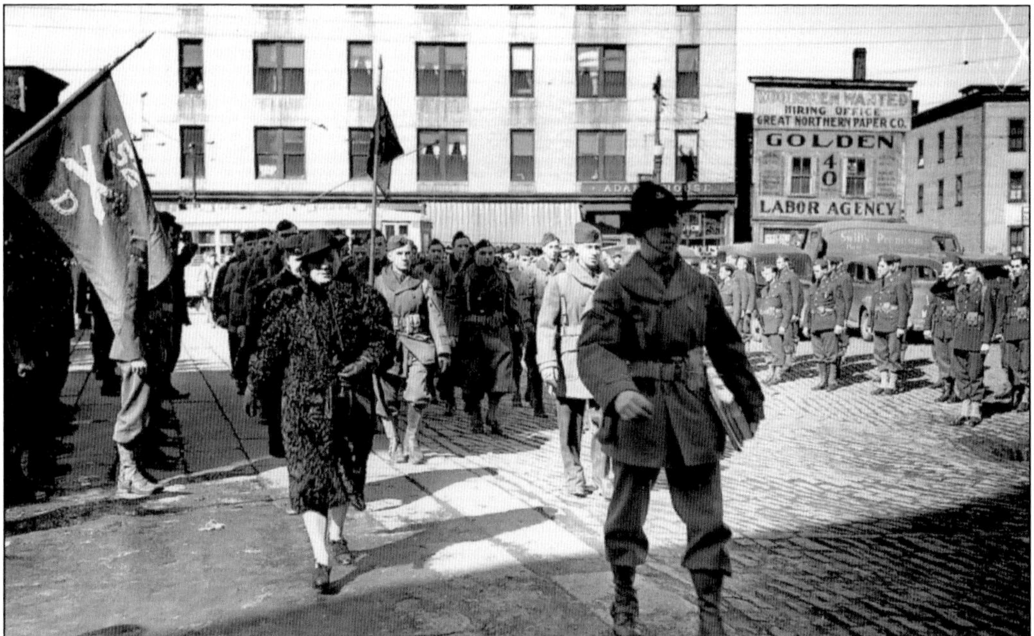

One cold morning in March 1941, several hundred National Guard enlistees marched from the armory on lower Main Street nearly two miles to Union Station. They bid farewell to family and friends before boarding trains bound for Camp Blanding, Florida, and other encampments. The 152nd guard unit is shown in this picture, taken by *Bangor Daily News* photographer Dan Maher. (BDN.)

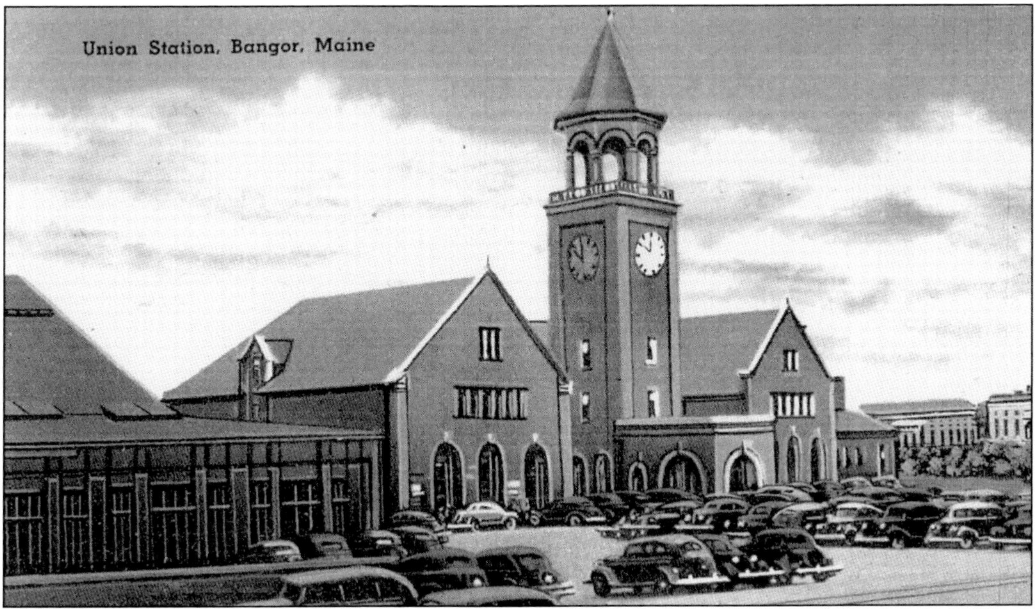

Bangor's most missed landmark may well be Union Station. Built in 1907 along the Penobscot River on Washington Street, the brick Maine Central Railroad passenger terminal was demolished in 1961, when rail travel was in decline and the land on which the building sat became more valuable than the station itself. Memories of wartime hellos and goodbyes were conjured up while saddened residents watched a wrecking ball knock down the station.

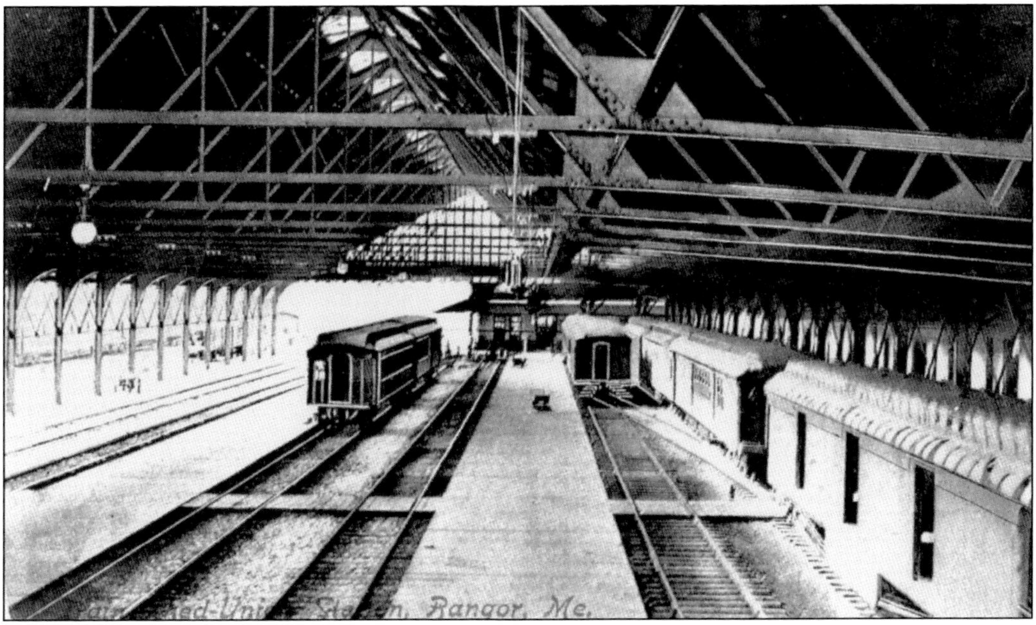

Generations of local people, in addition to the rich and famous, passed through Union Station's rail shed. Future president Franklin D. Roosevelt and his family came through Bangor each summer en route to their cottage in Campobello, New Brunswick. In 1912, trains returning to New York from Halifax, Nova Scotia, carried the remains of the *Titanic* disaster victims.

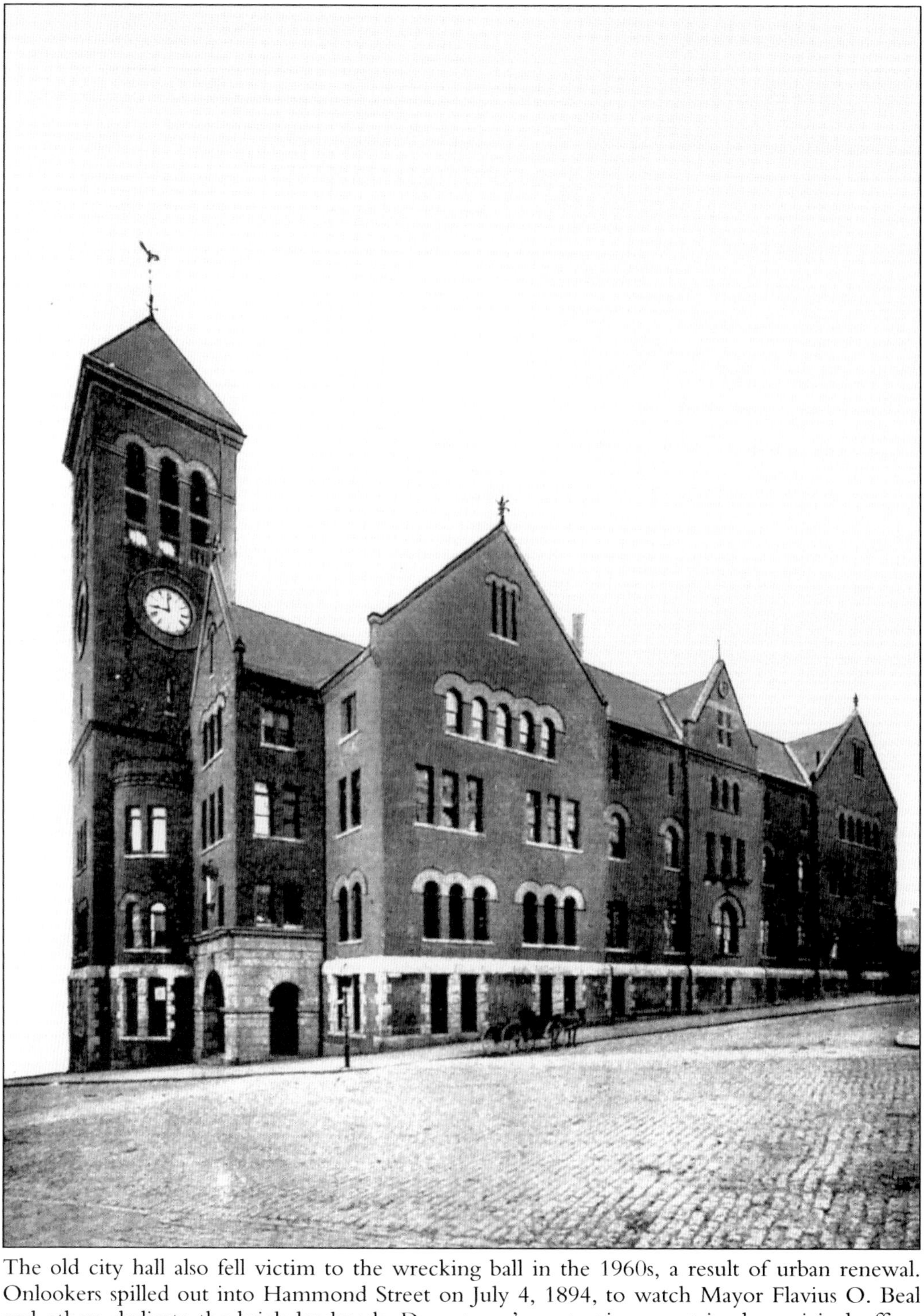

The old city hall also fell victim to the wrecking ball in the 1960s, a result of urban renewal. Onlookers spilled out into Hammond Street on July 4, 1894, to watch Mayor Flavius O. Beal and others dedicate the brick landmark. Downtown's centerpiece contained municipal offices and a 2,000-seat auditorium. Boxing matches were held here, along with concerts by the Bangor Symphony Orchestra and the Trapp Family Singers.

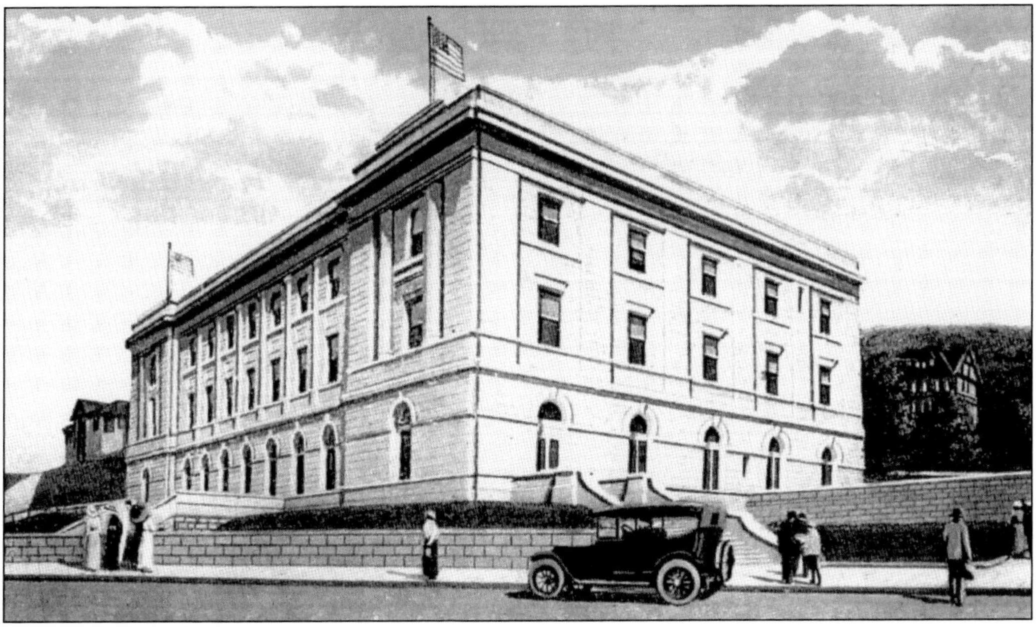

The former post office is downtown's only all-granite building. It rose from the ashes of the 1911 Bangor fire following the destruction of the old post office and custom house on nearby Kenduskeag Mall. After a new post office and federal building were opened down the street in 1969, city hall workers moved into the former post office and have been there ever since.

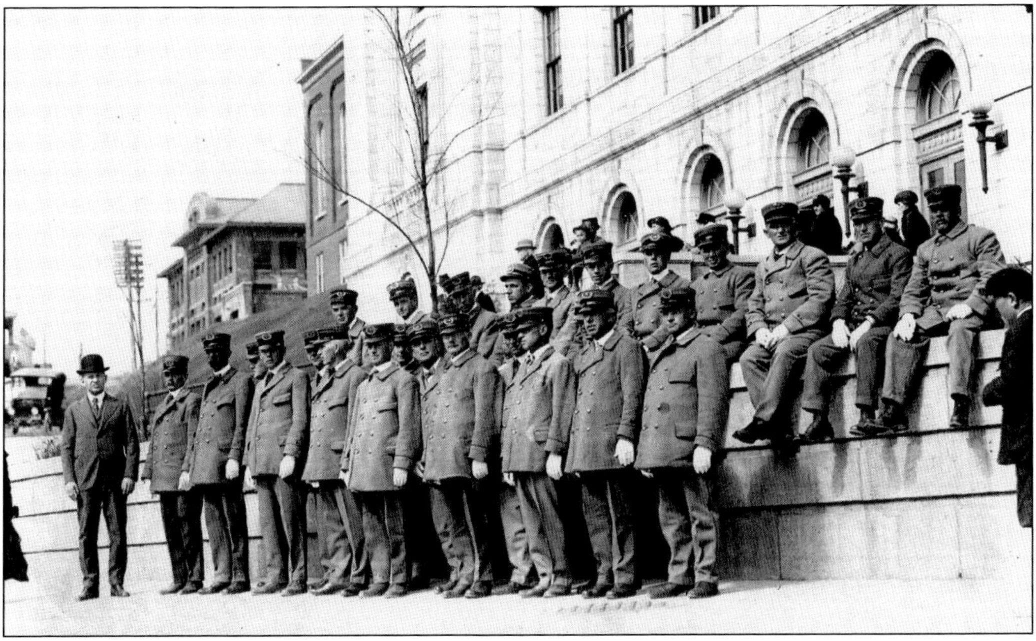

Bangor letter carriers pose outside the post office in this 1920s photograph. The man in the derby, or dip hat, on the far left was probably the postmaster. Center Street Hill, in the background, was called "post office hill" by earlier generations. Before that, locals referred to it as Baptist Hill, owing to the presence of the First Baptist Church, destroyed in the 1911 fire. It was located across from the post office.

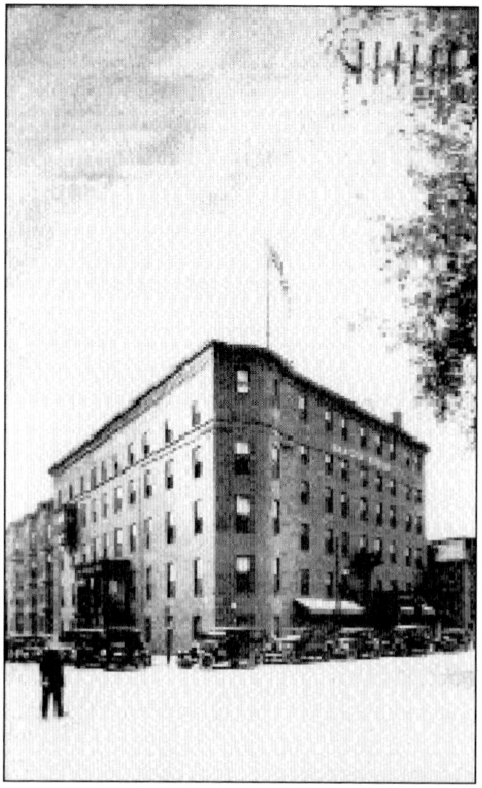

Since its dedication in 1834, this landmark has stood at the corner of Main and Union Streets. No longer a hotel, the Bangor House is home to senior and disabled residents. But the legacy of the city's leading hotel is part of Bangor history. Presidents stopped here, along with Jack Benny and Liberace. In 1934, aviator Amelia Earhart lunched at the hotel, and in 1941, First Lady Eleanor Roosevelt appeared here.

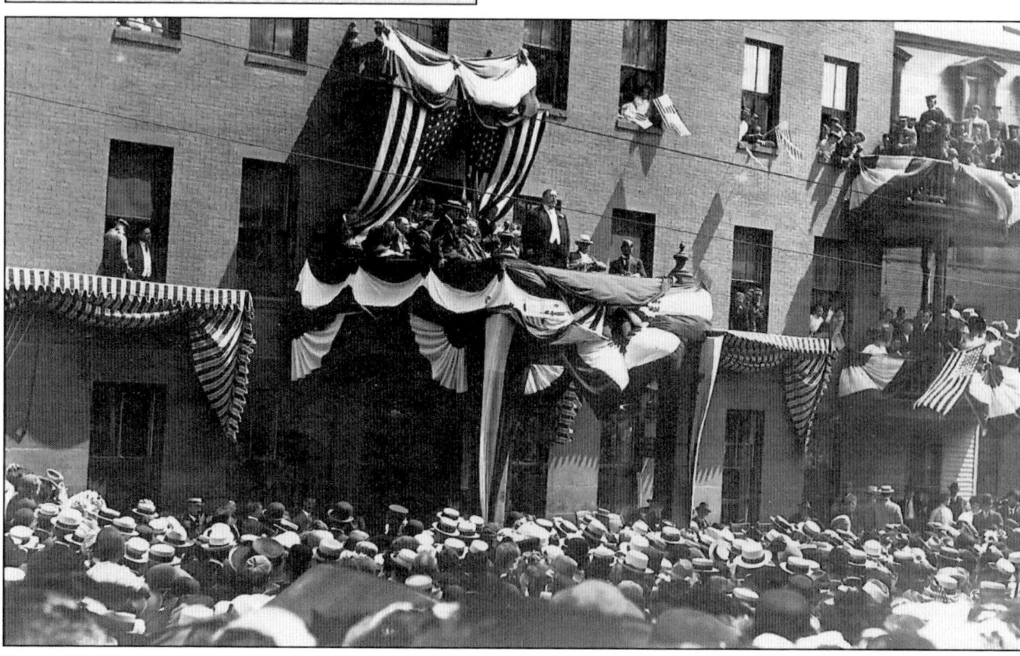

Pres. William Howard Taft addressed a large crowd in 1910 from the Bangor House's front portico. Before amplification, politicians such as the portly Taft knew how to project their voices. He spoke on agriculture and other topics before reentering the hotel and dining on Penobscot River salmon, broiled peas, chicken, and cake. (BMCH.)

Opened in 1827, the Penobscot Exchange predated the Bangor House by seven years. Bangor's first major hostelry, the "Penoby," as locals called it, never attained the other hotel's status, but it enjoyed a solid reputation well into the 20th century. This advertisement notes the hotel's 150 rooms, private baths, and showers, and perhaps its strongest selling point: its proximity to Union Station.

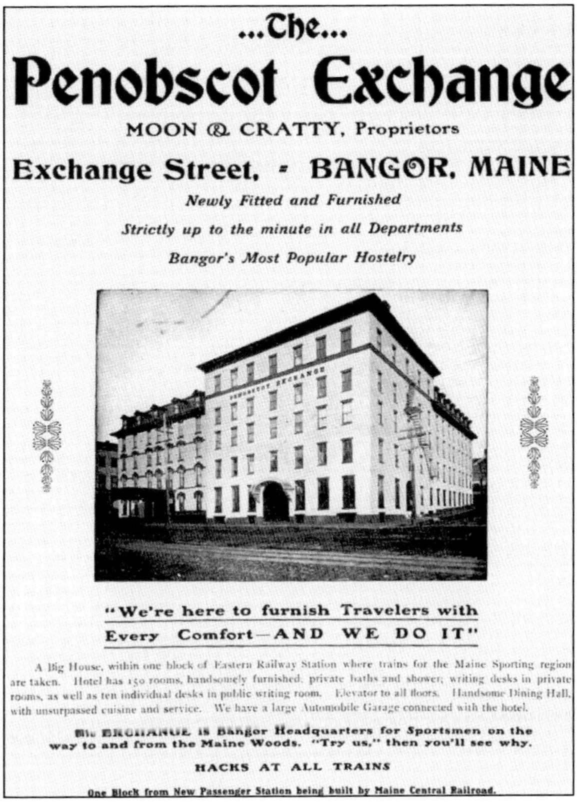

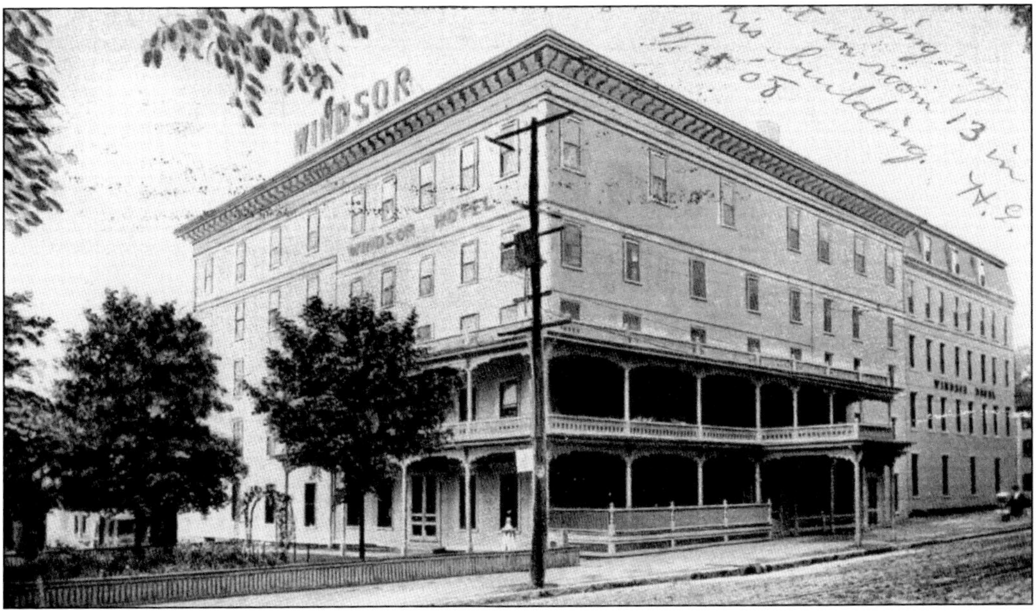

The Windsor Hotel was Bangor's third most desirable place to stay, behind the Bangor House and the Penobscot Exchange. Situated at Harlow and Franklin Streets, it derived its name from the elegant Windsor Hotel in Montreal. Owner Horace Chase was long associated with this hotel, which was destroyed in the 1911 fire. Room rates were $1.50, which included meals.

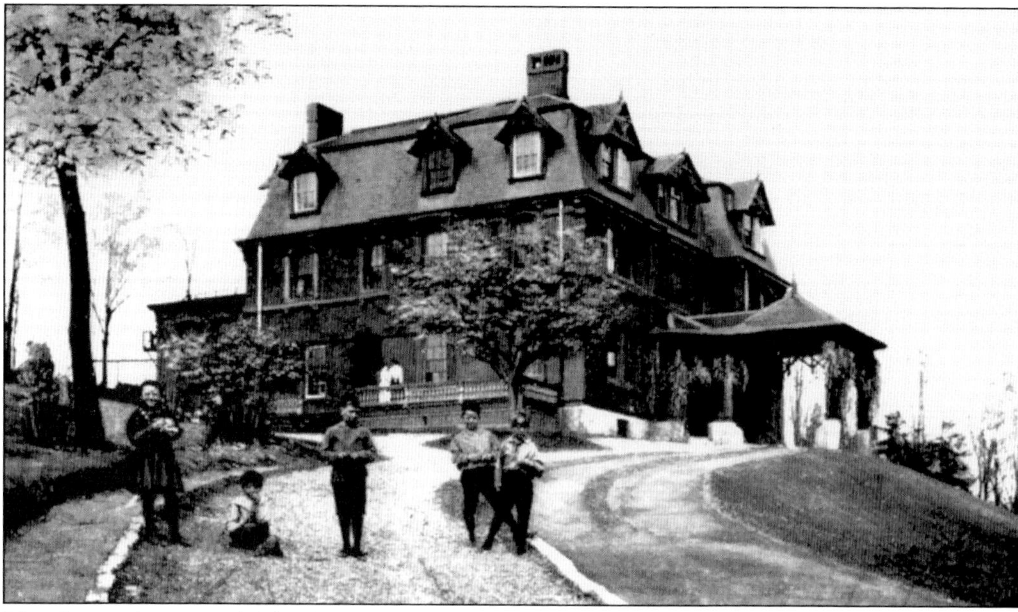

The former Bangor Children's Home sits like a fortress at 218 Ohio Street, down the hill from the standpipe. When this photograph was taken in the early 20th century, orphaned children were wards of the city here, many spending their entire childhoods in the edifice. Trudy Scee chronicled the home's history in the book *The Inmates and the Asylum: The Bangor Children's Home 1835–2002*. Now, the building is the Hilltop School.

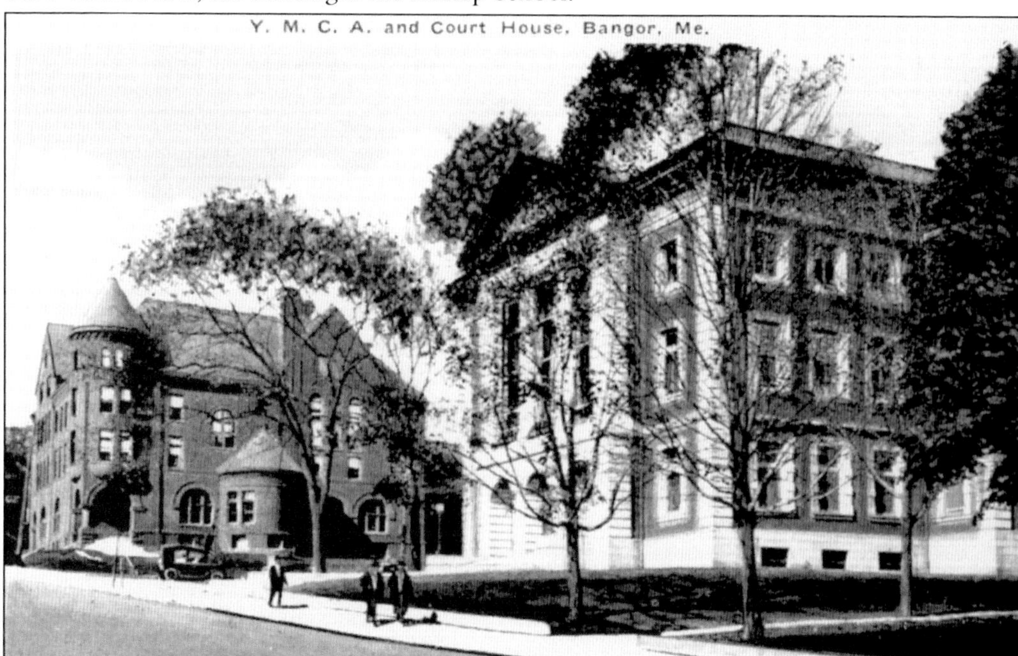

The old YMCA building and Penobscot County Courthouse stood in perfect symmetry at Hammond and Court Streets until the former was demolished to make way for a modern YMCA. Many famous murder trials, and other less newsworthy cases, were tried in this 1903 landmark. Architect Wilfred Mansur designed this second courthouse to stand on the site.

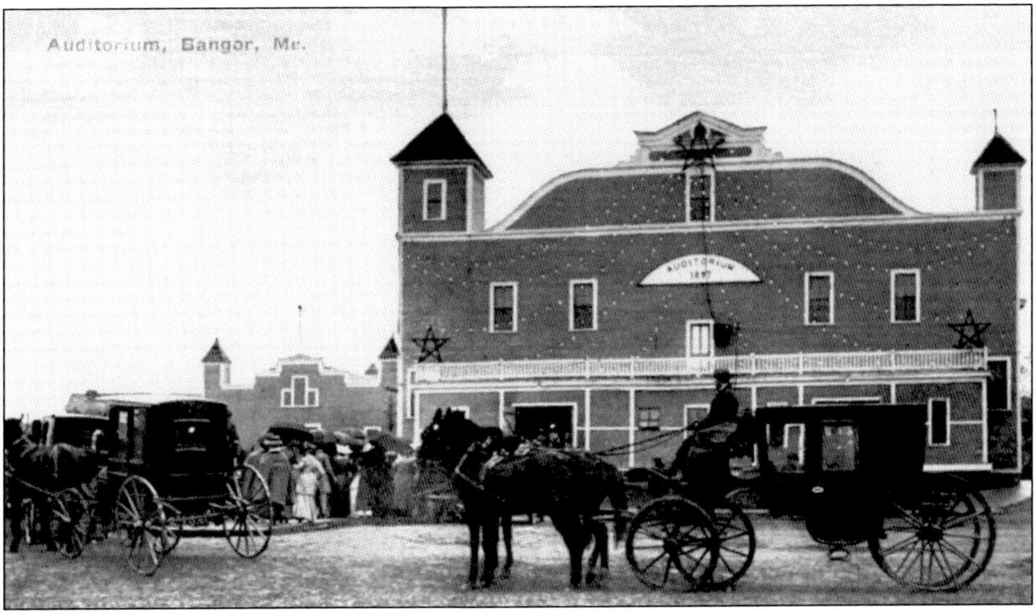

This barnlike building, which had near perfect acoustics, was the old Bangor Auditorium on lower Main Street. A 1913 postcard shows dignitaries arriving at the annual Maine Music Festival, which attracted crowds of 3,000. Maj. James M. Davis built this landmark in six months in 1897 before finishing the standpipe in a similar time period.

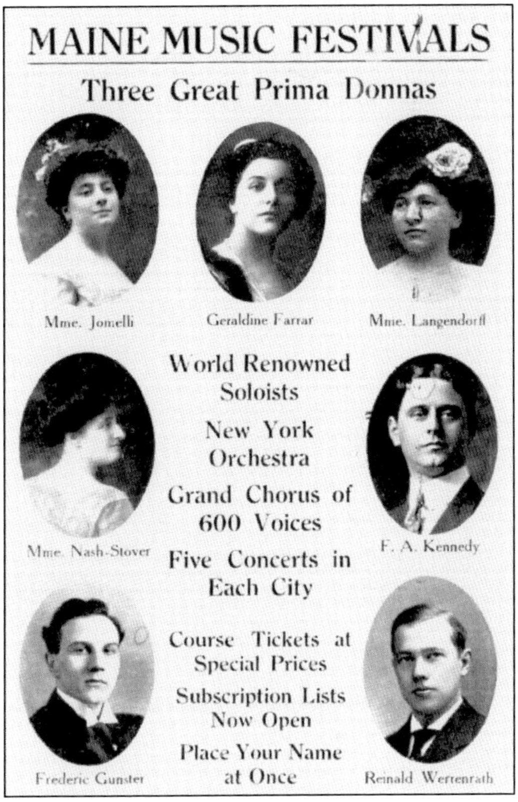

In 1909, performers at William Rogers Chapman's music festival included Geraldine Farrar, Reinald Werrenrath, and F. A. Kennedy. Lillian Nordica, of Farmington, Maine, also appeared at the festival. Whenever papers announced a Nordica performance, the excitement would build to opening night.

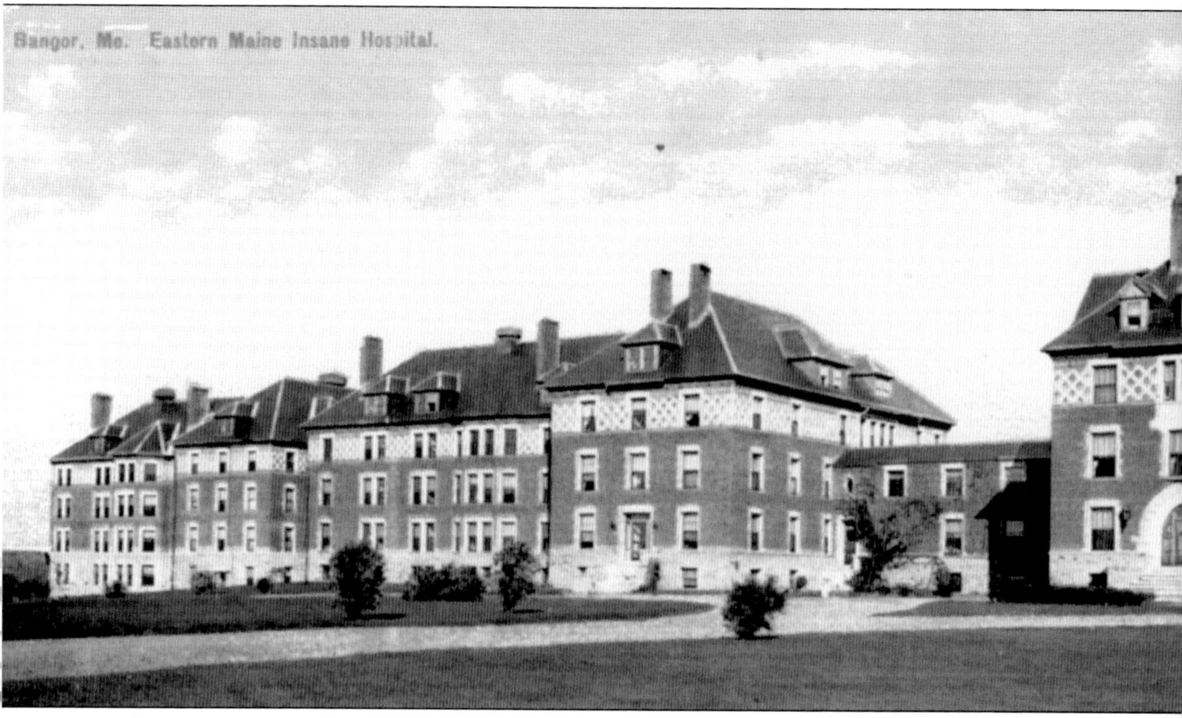

This double-sized postcard format was perfect for the imposing Eastern Maine Insane Hospital, located on outer State Street. Built in 1896, the hospital was later renamed the Bangor State Hospital and eventually the Bangor Mental Health Institute (BMHI), reflecting enlightened attitudes toward the treatment of the mentally ill. Although the institution's population has

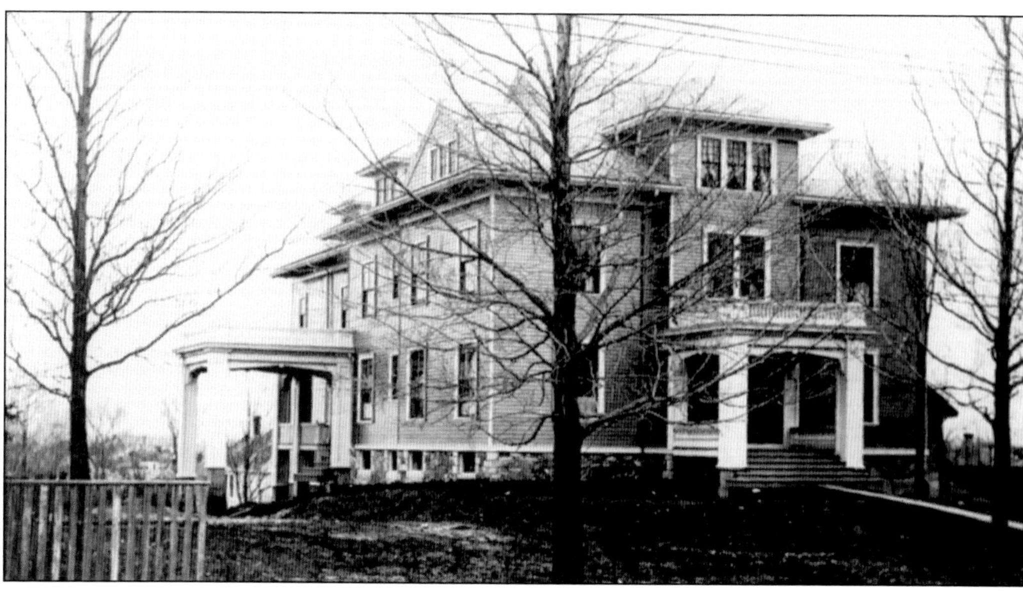

Before the construction of the modern St. Joseph Hospital, this simple wooden building was Bangor's principal east side hospital. The Paine Private Hospital on Center Street resembled a large home. The Felician Sisters of the Roman Catholic Church later acquired the property and continue to operate St. Joseph Hospital on this expanded property.

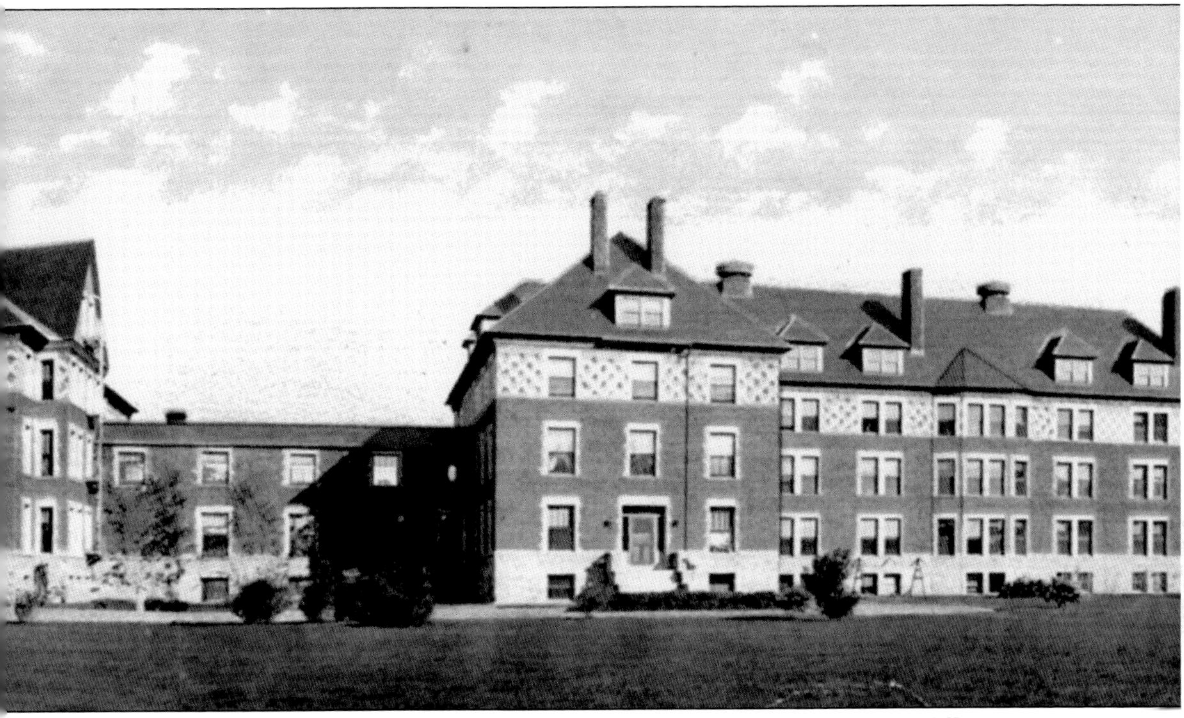

fallen in recent years, a result of residents moving into off-campus group homes, BMHI is still a functioning hospital that has lost none of its historic qualities. Former residents referred to this hillside property overlooking the Penobscot River as Hepatica Hill because of a plant that grew in abundance there.

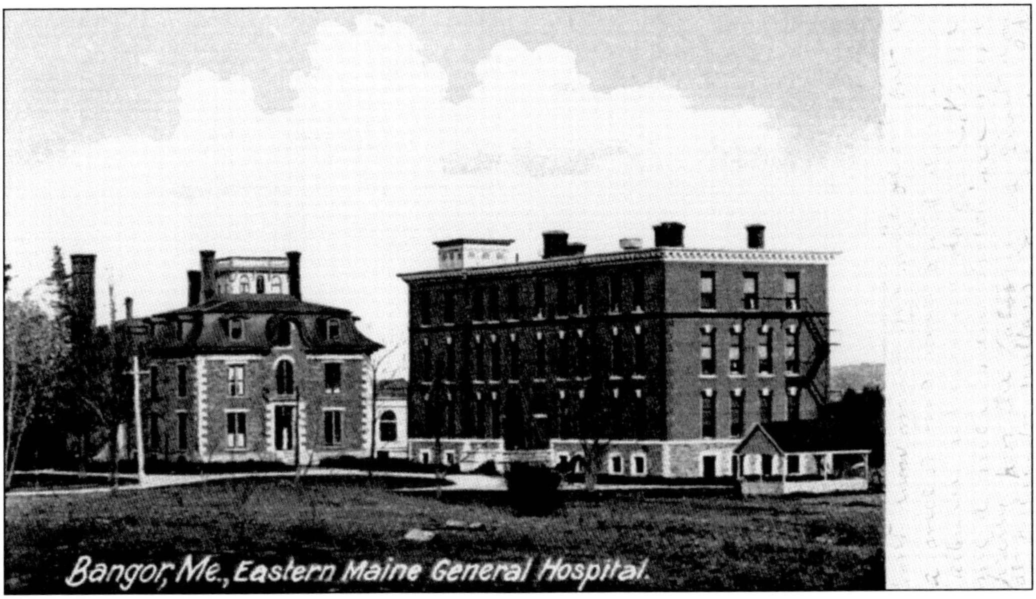

Nurses once lived and trained in the stone Mace House (left) of Eastern Maine General Hospital. The only other hospital building in existence in this *c.* 1910 postcard view was the main building, where surgical and hospital rooms were located. Today, Eastern Maine Medical Center, which includes oncology and cardiac units, dwarfs the two original buildings.

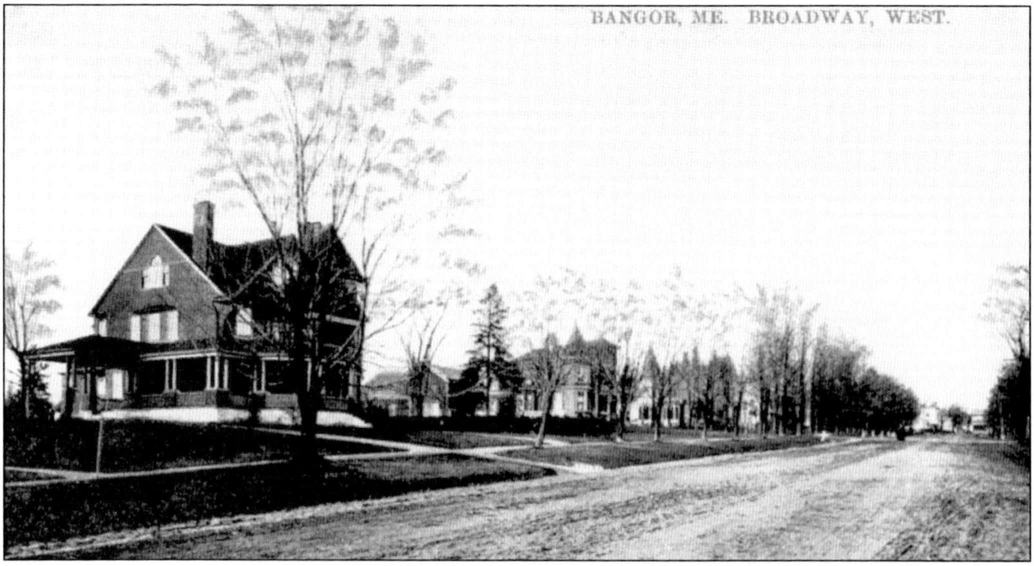

West Broadway is one of Bangor's finest neighborhoods. One 19th-century mansion contained a ticker-tape machine so its owner could monitor stock market returns. The gabled 1856 mansion at 47 West Broadway (center) was originally owned by William Arnold.

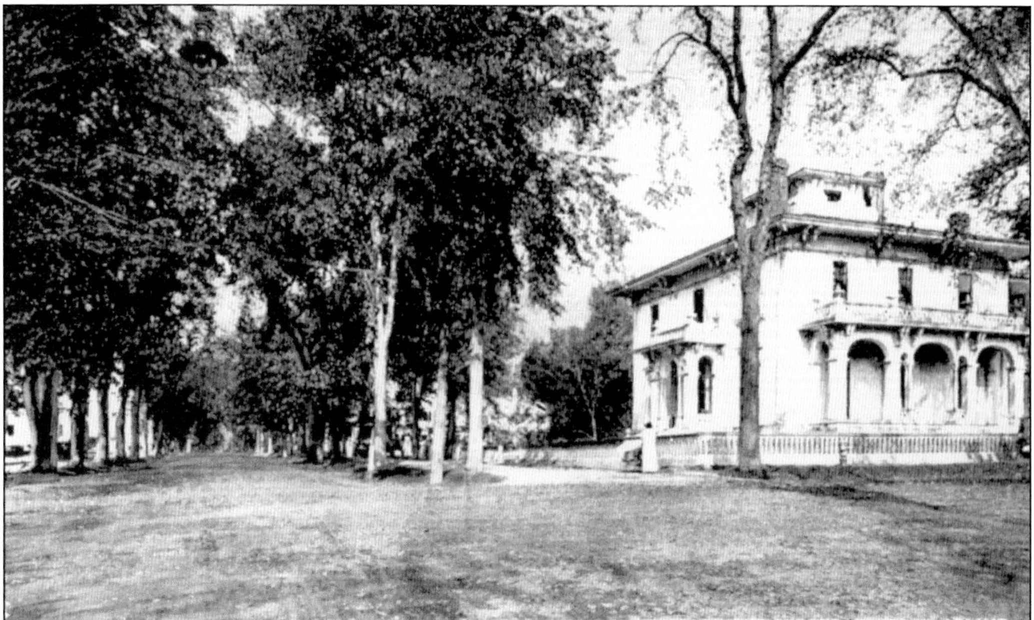

The late teacher and author James B. Vickery used to liken this Italianate home to old Southern antebellum mansions, so special was its place in Bangor history. Located at 113 Broadway and demolished in 1968, it was the residence of Ephraim Paulk and, later, banker George K. Jewett and lumberman Charles Stetson.

Two

Along the Penobscot River

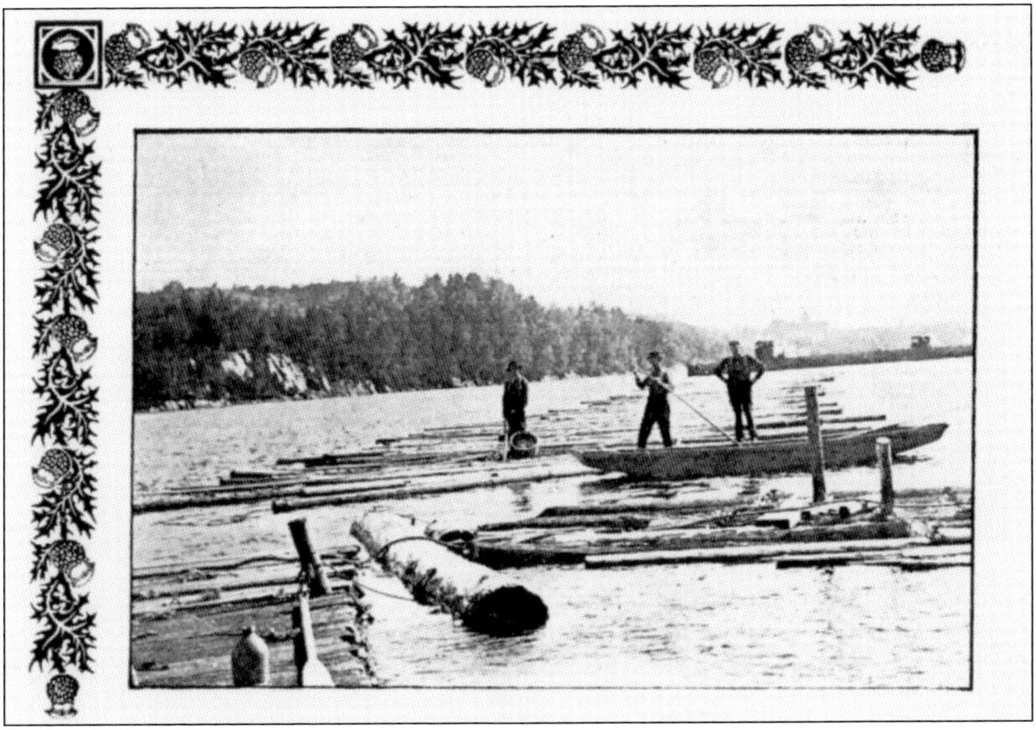

River drivers nicknamed "Bangor tigers" rafted logs on the Penobscot River throughout the 19th and early 20th centuries. This postcard shows three such men rounding up logs into rafts. Note the double-ended dory that two of the drivers are standing in. Before the logs were driven down the West Branch of the Penobscot and into Bangor, they were stamped with each forest owner's mark to prevent mix-ups farther downriver.

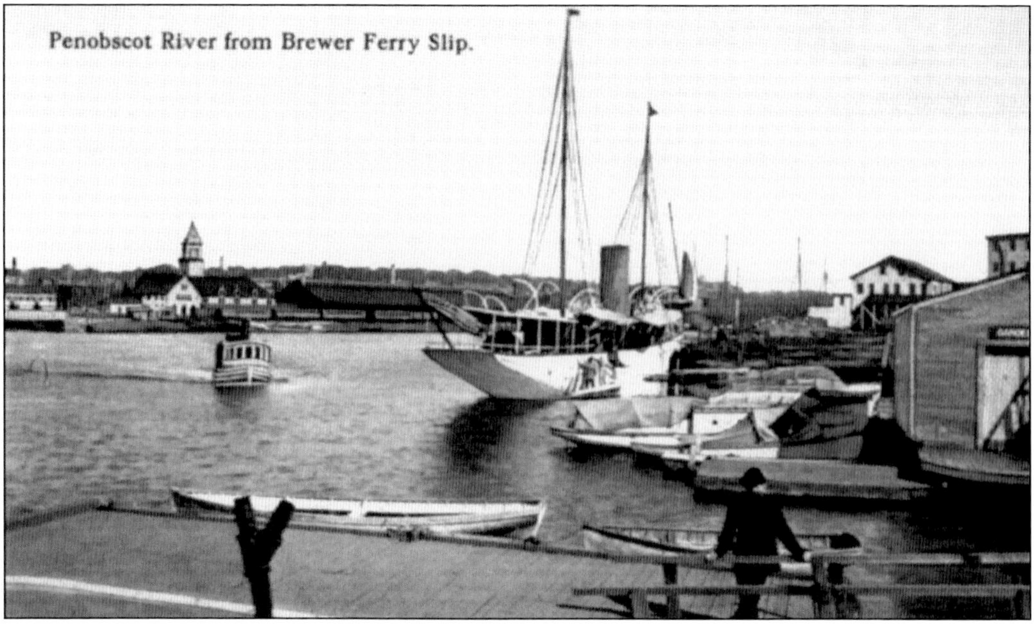

This view, dated January 15, 1913, says a lot about the harbor shared by Bangor and Brewer. Towering above the other boats is a private steam-powered yacht. Making its way toward the Brewer side is the *Bon Ton* ferry boat. Assorted smaller boats are tied up at the ferry slip on Wilson Street in Brewer.

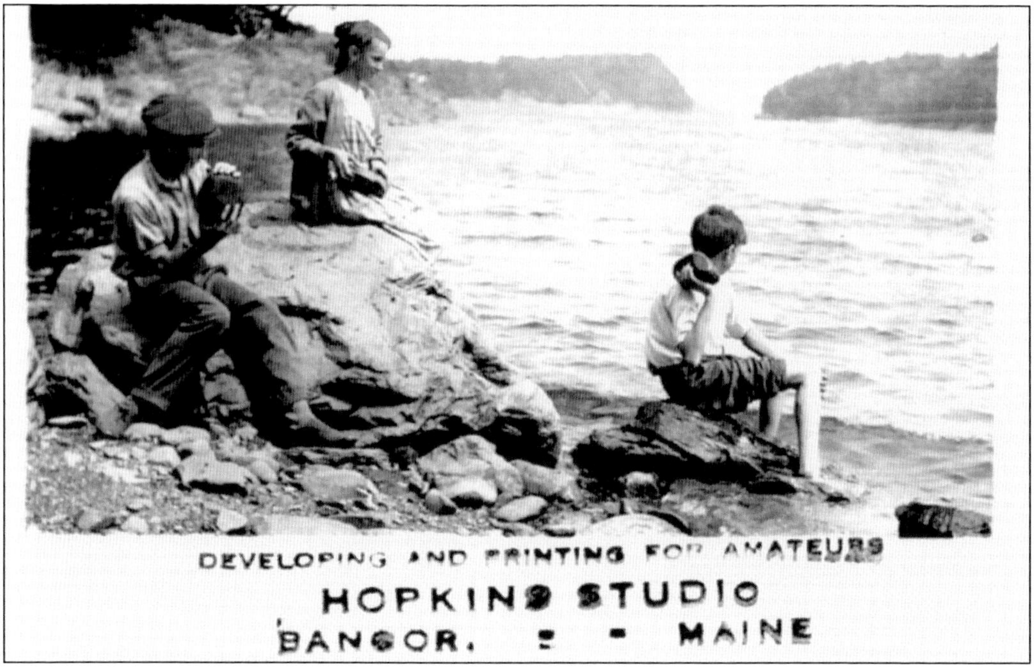

A trio of children, two brothers and their sister perhaps, toss rocks into the Penobscot River in Hampden, the next town to the south after leaving Bangor. The bluff in the distance was known to travelers as High Head. Our ancestors traveled the river far more frequently than today's residents, many of whom have never taken a sightseeing trip on "the Rhine of Maine."

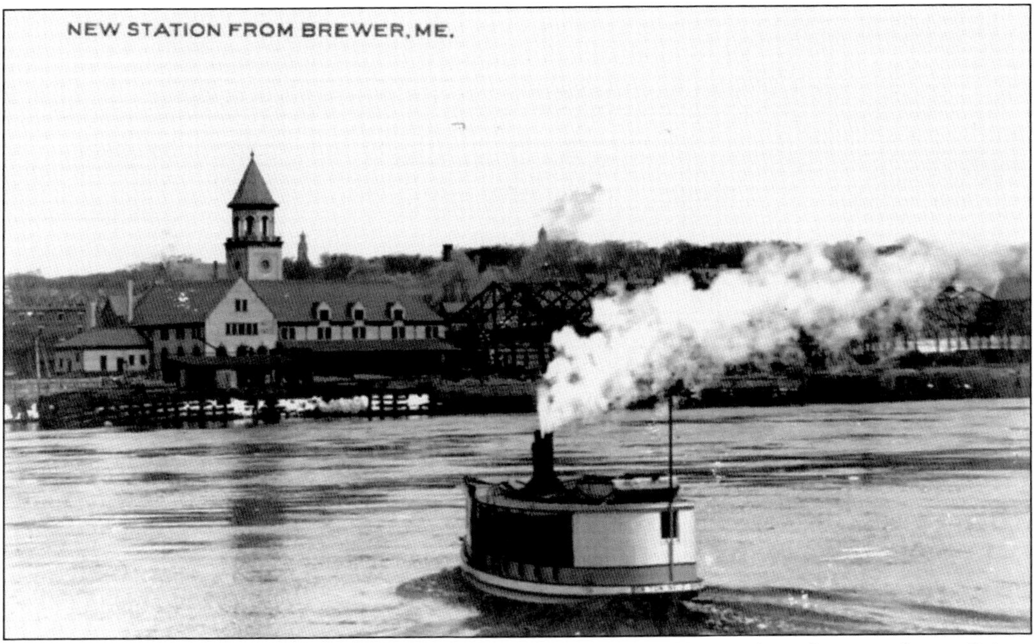

The second of the Bangor-Brewer passenger ferries, *Bon Ton II,* plies the Penobscot River between the twin cities in 1907. The boats began running in 1884, and service ended in 1939, when a fire destroyed *Bon Ton III.* The trip lasted five minutes, and the fare was initially 1¢. When it spiked at 5¢, irate passengers cried inflation.

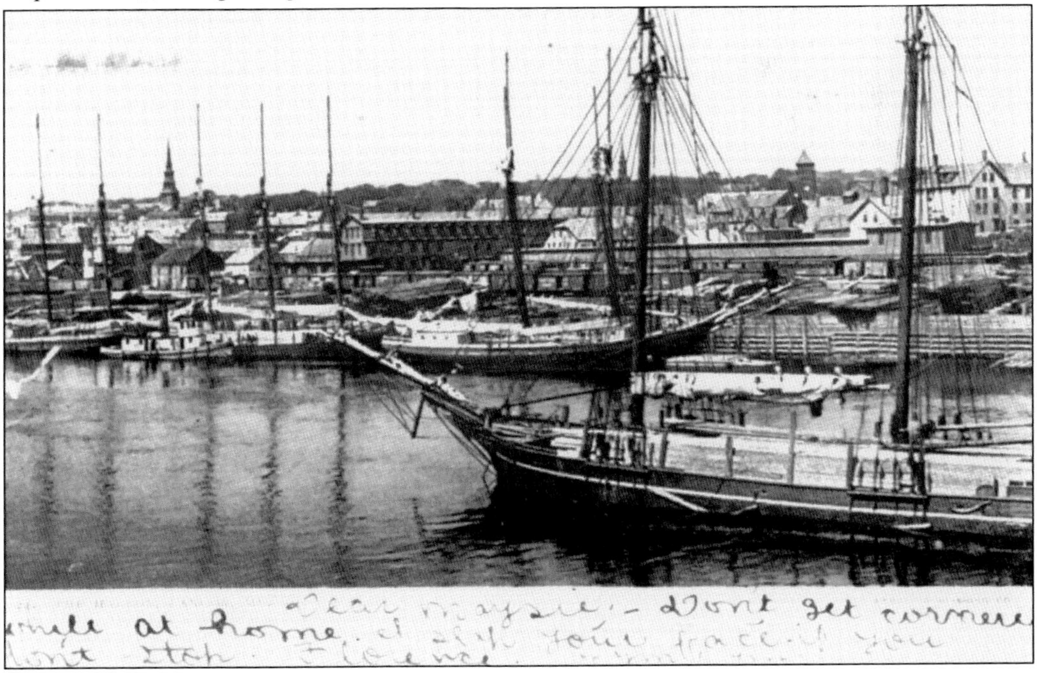

You may have heard the tales of hopping across the river from Bangor to Brewer on the decks of boats without getting your feet wet. This postcard proves how busy the harbor was even in the waning days of shipping in the early 20th century. Schooners called "coasters" were the workhorses of the maritime trade since they delivered a variety of goods along the Maine coast.

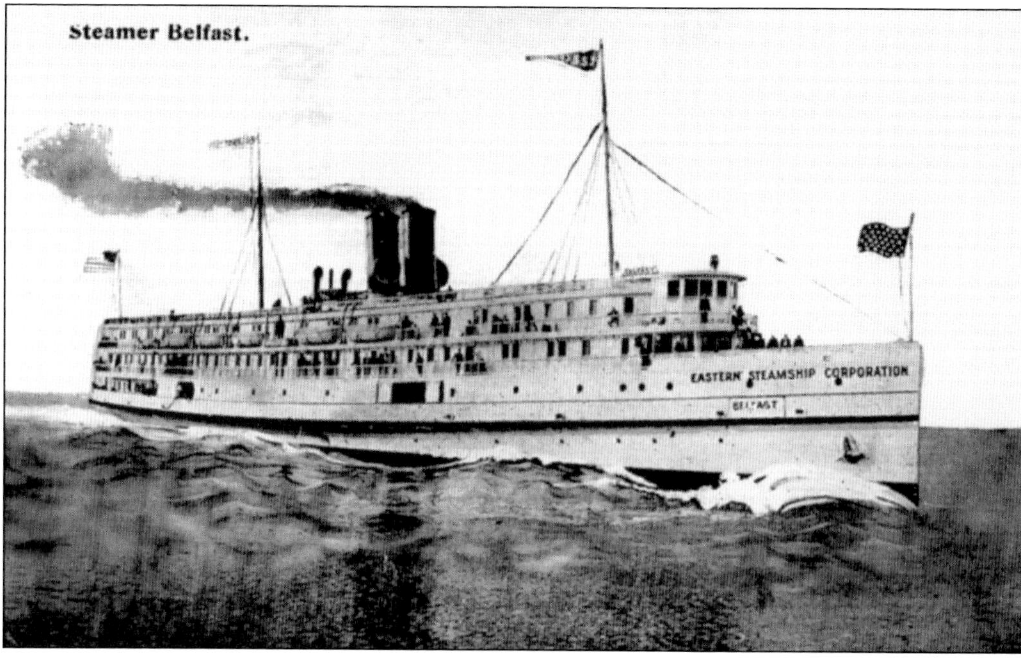

The shrill whistle of the Boston steamers was a familiar sound from the 1830s until 1935, when the last of the boats visited Bangor. The steamer *Belfast* was a favorite, carrying passengers and cargo as near as Hampden and as far away as Boston. Children loved the steamers since they left a wide wake perfect for river swims at the Tin Bridge near the East Hampden town line.

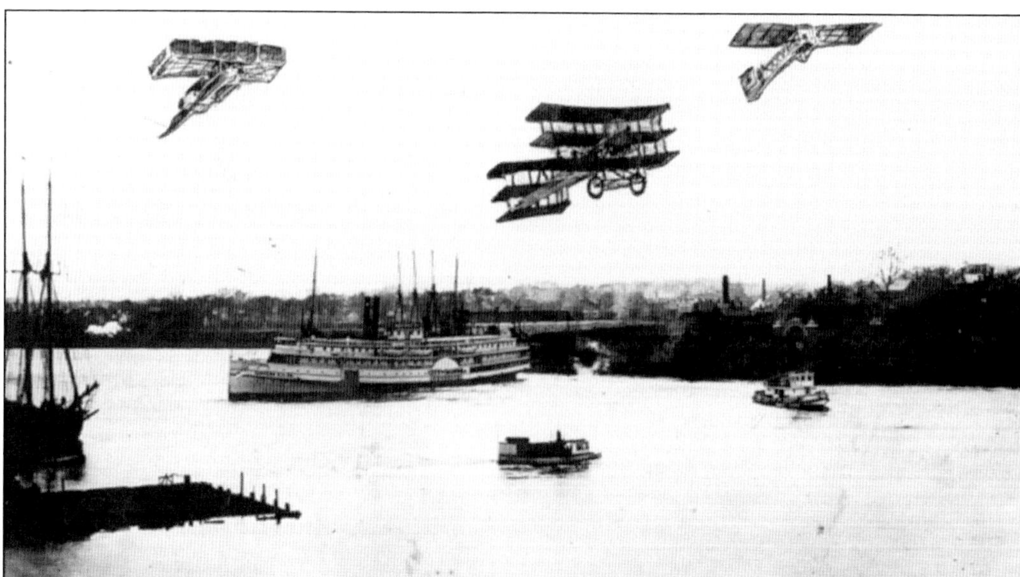

This postcard view is titled "Airships Passing over Bangor, Me.," but the view is a photographic fabrication that exploited the aeronautical craze around the time of World War I. The boats are real, though, including a Boston side-wheeler and the *Bon Ton* ferry in the center foreground.

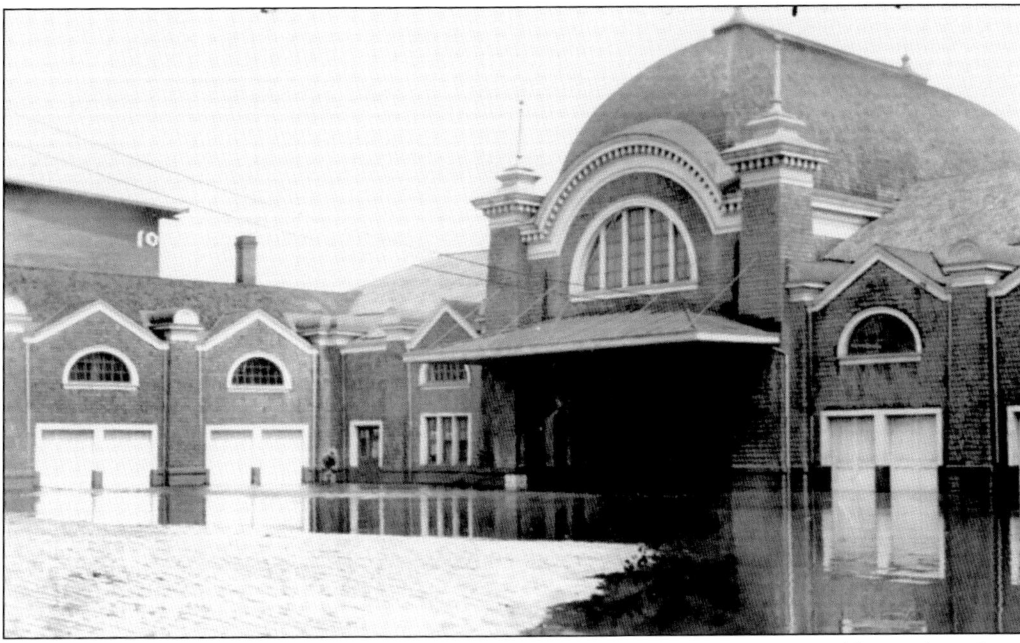

Passengers boarding the Boston steamers entered through this opulent terminal located on Front Street. The Eastern Steamship Company headquarters spared no expense to impress travelers. This view, probably taken during the spring freshet of 1923, shows the terminal partially submerged by Penobscot River water.

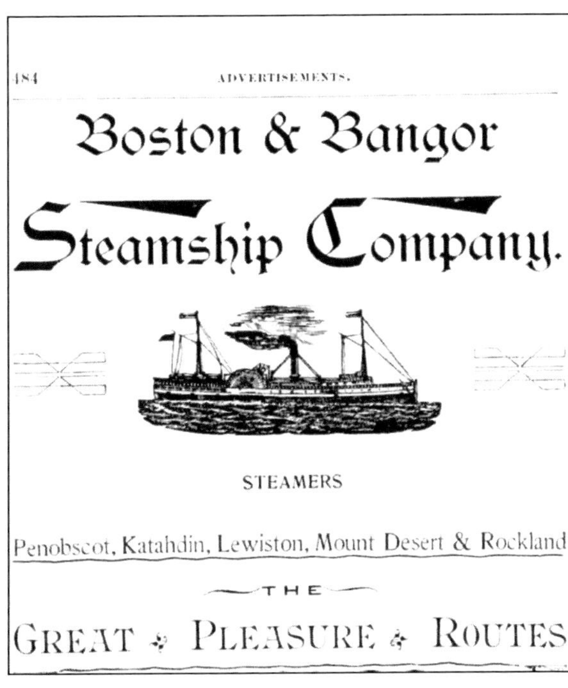

Advertisements such as this lured customers to the "great pleasure routes" of the Boston & Bangor Steamship Company of the late 1800s. Five steamers went as far as Boston, in addition to offering excursion routes to Frenchman Bay off Bar Harbor and Penobscot Bay. The long steamer pictured in this advertisement was used for longer routes.

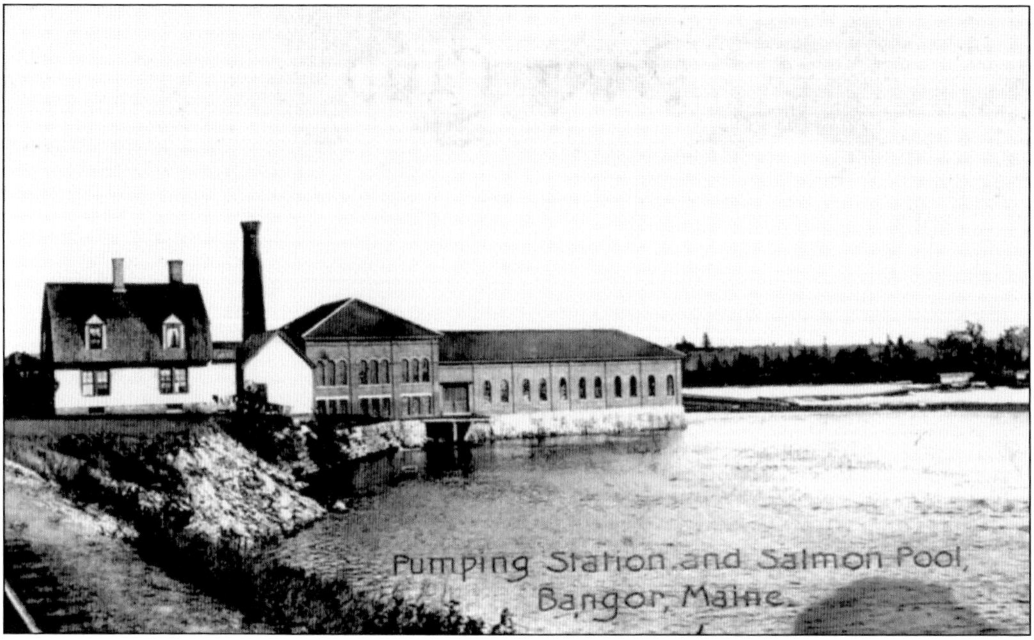

Since 1875, the Bangor waterworks property on State Street has been a river landmark. Built to pump water throughout the city, the huge indoor turbine was powered by a dam. The superintendent lived with his family in the wooden house on the left. After the buildings were vacated, the property fell into disrepair. Plans to renovate the buildings as apartments were proposed in 2003.

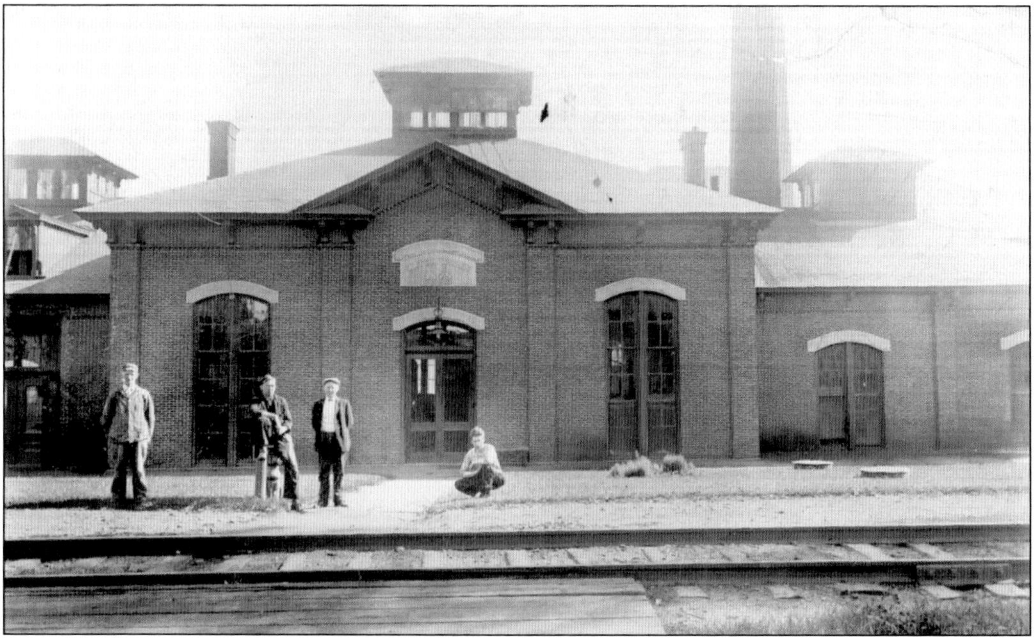

This real-photo postcard shows four men standing in front of the waterworks building. They are unidentified, but the man on the far left may be wearing a railroad uniform. Railroad tracks bisect the waterworks property. The Holly waterworks system installed fire hydrants throughout the city. (MHPC.)

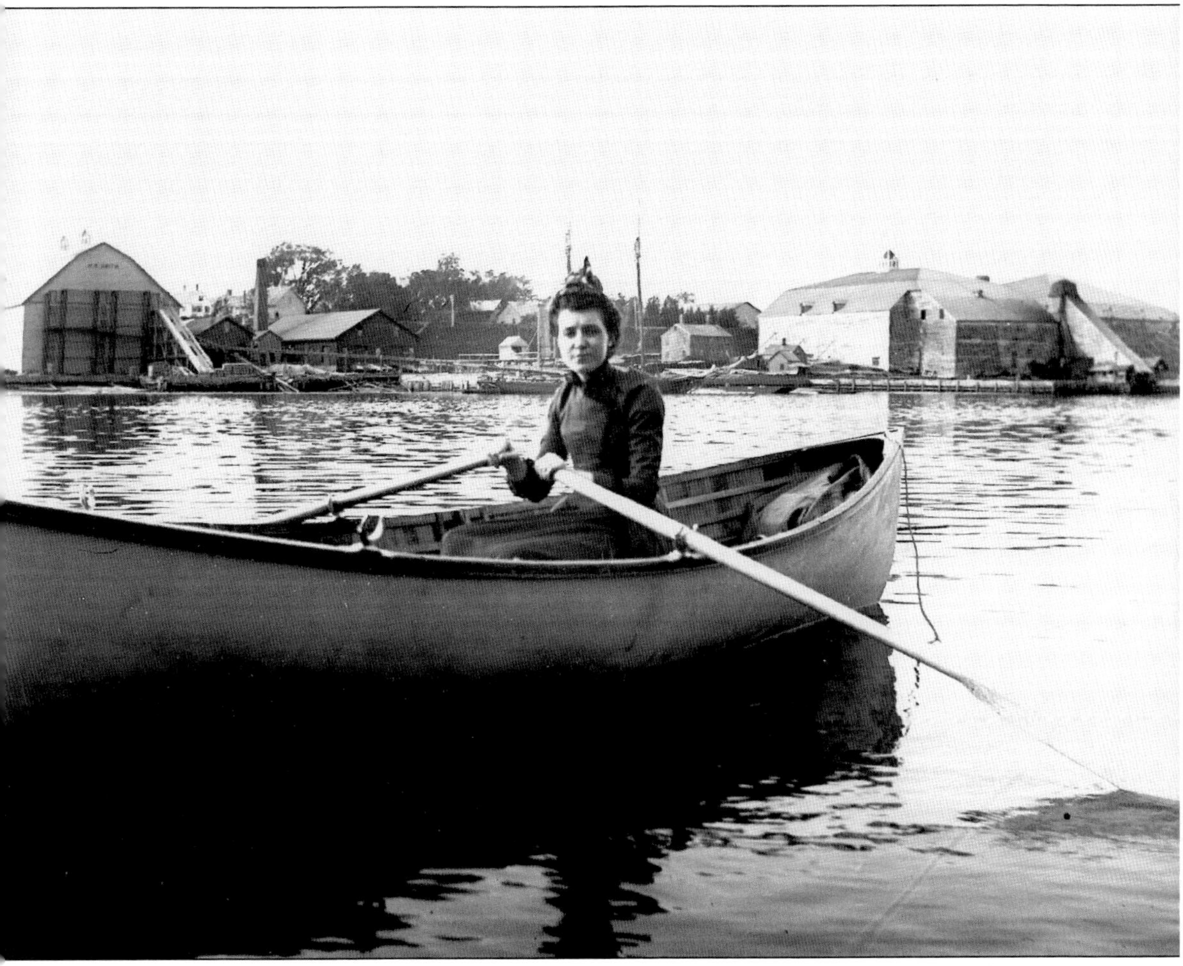

Anyone who met Jennie Sullivan never forgot her. The feisty, independent woman could handle a boat as well as any man could. Here, she is attired in a black dress buttoned to the neck, standard fashion for a woman in 1892 even while paddling a pea pod–style boat manufactured in Bangor. Sullivan and her father lived at the salmon pool, where her father was the dam keeper. Tom Hennessey, the *Bangor Daily News* outdoors columnist, said Sullivan caught a presidential salmon. She was the only woman to hold that honor. Beginning in 1912, people gathered at the Penobscot Salmon Club in Brewer to try and catch the first fresh-run salmon. It would be carefully packed on ice at a Bangor fish company and shipped to the White House. There, a ceremony would typically feature a smiling president either holding the fish or looking at it from a respectable distance. Pres. Herbert Hoover's encounter with the presidential salmon was amusing, in retrospect. Prior to its presentation to the chief executive, the salmon's head fell off, necessitating its reattachment before Hoover even saw it.

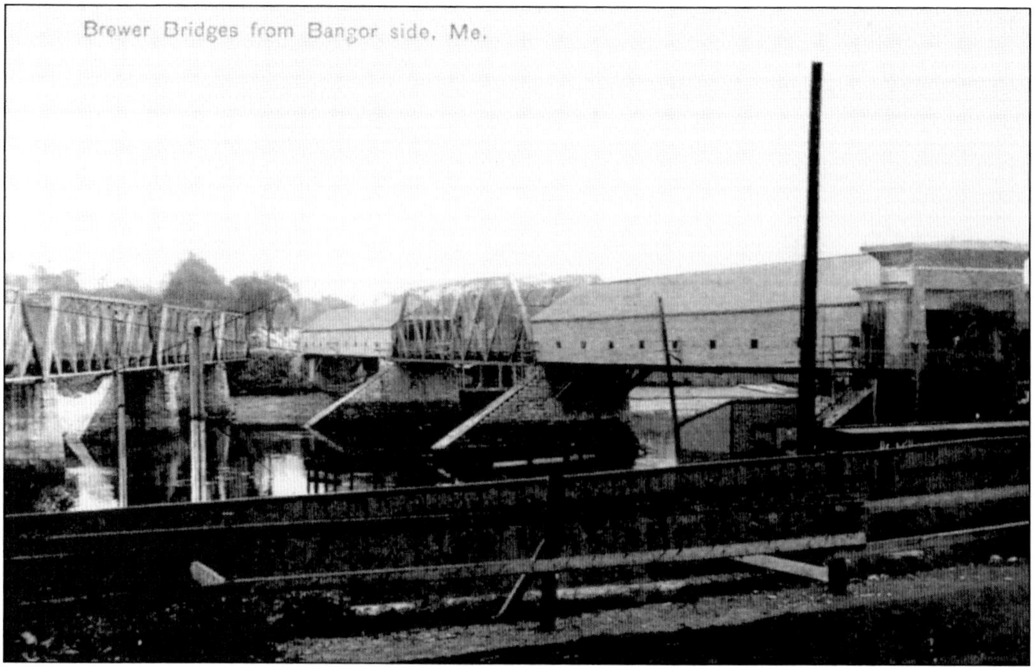

This old covered bridge once linked Bangor to Brewer. It replaced a similar bridge that washed out in 1846. This bridge lasted until 1902, when ice floes knocked out the center span. An iron section joined the existing wooden bridge ends until 1912, when an all-iron bridge was built, lasting until the present Penobscot Bridge replaced it in 1997.

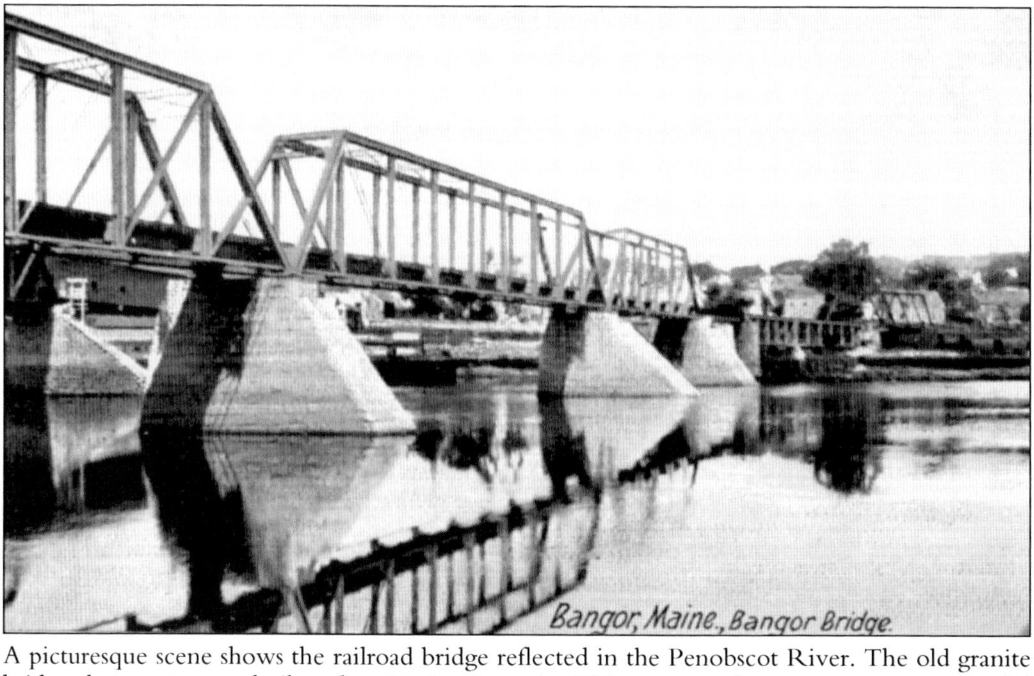

A picturesque scene shows the railroad bridge reflected in the Penobscot River. The old granite bridge abutments were built to last. Dating from the 19th century, they are a testament to solid workmanship by men who knew how to pile into the riverbed and make a structure last. Freight trains still rumble through Brewer across the narrow bridge into Bangor.

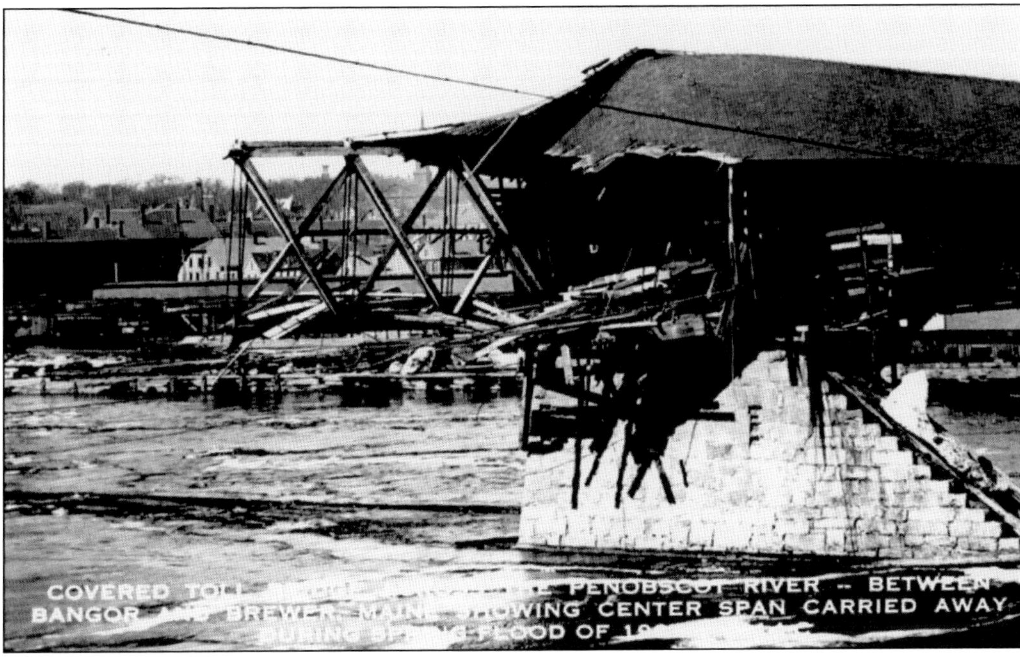

Mother Nature's fury is on display in this real-photo postcard picturing the old Bangor-Brewer toll bridge following the flood of March 1902. A mighty wall of ice swept downriver, sending pedestrians on the bridge scrambling for their lives. No one was injured in what was some of the city's worst river flooding. Property damage was extensive.

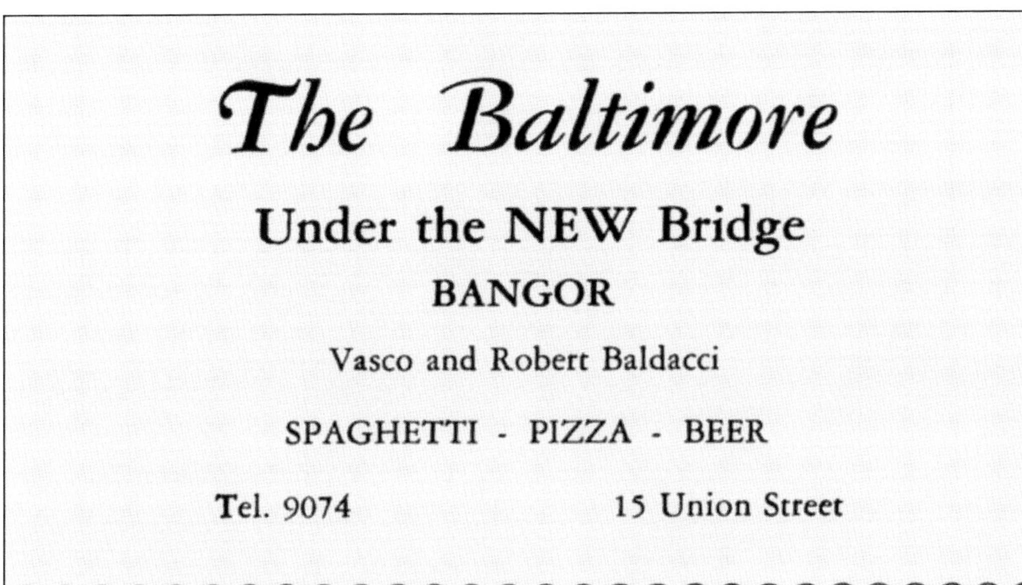

Restaurateurs Vasco and Robert Baldacci carried on a family tradition that began at 15 Union Street in the 1930s. There was no bridge to meet under in the early years, only a cozy restaurant and bar that served spaghetti, pizza, and beer. The Joshua Chamberlain toll bridge, under which the Baltimore sat, was built in 1959. Robert Baldacci, whose son John was elected Maine governor in 2002, later operated Momma Baldacci's restaurant at 12 Alden Street, now run by Paul Baldacci.

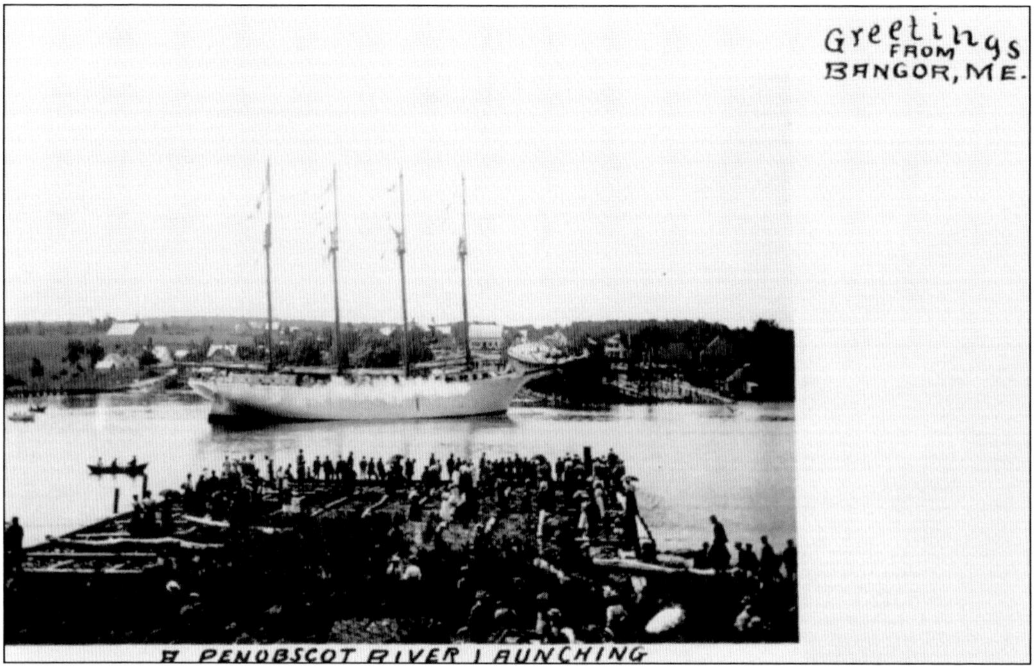

Ship launchings were occasions of high drama in many river towns. This four-masted schooner attracted a throng on the opposite shore. Brewer was home to many shipyards that saw renewed activity during World War I, after the federal government subsidized the building of wooden ships. Steel-hulled vessels were greatly favored by then, however, and big wooden boats faded into the past.

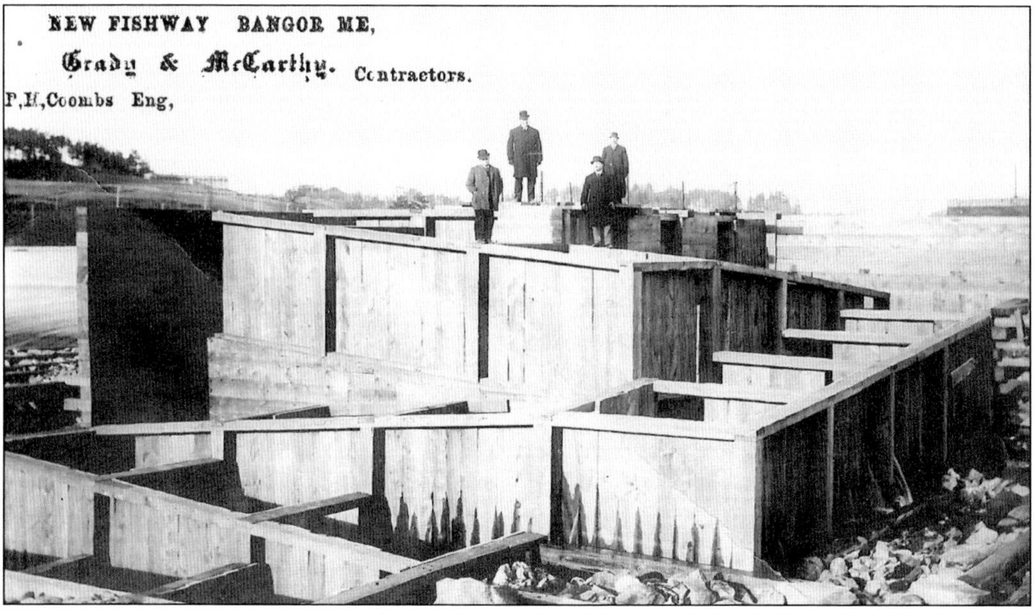

This unusual postcard view shows the new fishway located on the Brewer end of the salmon pool. The federal government mandated fishways at all salmon fishing areas. City engineer Philip Coombs, presumably the man standing at the very top of the wooden contraption, designed it. It was built by Grady & McCarthy, contractors. (BMCH.)

Three

Schools, Public and Parochial

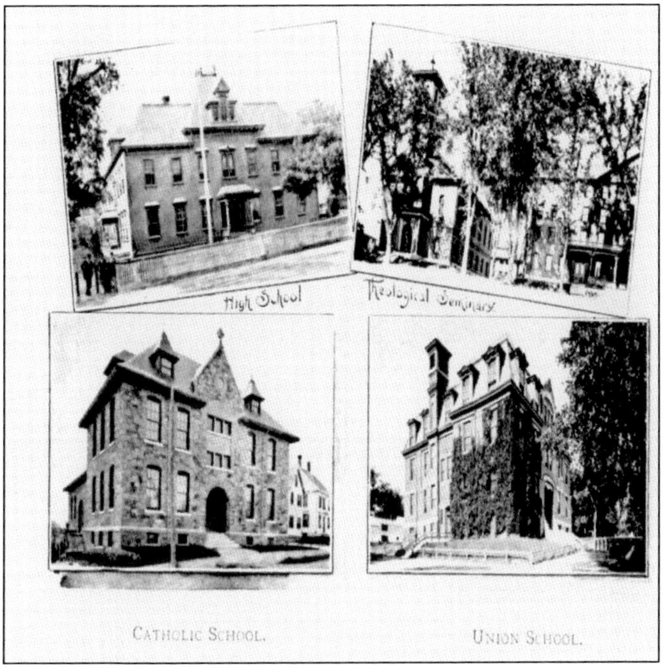

Bangor has always prided itself on a first-rate school system. This photograph montage done just prior to the beginning of the 20th century pictures the old high school building, located in Abbott Square; the theological seminary chapel, still in use today; St. Mary's Catholic School on First Street, now home to Community Health and Counseling Services; and the Union Street Grammar School. Schools used to be located in every neighborhood in the city.

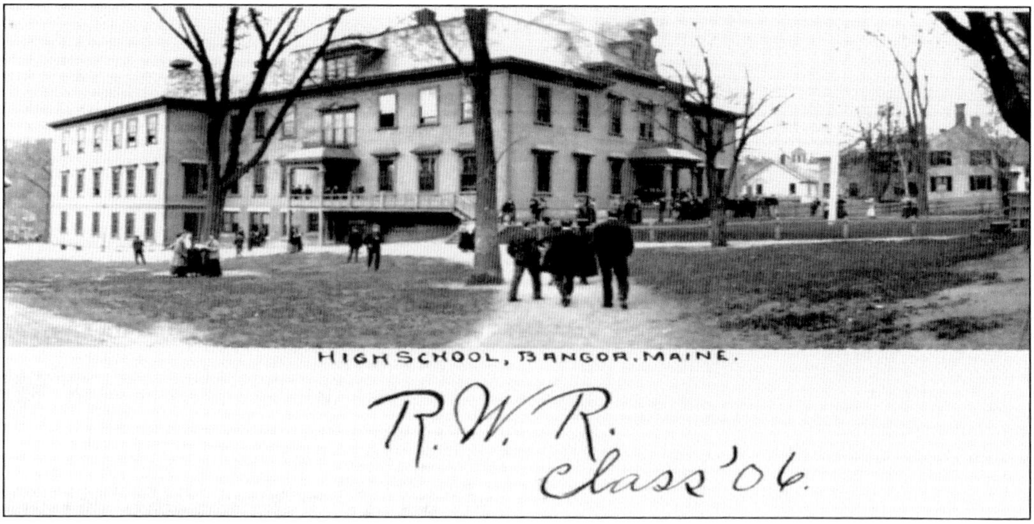

The old high school building sat on Abbott Square. An early postcard sent by a graduate of the class of 1906 shows a side view of the high school. Originally, girls attended a separate school behind the boys' building. The fire of 1911 claimed this and many other Harlow Street treasures, ending an era when the street was lined with private residences and homey-looking hotels and businesses.

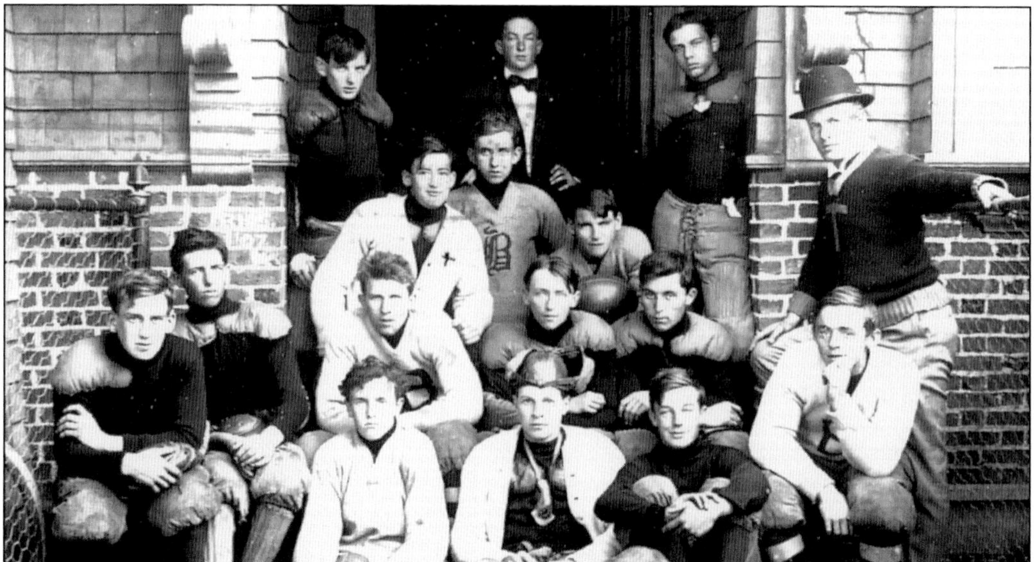

"Can you beat this?" scribbled Heyward S. Boyle on the back of this card, postmarked October 28, 1907. "I bet you can't see my picture there. I will put a cross on my sweater. We have your 'bunch' scun a mile for good looking players." The recipient lived in Foxcroft, whose academy was probably scheduled to play against Bangor High School's football team.

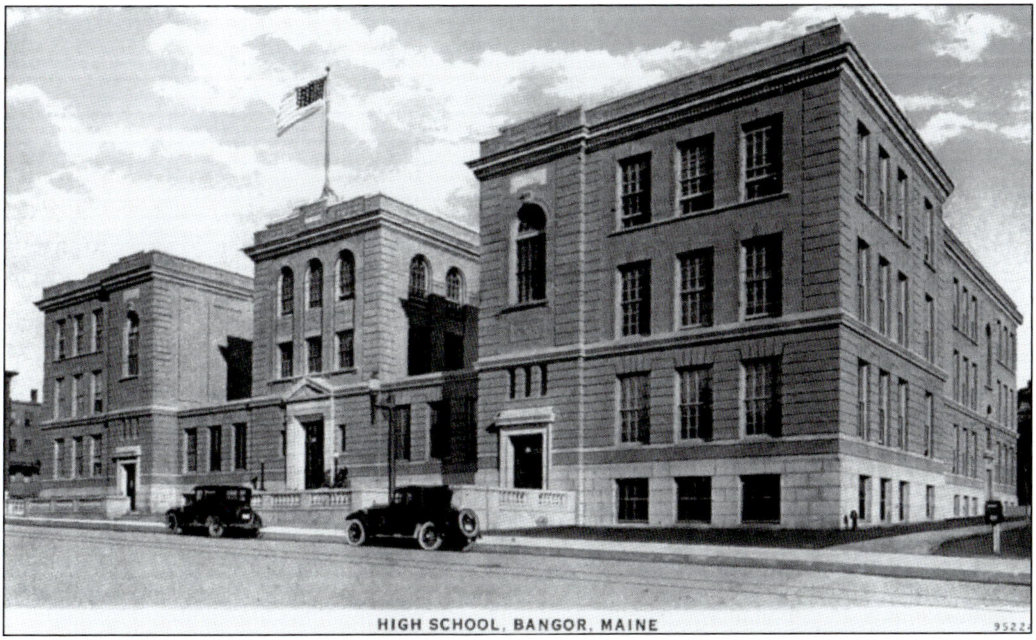

You are dating yourself if you admit having attended the old high school building on Harlow Street. The last class was graduated in 1964, before the new school on Broadway was opened. This school was state of the art when it opened in 1913, complete with science laboratories and study halls.

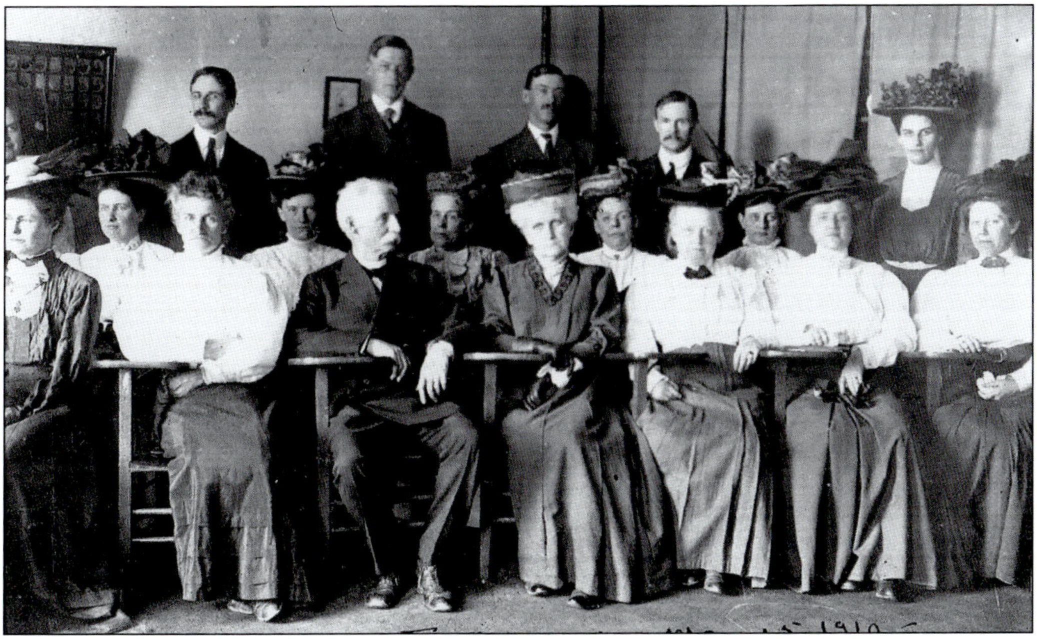

Faculty members of the old high school had their portrait taken on May 15, 1910, less than a year before the April 30, 1911, fire would claim their landmark. All women wore floor-length skirts and lacy white blouses. The elderly couple (front, center) must have had seniority over the rest. This picture was reproduced on a reunion invitation for the Bangor High School class of 1909, which met in Bucksport, Maine, on June 23, 1960.

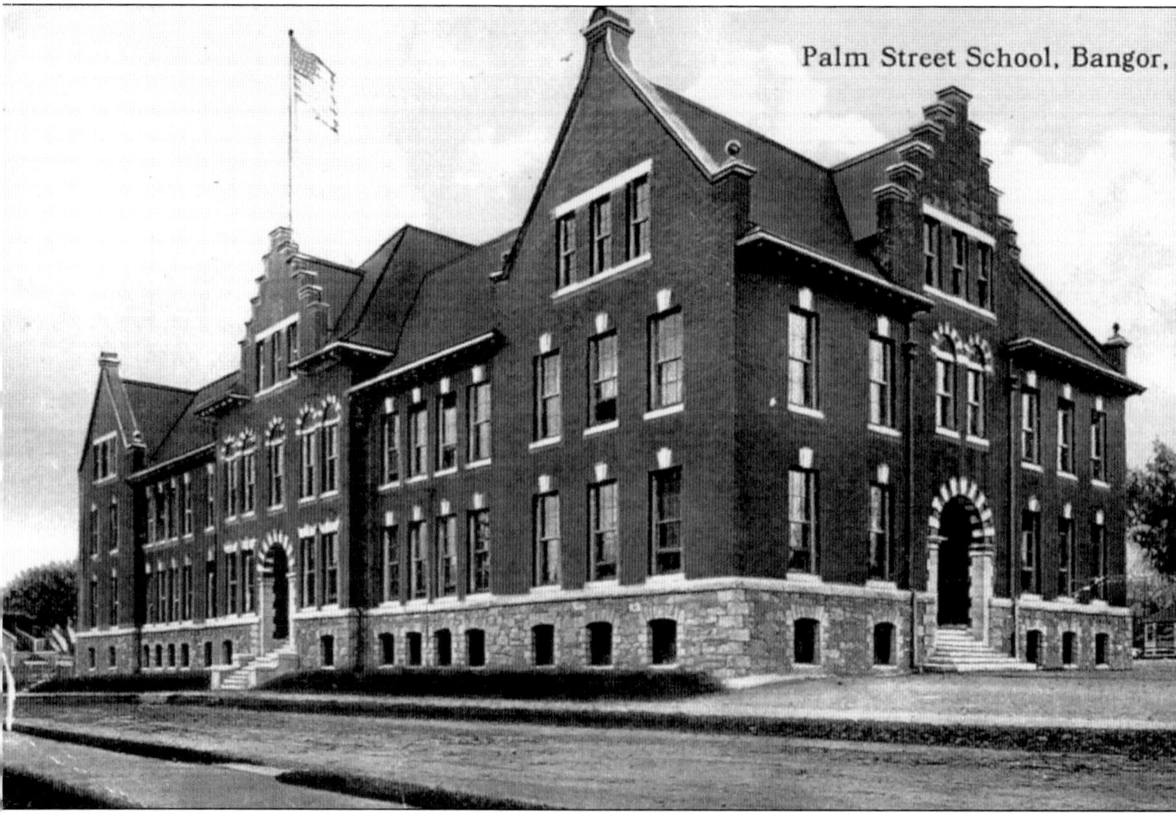

The Palm Street School holds a most special place in graduates' hearts. Built in 1895, the school, later renamed Abraham Lincoln, was a neighborhood favorite. The elementary building resembled a fortress but also invited students into its large, sunny classrooms and third-floor assembly hall. A new Abraham Lincoln School sits on the property today.

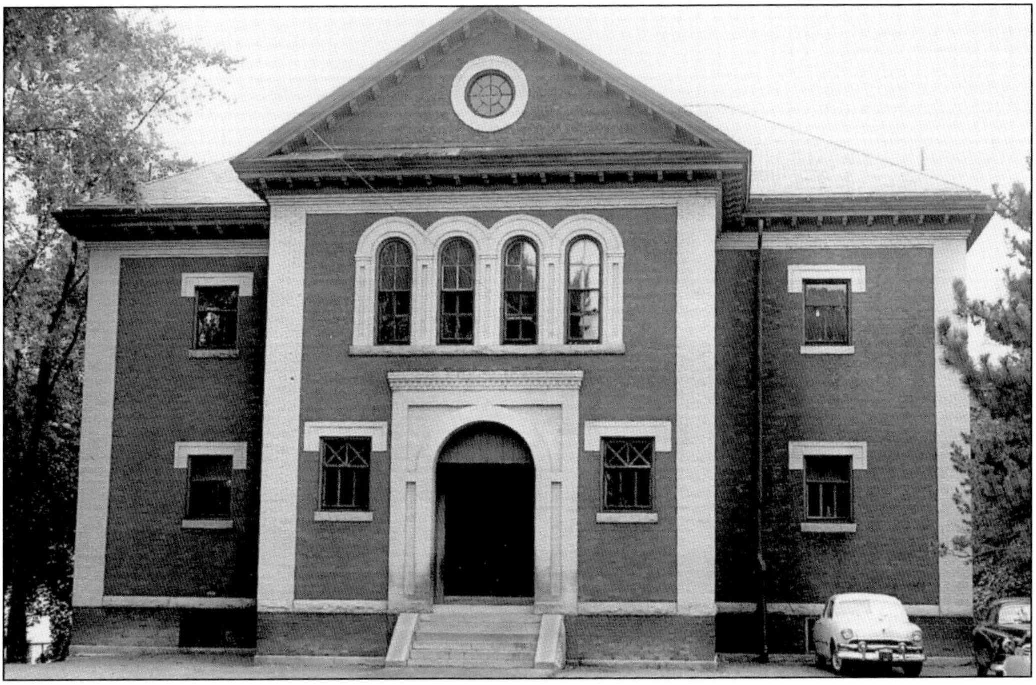

Tiny Longfellow School on Center Street had two kindergartens on the first floor and two first-grade classrooms on the second floor. Louise Ness was a first-grade teacher in the 1950s and 1960s, while also serving as principal. Cold war air-raid drills were held in a dank basement. The school was razed in the 1960s, and St. Joseph Hospital acquired the property. (BDN.)

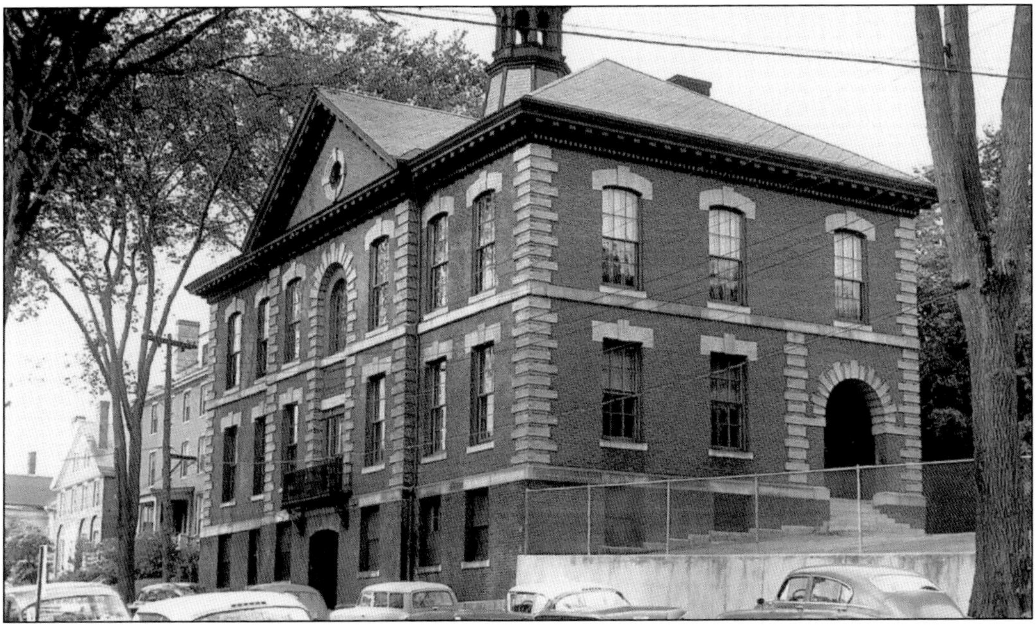

The Valentine School always seemed like a romantic name for a house of learning. West side students walked to the brick building, designed by Wilfred Mansur. He also designed the Longfellow and Palm Street schools. Valentine was later purchased by the American Legion and, still later, became the Shaw House, a home for teenagers. (BDN.)

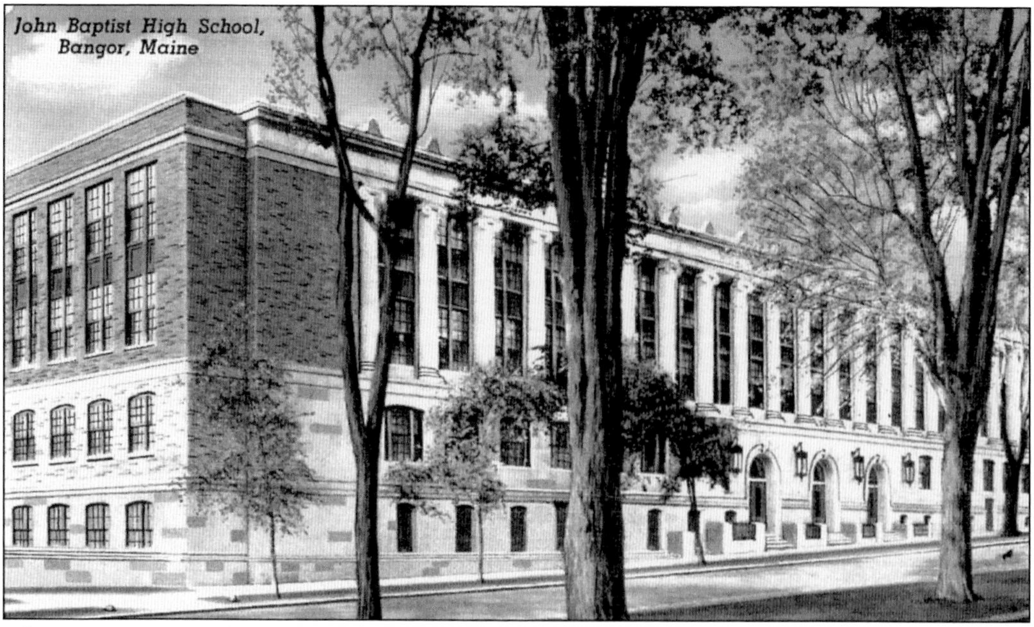

John Bapst Memorial High School stretches nearly an entire block on Broadway. Named for a Swiss Jesuit priest at St. John's Catholic Church in Bangor, the school opened in 1928 for the city's Catholic students. The former parochial school is now a distinguished regional private high school with an admirable academic record and athletic teams.

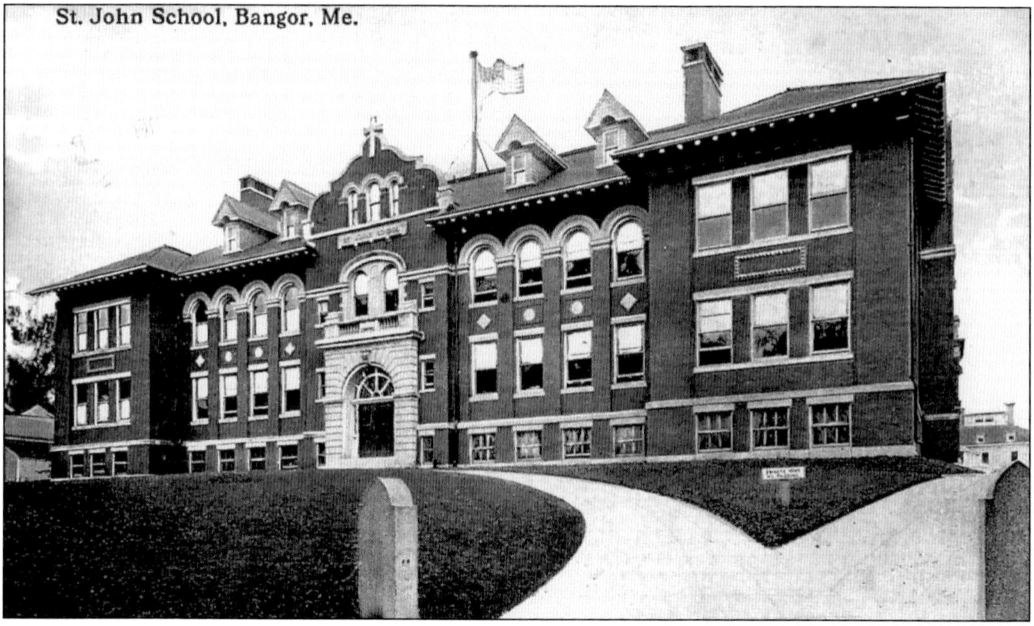

St. John's Catholic School on State Street was dedicated on June 16, 1912, and contained kindergarten through eighth grade. Most students entered John Bapst High School after graduating from St. John's. Nuns taught at St. John's, along with such beloved teachers as the late Constantine "Nick" Albans. A modern building on Ohio Street named All Saints Catholic School now educates younger students while students through grade eight still attend the former St. John's School, also part of All Saints Catholic School.

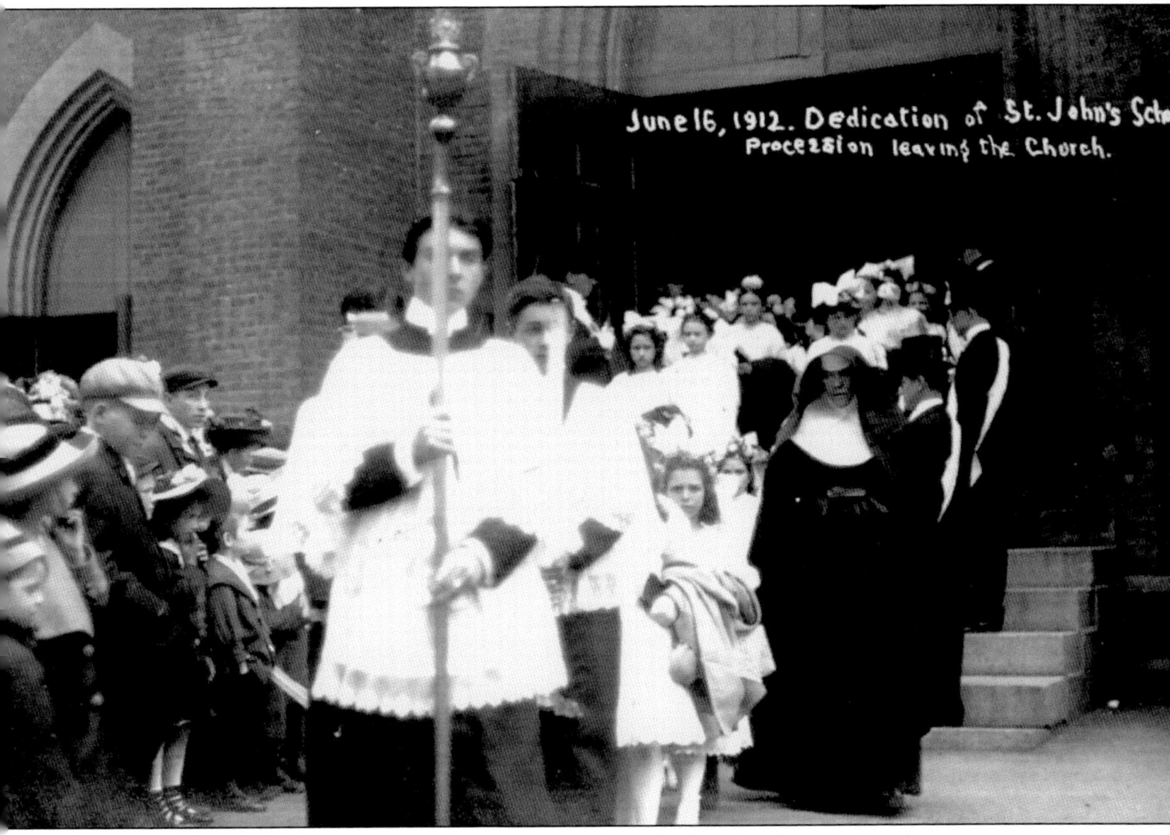

This rare postcard shows the 1912 dedication of St. John's School. An altar boy, numerous children, nuns, and the Knights of Columbus participated in the solemn springtime procession, which proceeded from St. John's Church on York Street to the newly built school on State Street. Newspaper accounts spoke of the Right Reverend Lewis S. Walsh being in attendance.

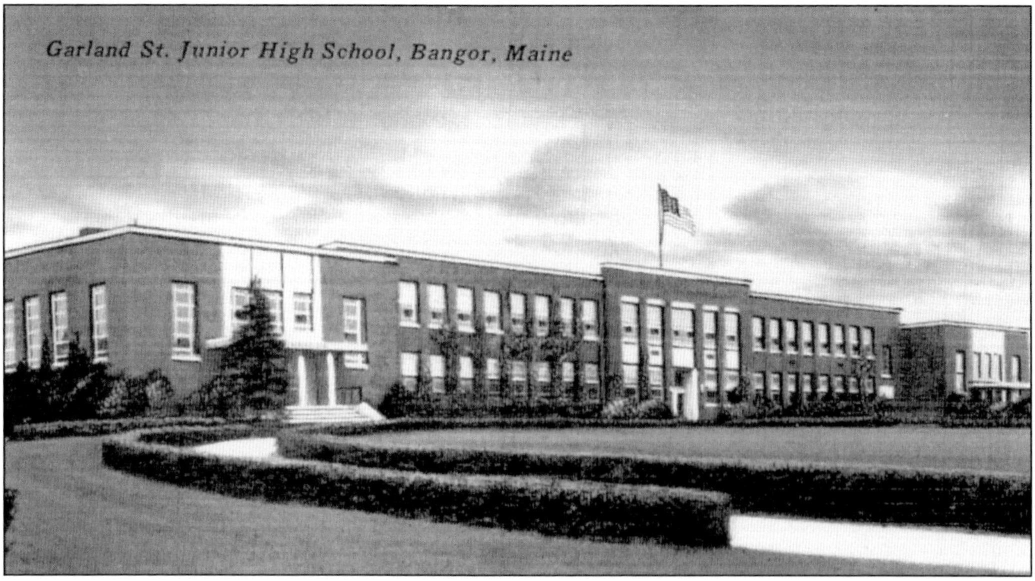

Built in 1939, the Garland Street Junior High School was a remarkable school for its time. The two-year junior high, which included grades seven and eight (a ninth grade was later added), featured a gymnasium on the left side and an auditorium on the right. Male students could take wood and metal shop, and girls could take home economics. Today, this is the modernized and expanded three-year William S. Cohen Middle School, named for perhaps the school's most famous alumnus, who went on to become a U.S. senator and the secretary of defense.

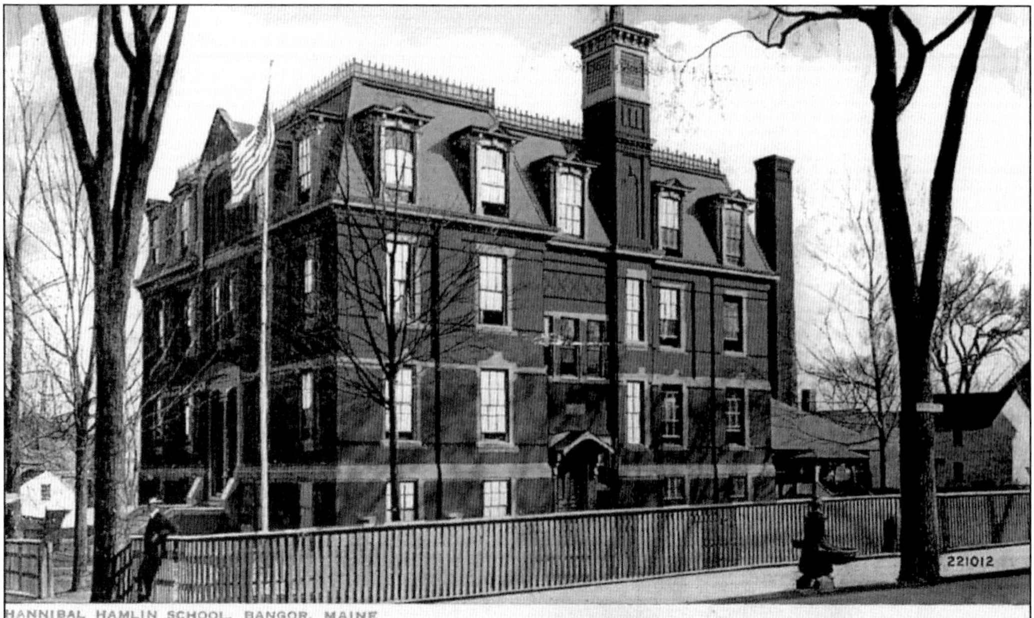

The Hannibal Hamlin School on Union Street was the west side's main elementary school. The square brick building, constructed in 1875, was within walking distance of many neighborhoods, so walking to school began a daily ritual for young students. Originally named the Union Street Grammar School, this landmark was probably renamed when its east side counterpart, the Palm Street School, became the Abraham Lincoln School.

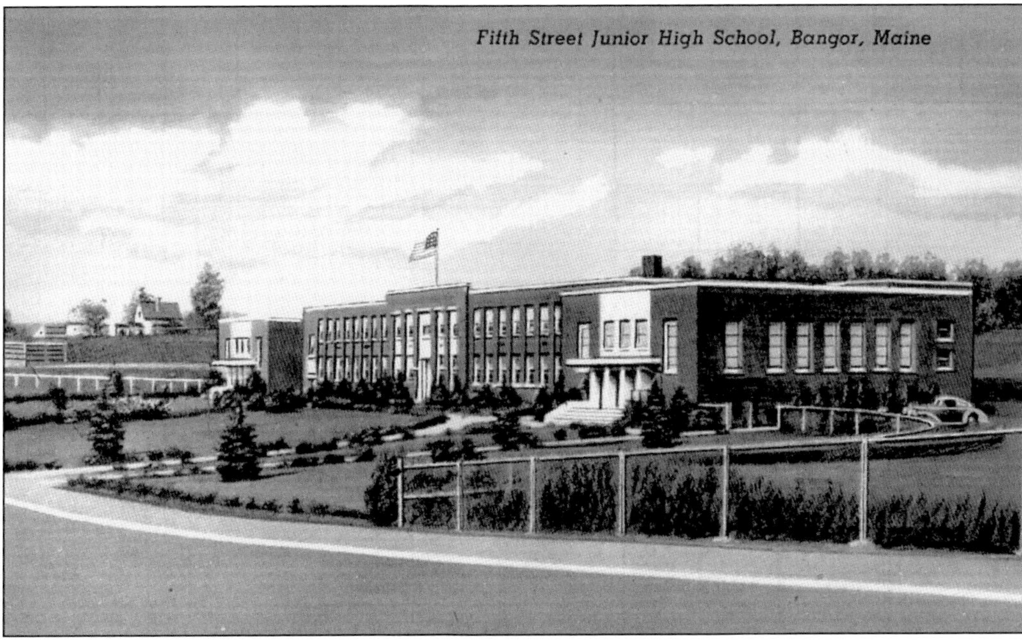

A mirror image of the Garland Street Junior High School, Fifth Street Junior High was the west side's counterpart, as it was virtually identical to its east side twin. Like the Garland Street school, the Fifth Street school is also a middle school including grades six to eight. It was named for a William S. Cohen contemporary named James F. Doughty, who attended this school. Doughty later became superintendent of schools.

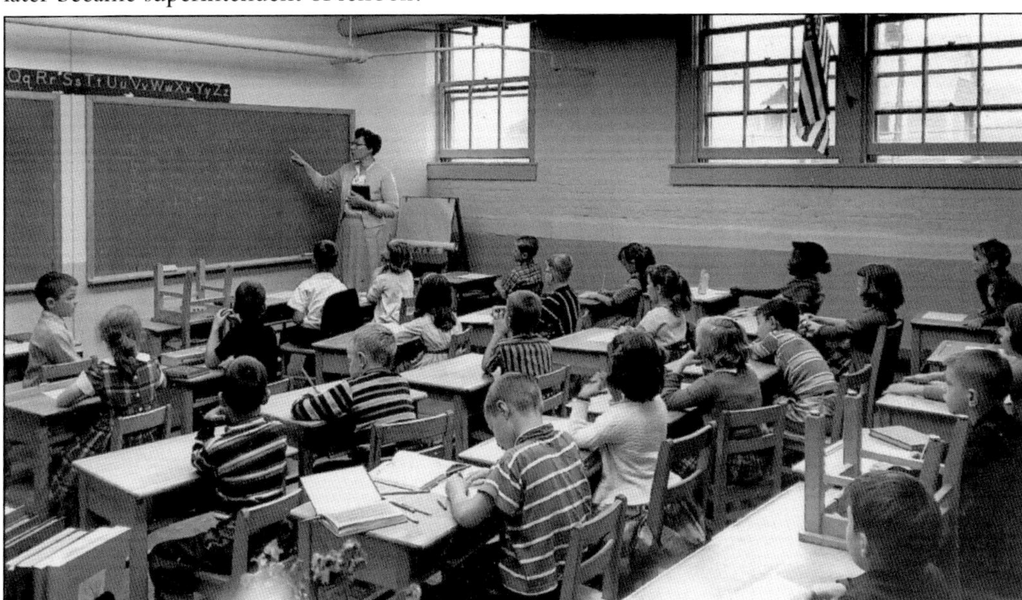

Sometimes Bangor students had to learn in less than ideal environments. Bertha Booker's second-grade classroom at Fairmount School was located in a former basement voting room. The 13th Street elementary school was crowded in 1958, when this *Bangor Daily News* photograph was published. One reason for the crowding may have been the influx of students whose U.S. Air Force fathers were stationed at Dow Field. (BDN.)

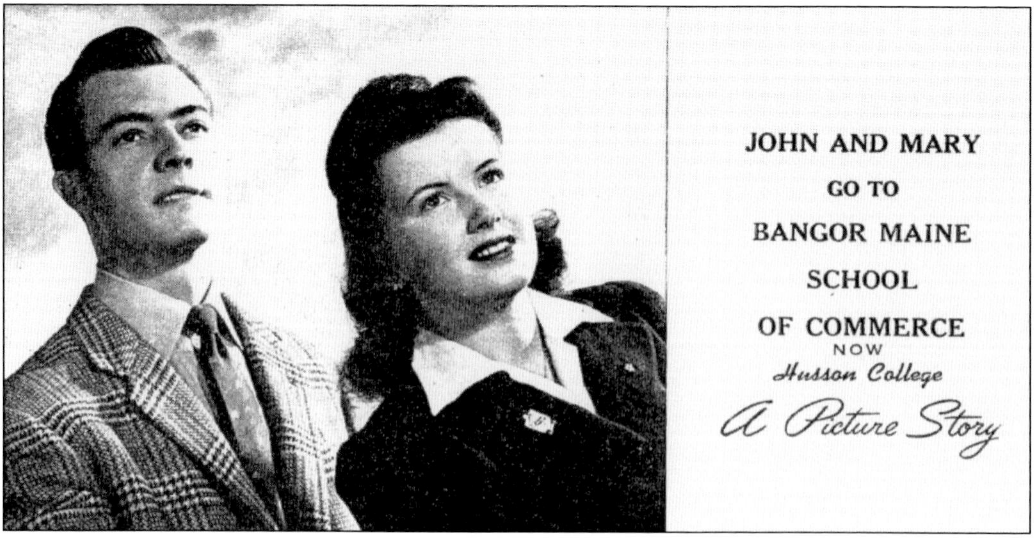

Husson College's roots extend deep and wide in Bangor. Founded as the Maine School of Commerce, it was originally located downtown on Columbia Street. In 1940, it relocated to a new building on Park Street. In 1968, a new campus was built off Kenduskeag Avenue. John and Mary in this *c.* 1949 college "picture story" would have attended the gold-brick building on Park Street, with president and founder Chesley Husson in charge of operations.

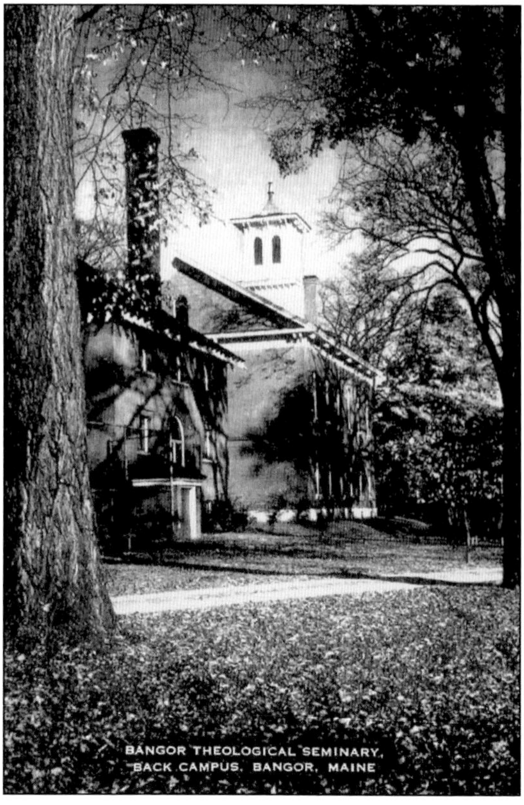

Founded in 1816, the Bangor Theological Seminary is almost as old as the city itself. In fact, it was founded less than 50 years after Bangor's first settler arrived in 1769 and less than 20 years before Bangor received its city charter. The chapel of its Union Street campus has long been a downtown landmark. Its students, by both age and discipline, are very diverse, taking a variety of courses for which they receive college degrees.

Four

Monuments, Parks, and Squares

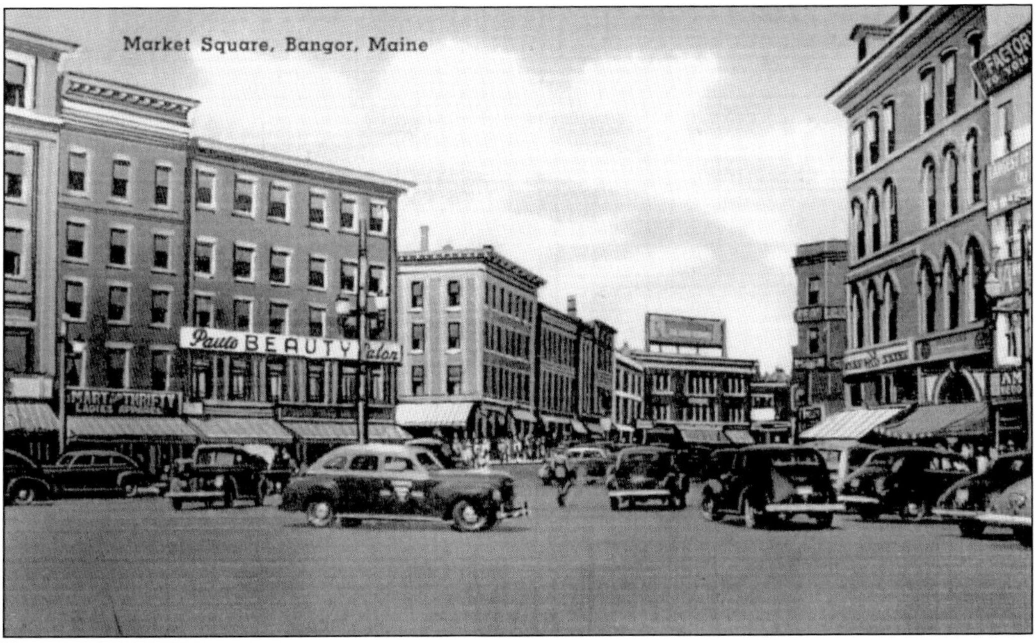

West Market Square is in the very heart of Bangor, squeezed into the junction of Broad and Main Streets. Today, it is lined with The Charles Inn, the Whig and Courier Pub, and the Grasshopper Shop, an emporium housed in the Wheelwright and Clark Block. In the late 1940s, the era of this postcard view, the square was home to clothing and jewelry stores. A modern park with a fountain and sculpture encloses part of the square today.

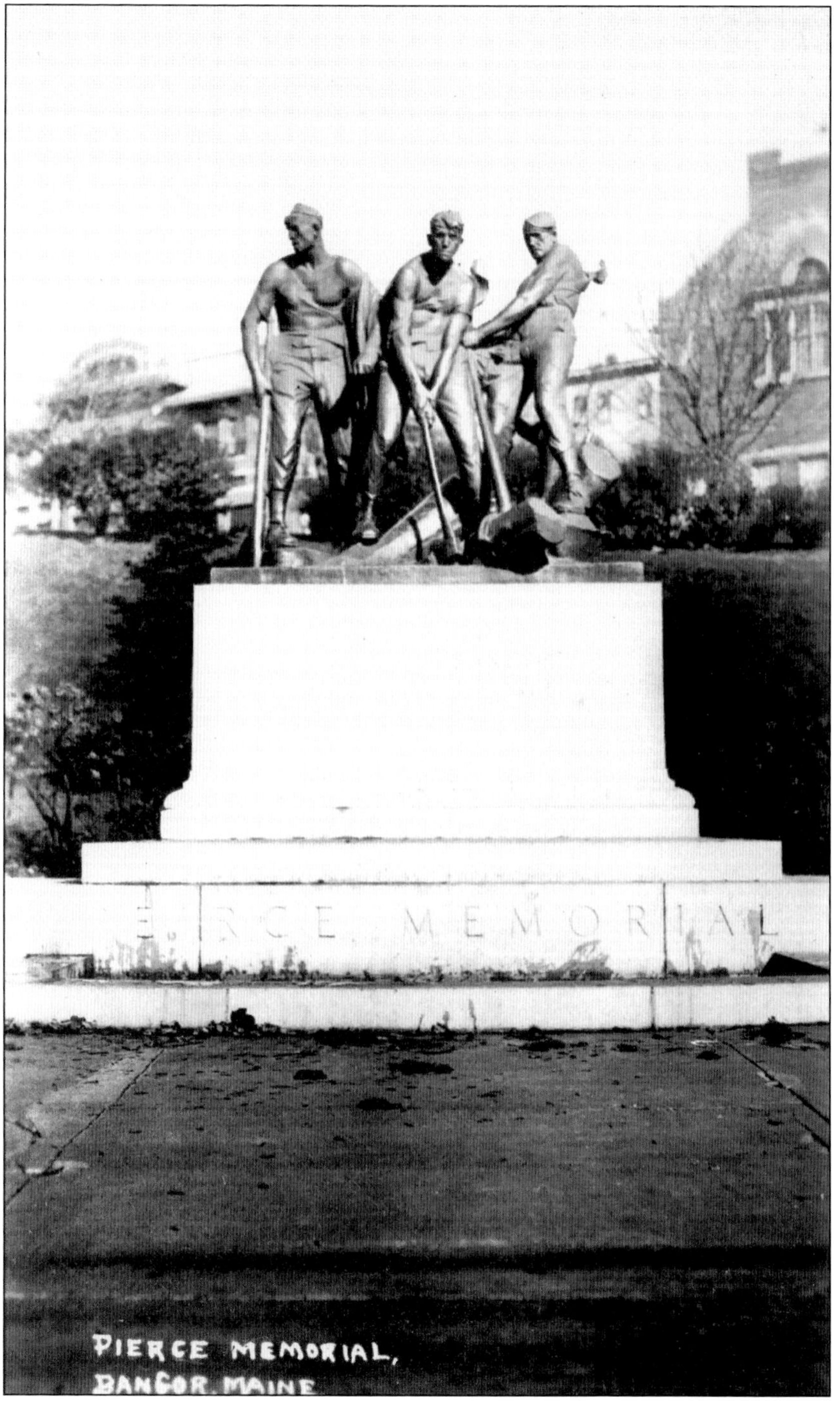

"Unquestionably the finest piece of sculpture in Maine," the late Bangor historian James B. Vickery was fond of saying. Brewer architect Charles Tefft created a graceful, larger-than-life masterpiece in *The River Drivers,* part of the Pierce (or Peirce) Memorial on Harlow Street next to the public library. Tefft hired actual Penobscot log drivers into service as they posed for his sculpture, dedicated in 1925. (BPL.)

Sculptor Tefft also created this bronze statue of statesman Hannibal Hamlin, which has stood proud on the Kenduskeag Mall since its dedication in 1927. Tefft used to say that he wanted to capture Hamlin, a former U.S. senator and vice president under Abraham Lincoln, in full stride, as he looked while marching in a parade. Pranksters used to steal his cane, but that does not happen now, as it was welded into place. This postcard pictures a young visitor by the statue and shows its true scale.

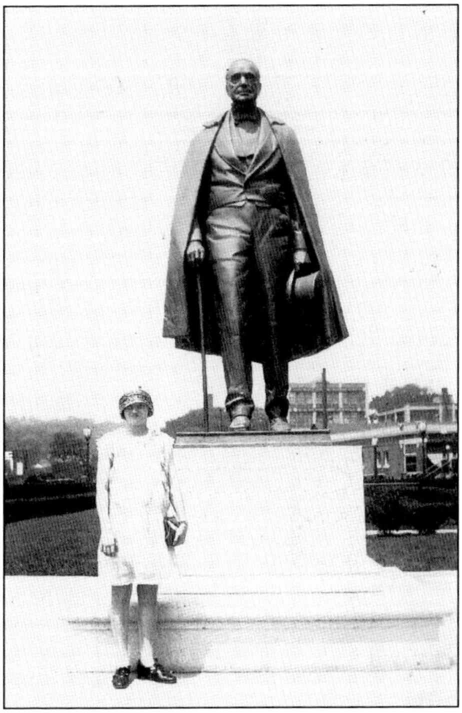

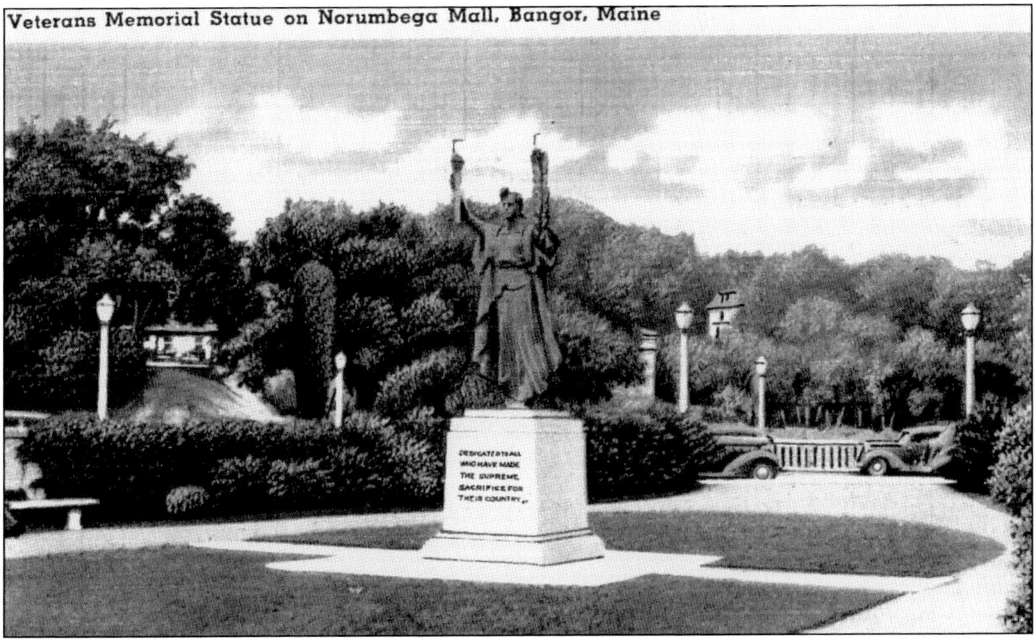

The third of Tefft's downtown sculptures is a veterans memorial titled *Victory*. Dedicated in 1939, it is reminiscent of the Statue of Liberty, but this female holds both arms in the air, bearing lighted torches. Located on Norumbega Mall downtown, the statue answered the needs of a local populace that was thinking again of war as storm clouds mounted in Europe and Asia. As with his other creations, Tefft employed an actual model after which to fashion his larger-than-life sculpture.

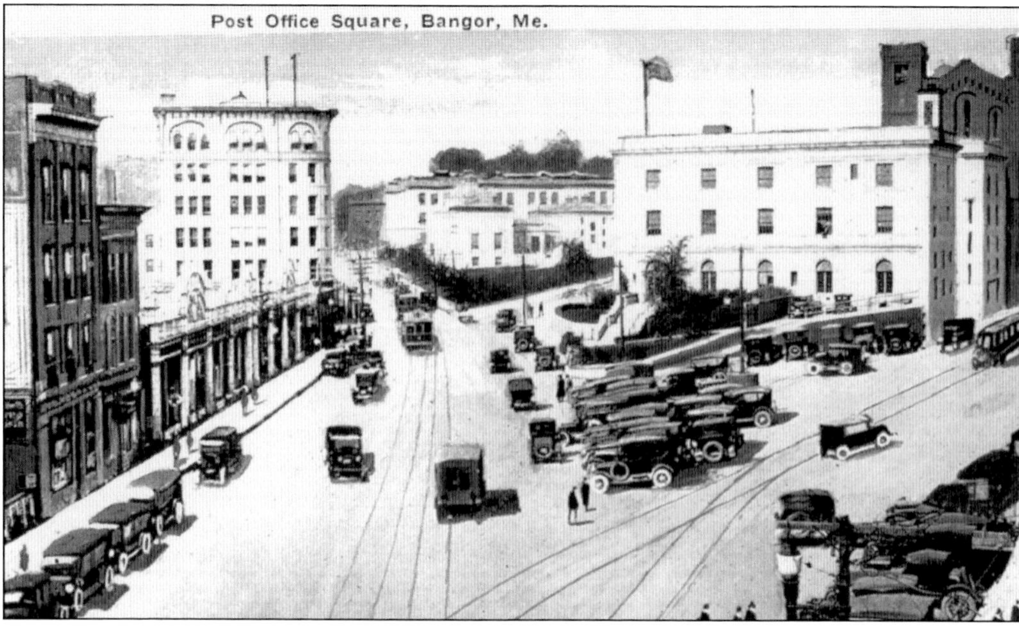

Remove the 1920s-vintage cars and the streetcar tracks and this scene of Post Office Square might have been taken today. The only difference is that few residents call it by that name anymore, since the post office moved out of the large granite building on the right and the city hall moved in. Sears Roebuck and Company occupied the long, low, fancy building on the left long before it left downtown and moved to the Bangor Mall.

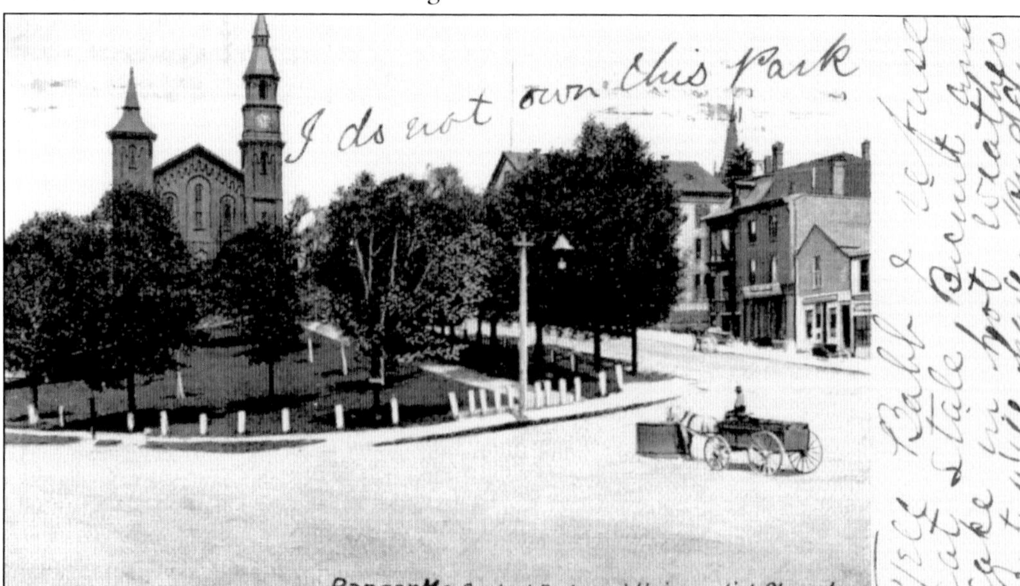

Before there was Post Office Square, this square was known as Central Park. A "punch-bowl" watering trough was a welcome oasis for horses and other livestock in 1910, one year before the great fire gutted the brick Universalist church (see page 105) in the background. It was rebuilt, but with smaller steeples. A wooden bandstand just out of range of this postcard view was a lively place on holidays and during political campaigns. The Bangor Band performed there numerous times, and presidential candidate James G. Blaine of Maine stumped there in 1884.

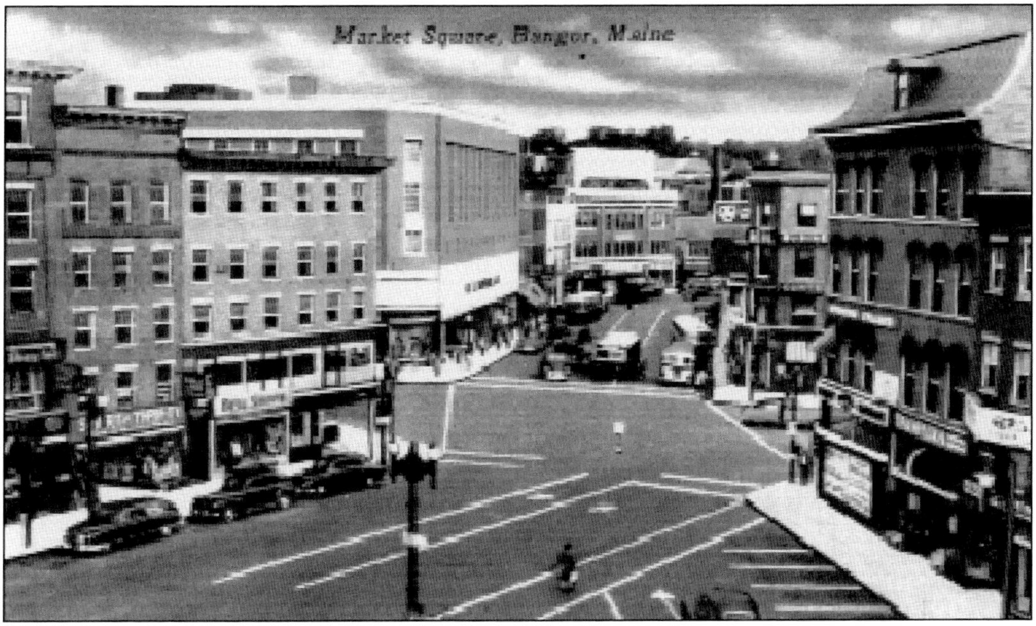

An elevated view of West Market Square shows the new W. T. Grant department store block at Hammond and Central Streets and the buildings lining Central Street in the distance. Four streets converge on this square, making for some interesting traffic squabbles in the days when Bangor traffic cop John "Mittens" Burke stood in a high booth and directed traffic. In recent years West Market Square has experienced a renaissance. Many buildings have had facelifts.

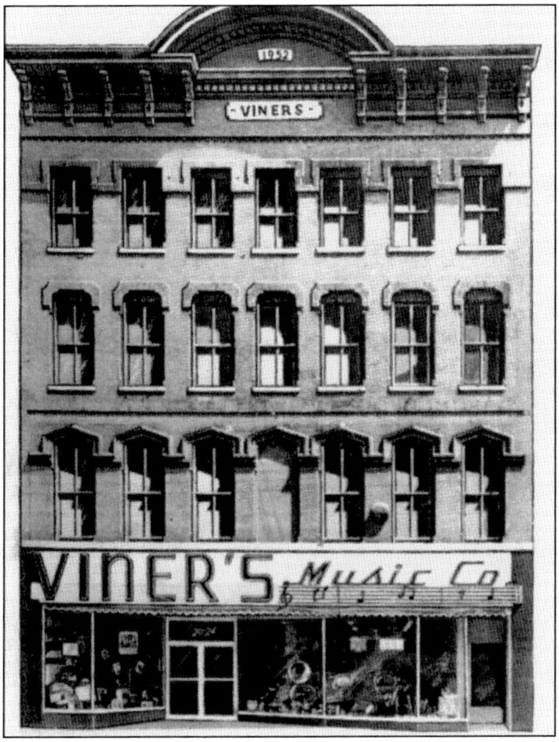

Sam Viner and his family loved to demonstrate musical instruments, and the latest televisions and stereos, at Viner's Music Company, located on West Market Square. In the 1930s, Viner sold shoes manufactured by his family, along with music and instruments across the street in a walkup store. It was quite a step up when the family bought the Phenix Block on Broad Street. In the 1960s, record buyers spent hours poring over the latest Beatles and Rolling Stones LPs.

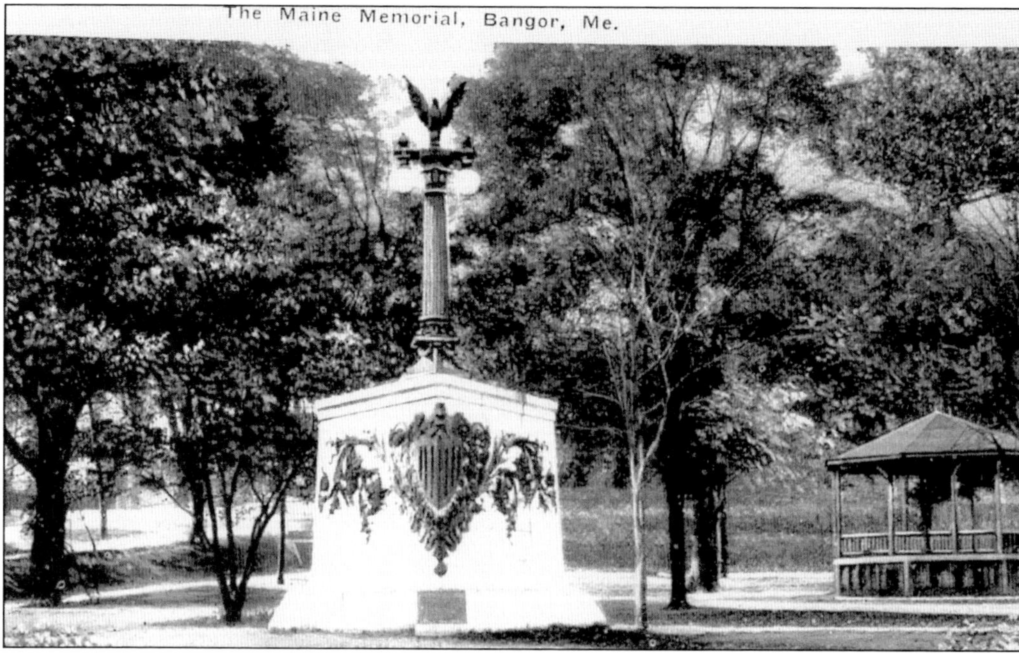

The USS *Maine* memorial is located in Davenport Park at the corner of Main and Cedar Streets. Dedicated in 1922, the stone base displays the shield and scrollwork removed from the battleship that exploded in Havana harbor in 1898. The Spanish-American War began soon afterward as a result of this tragedy, now believed to have been the result of an accident. Wreath-laying ceremonies are held here at the recently renovated park and monument each year on Memorial Day and February 15, the anniversary of the tragedy that killed 266 men.

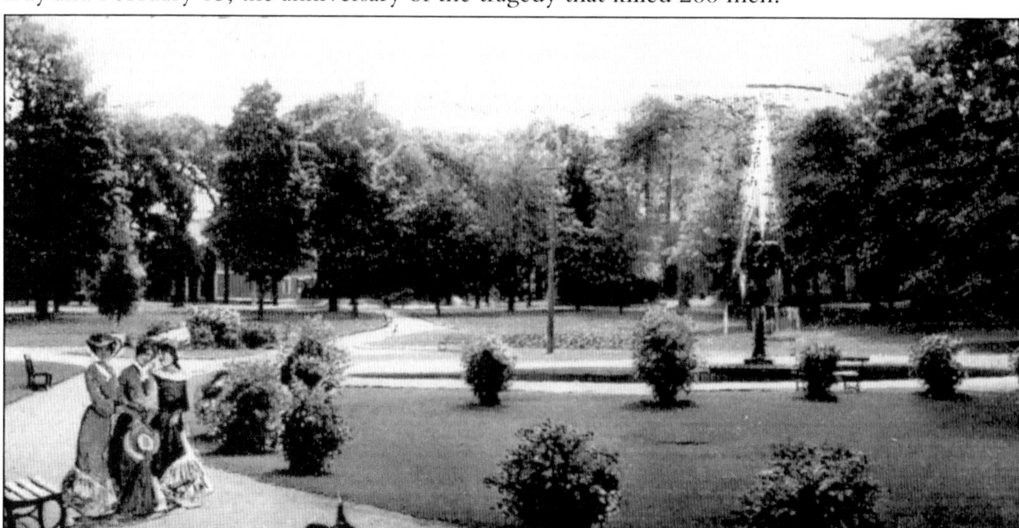

Chapin Park dates to the 1830s, when architect Charles G. Bryant designed a city common to enhance the growing east side neighborhood. An iron fountain provided a centerpiece in the park. While those seen here were drawn on to the postcard, people and their pets still enjoy strolling through the well-manicured park. Each summer the Bangor Band hosts a block party here, sponsored by Miller Drug, Frank's Bakeshop, and other area businesses. Ice cream is served, music is played, and people see old friends again, just like in the old days.

This two-block grassy median has separated lower Broadway since Bangor's earliest days. Earlier photographs show men shaking hands in the middle of the strip while standing under a canopy of elms that, before succumbing to Dutch elm disease, stretched from State to Somerset Streets. The width of Maple Street, West Broadway, and other neighborhood streets suggests city planners once envisioned grassy medians there, too, but abandoned the idea, perhaps because of cost and changing tastes. Dunning Boulevard off Union Street contains the city's only other median.

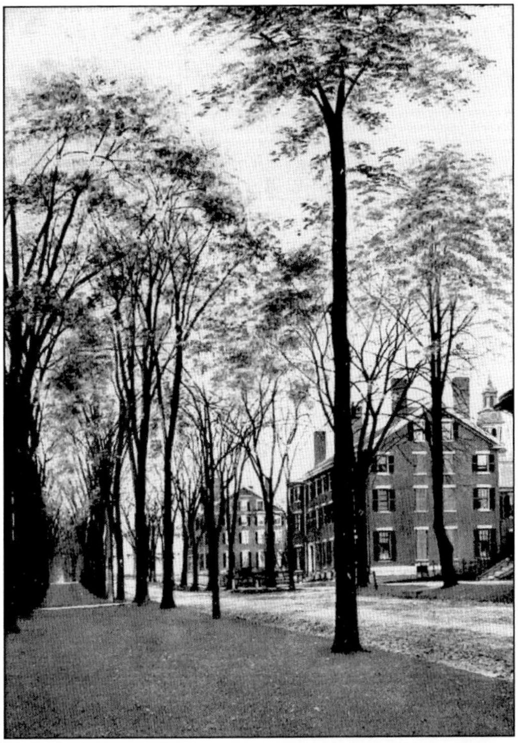

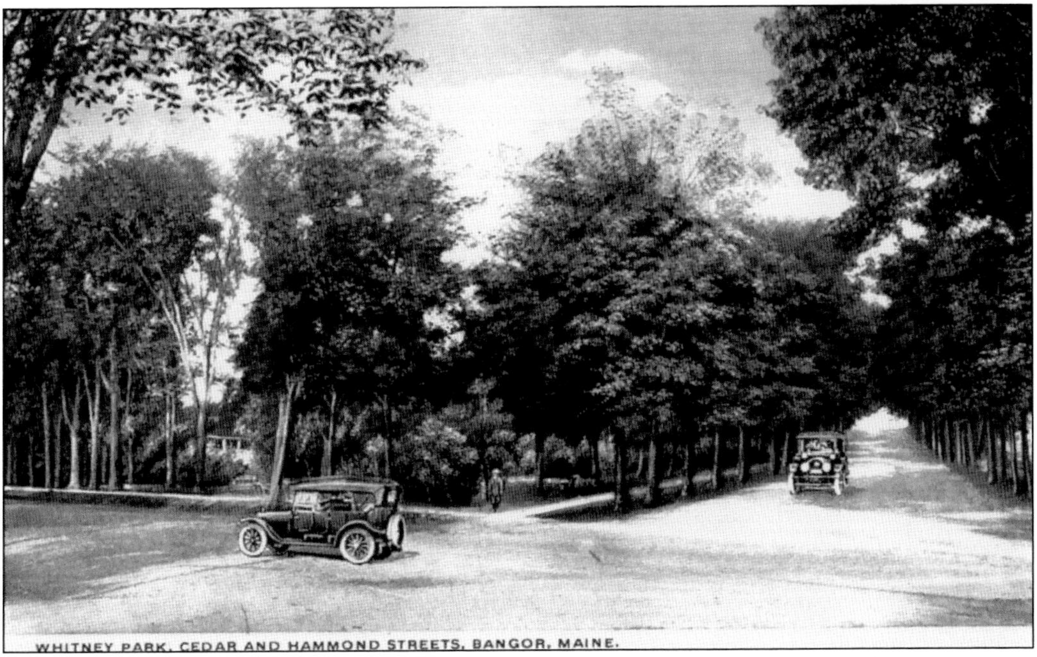

Whitney Park is a small, pie-shaped piece of greenery located at the corner of Hammond and Cedar Streets. This 1920 postcard view is remarkable because of the many trees that have long since been taken down and the phony cars that were superimposed in a studio to add movement to the picture. Some of the same vehicles crop up in local views. Most people never caught on to the joke.

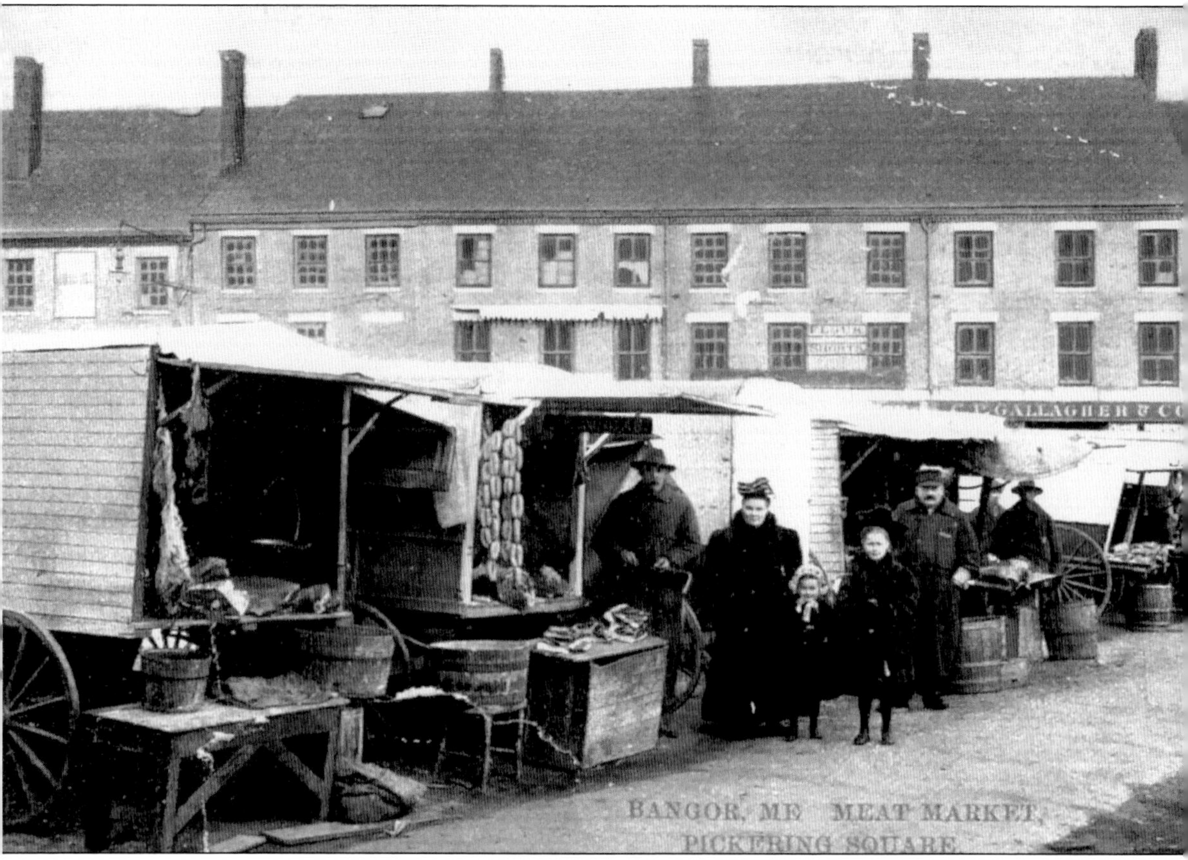

If you lived in Bangor a century ago, this would have been a common sight in Pickering Square, the city marketplace located between Main and Broad Streets. Every day before the sun rose, meat and poultry merchants drove their horse-drawn market wagons into the city center, opened up the rears, and hung out their merchandise. The men, women, and children in this early postcard view seem to be advertising their meat products. Note the sausage hanging from one wagon and the wooden barrels standing up at the end of others. The building in the background was the ancient flatiron block, which was razed in the 1960s during urban renewal demolition. Today, Pickering Square, named for prominent merchant George Pickering, is the site of the multilevel Pickering Square parking garage and a modern brick courtyard with a waterfall. The tiny Midget Lunch, a long-ago doughnut and breakfast shop that opened in the wee hours of the morning, and the first Pine Tree Restaurant were located in Pickering Square. Both catered to the early-morning meat, poultry, and vegetable merchants who wanted a hot, nutritious meal for a dime or maybe a quarter.

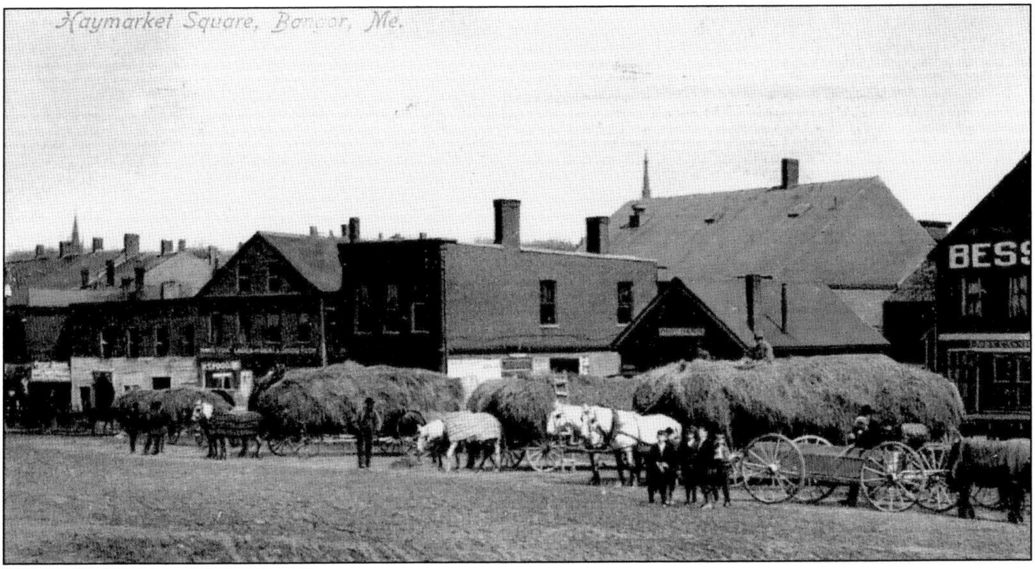

Hay wagons filled nearly to overflowing were common sights on Haymarket Square next to Pickering Square. This card, postmarked 1910, shows horses, hay, wagons, and the people who drove the wagons. Also shown are the long vanished sheds and offices that once hugged the square. Long forgotten by most residents today, the Haymarket Square site is the approximate location of today's Key Plaza bank complex.

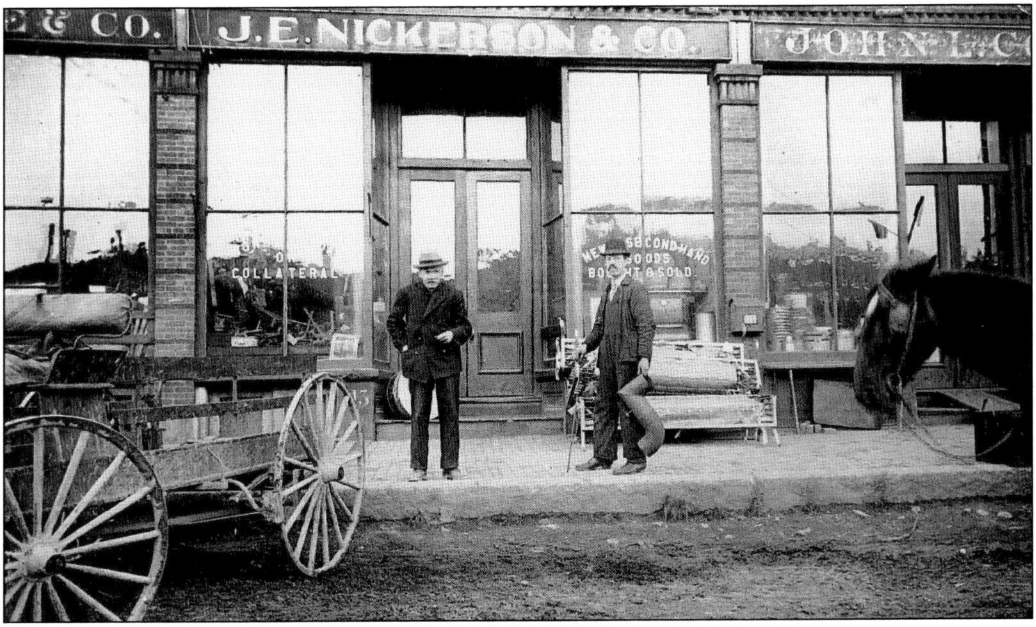

J. Edgar Nickerson was an enterprising merchant who sold new and secondhand furniture in a store located at 113 Pickering Square. This real-photo postcard, selected from the James B. Vickery postcard collection at the Bangor Public Library, dates from *c.* 1919. Nickerson's storefront windows mention collateral and that the owner bought and sold furniture. The wagon on the left seems to have been backed up to the granite curbing for either a delivery or a purchase. (BPL.)

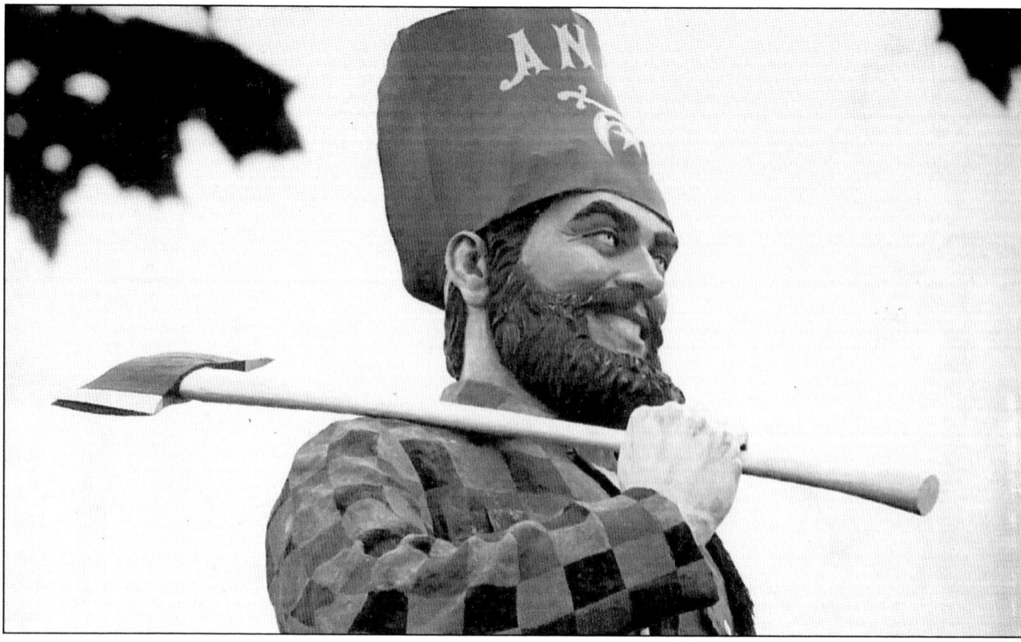

Since 1959, the Paul Bunyan statue at Bass Park on Main Street has stood watch over passing traffic and curious photographers. Sometime in the 1960s, the Anah Temple Shrine, based in Bangor, imagined how the mythical lumberjack would look in a fez. So, up went a worker on a cherry picker who slipped one on, intending to advertise a Shriners gathering in Bangor. Later, the statue was adorned with a king-sized bandana to publicize an upcoming Willie Nelson concert. Several years later, the city council nixed a local radio station's scheme to adorn Bunyan with one of their T-shirts to tout a Don Imus radio program broadcast live from the nearby Bangor Civic Center. (BDN.)

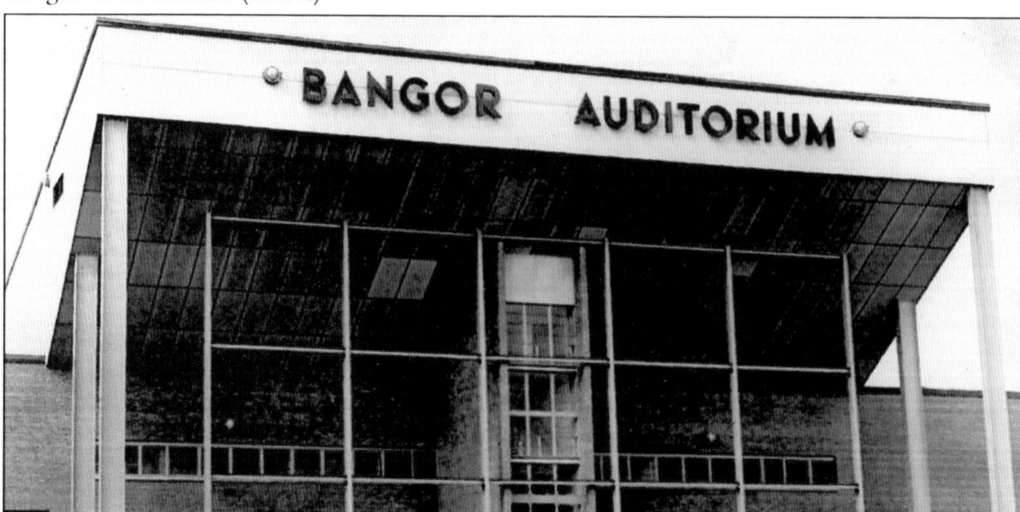

With its inverted roof and poor acoustics, the Bangor Auditorium, opened in 1955 in Bass Park, has been the butt of many jokes. But few can argue that the city did not get its money's worth after the 6,700-seat auditorium was completed. Many have enjoyed a basketball tournament in this building, or perhaps a Bob Dylan or Jethro Tull concert. Ice-skaters also enjoyed weekend activities here. (BDN.)

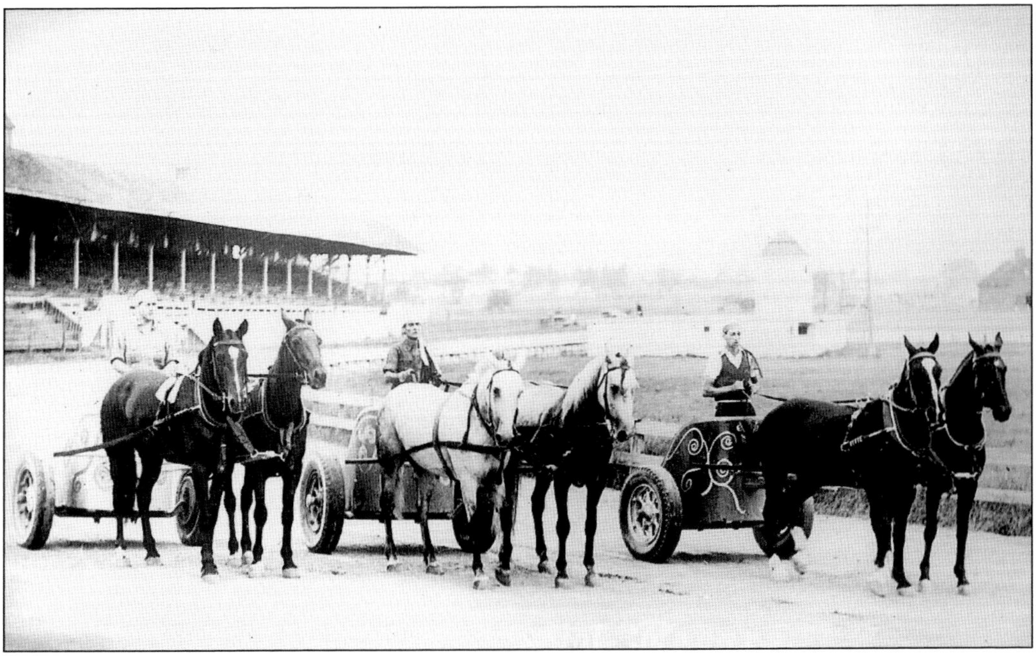

This rare real-photo postcard pictures an undated Ben-Hur chariot race at Maplewood (now Bass) Park. Note the three chariots and the old wooden grandstand in the background. The racers had a ready-made audience since crowds packed the old Bangor Opera House in 1904 for a live performance of *Ben-Hur.* A revolving stage that brought actors, horses, and chariots whizzing past the audience was an immediate sensation. (BPL.)

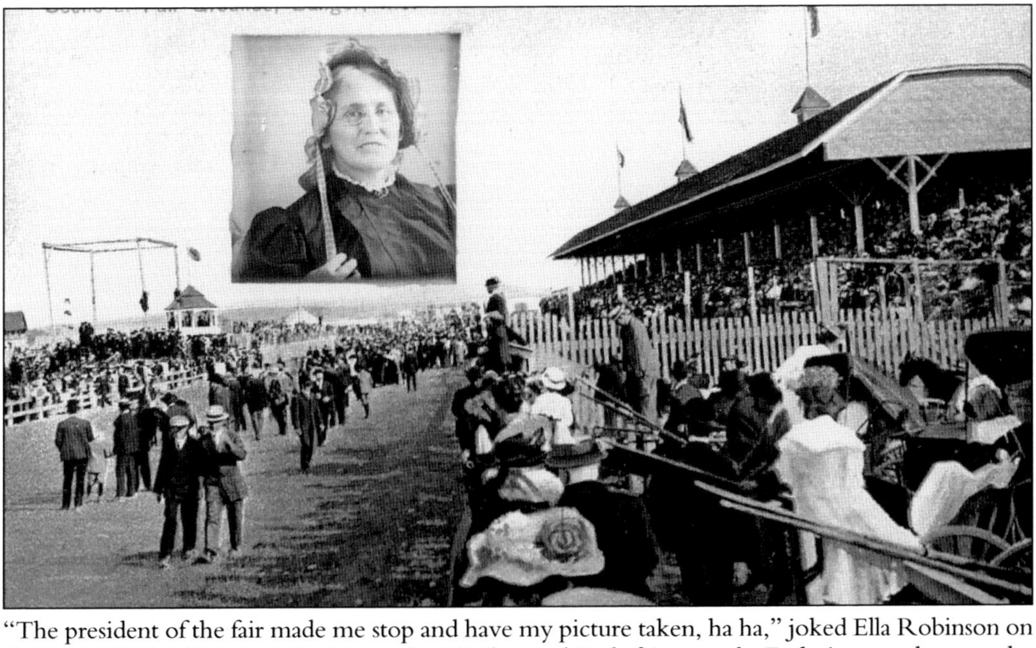

"The president of the fair made me stop and have my picture taken, ha ha," joked Ella Robinson on the back of this old postcard taken at the Maplewood Park fairgrounds. Early instant photography made possible a carry-out postcard made right on the spot. Harness racing is still held at Bass Park, along with a summertime fair that draws large crows from northern and eastern Maine.

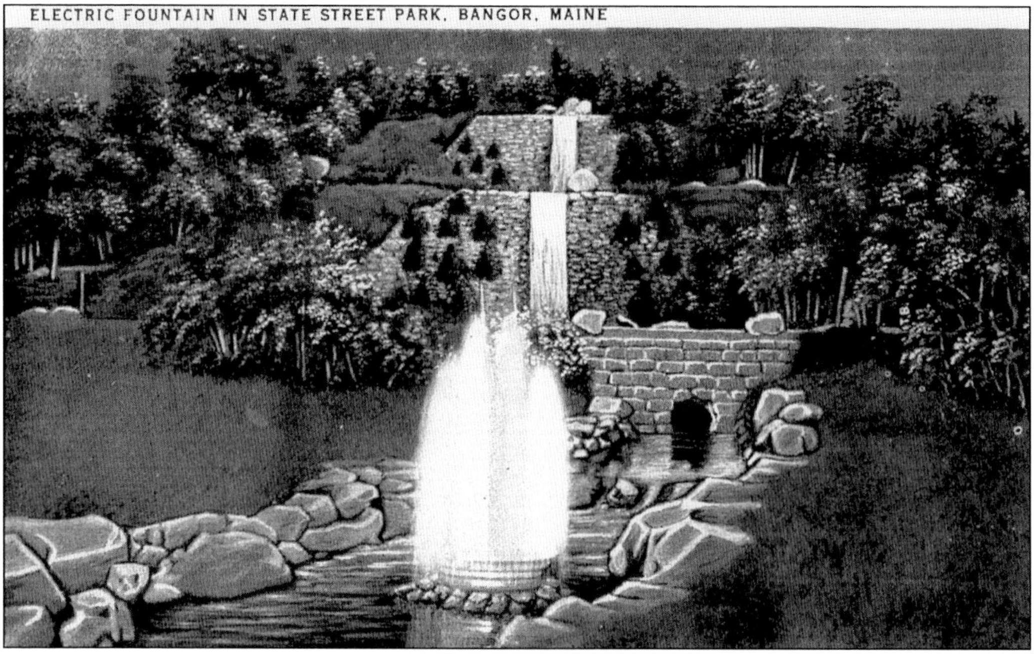

The lighted waterfall and fountain at Grotto Cascade Park have enchanted children and adults since the little park was opened in the early 1930s. Located on State Street across from the Bangor waterworks, the park fell into disrepair in the early 1990s but was renovated and reopened sometime later. Weddings and picnics are regular activities here, along with a Labor Day festival.

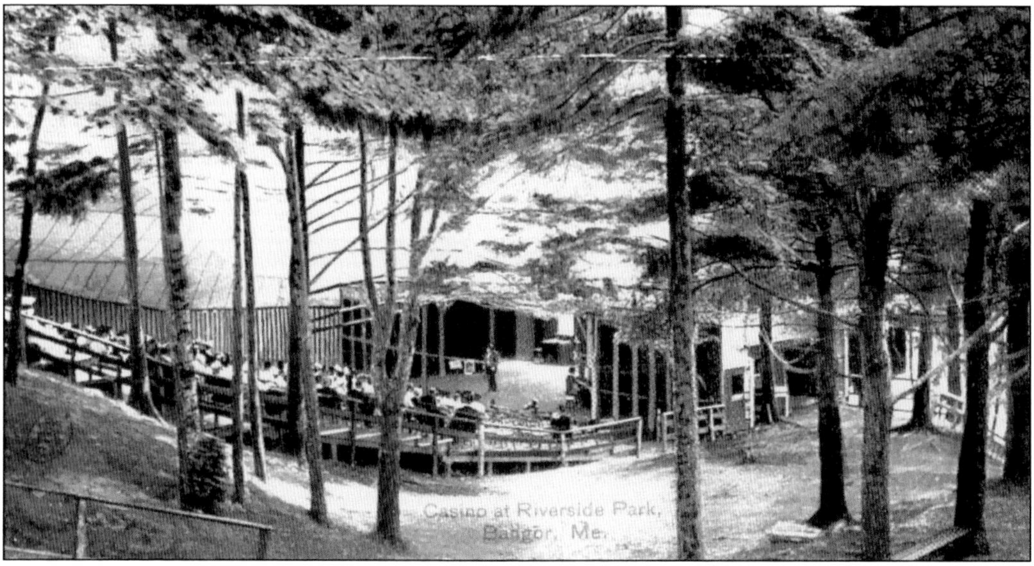

Riverside Park was located not far from Bangor in neighboring Hampden. With its natural amphitheater, pine trees, and river frontage, Riverside was an instant hit with summer enthusiasts. Buster Brown variety shows were favorites here, along with fresh-roasted peanuts and popcorn. Like many amusement parks in America in the late 19th century, Riverside was owned by the local street railway company, which provided free admission if one paid a nominal fee to ride to the park in an open-air trolley.

Five

Kenduskeag Stream Attractions

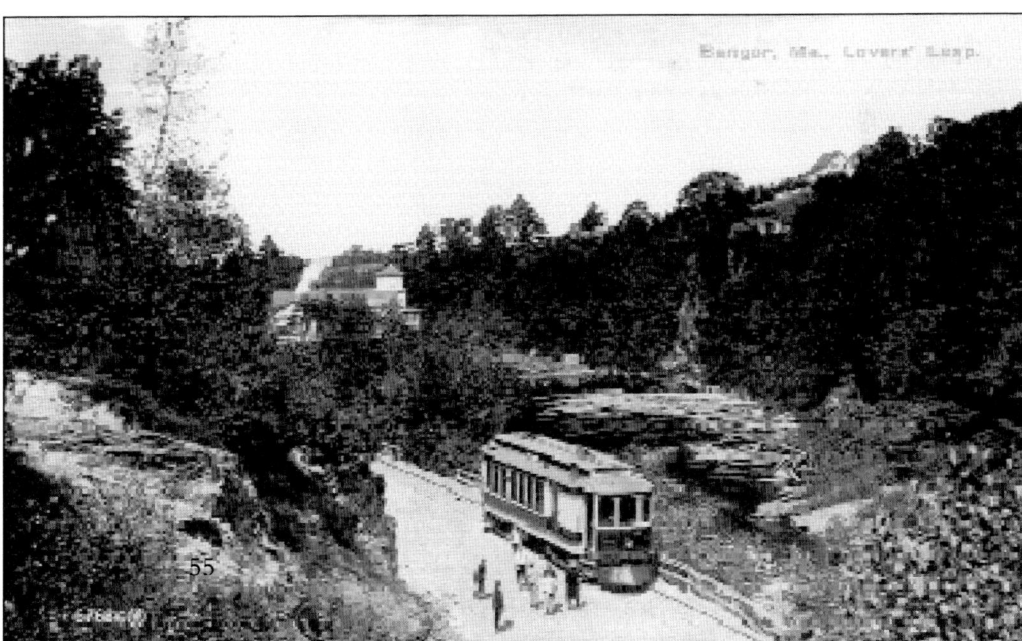

Did you ever wish you could transport yourself back in time, if only for a day, or take a trolley ride along Valley Avenue, a quiet, picturesque place even today? Trolleys carried passengers through two covered bridges over the Kenduskeag Stream as far as Corinth and Charleston, 26 miles to the north. Note the pulpwood and Maxfield tannery in the background. High above the scene are buildings located on Kenduskeag Avenue.

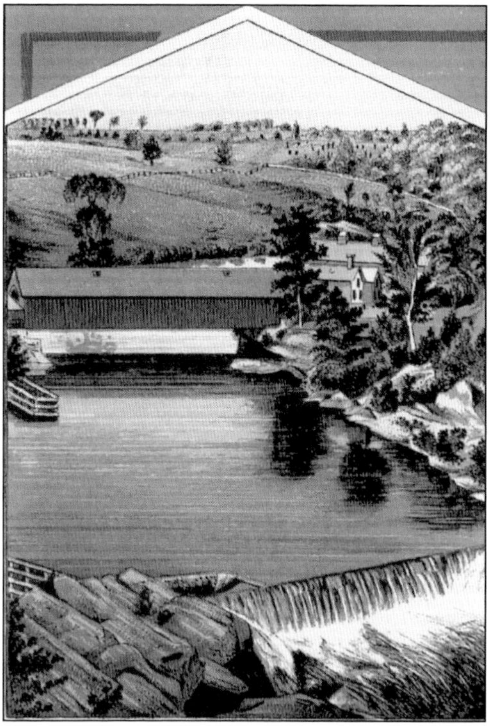

This Victorian-era view shows the Maxfield covered bridge and dam on the Kenduskeag Stream. The romanticized picture shows a crystal-clear stream when in reality it was badly polluted by the nearby Maxfield tannery, which also fouled the air. Maxfield's was a single-span bridge, with no support between the two abutments on the shore. Like nearby Morse's Mill, Maxfield's tannery had its own covered bridge; it just was not as long as Morse's. The bridge pictured here was destroyed by fire in 1944.

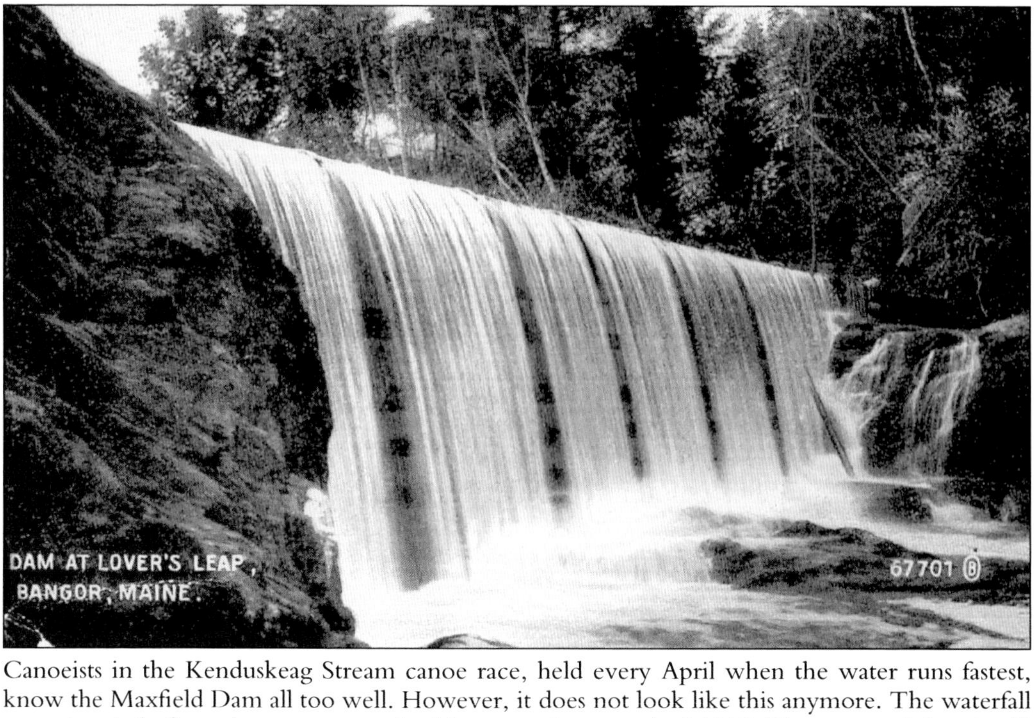

Canoeists in the Kenduskeag Stream canoe race, held every April when the water runs fastest, know the Maxfield Dam all too well. However, it does not look like this anymore. The waterfall scene is strictly from the past, as seen in this postcard postmarked 1919. The removed dam is still a dangerous prospect for springtime canoeists. It marks one of several portages that have them scrambling across Valley Avenue, trying not to waste time.

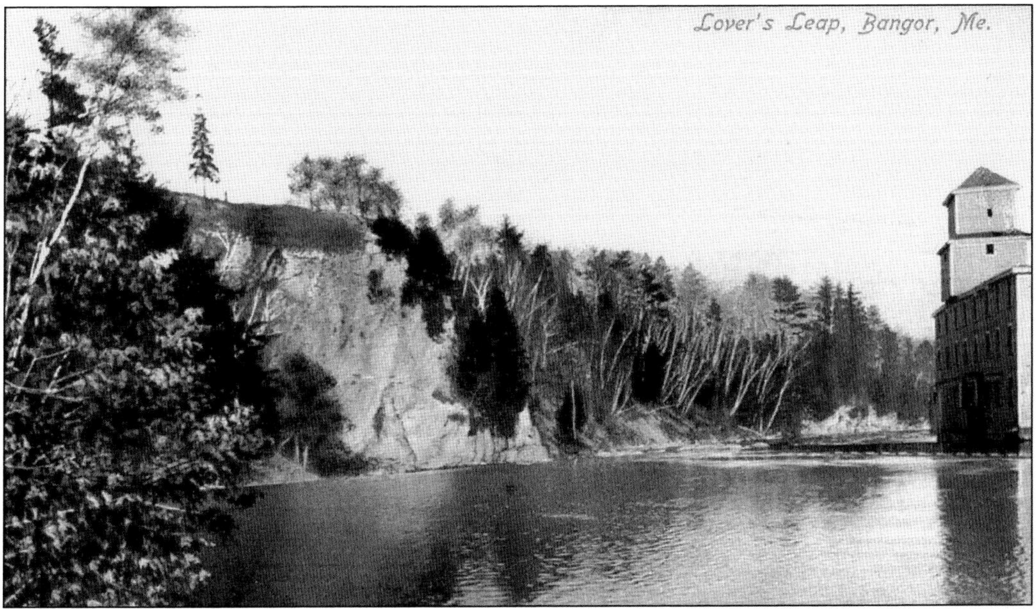

Lover's Leap and a corner of Maxfield's Mill helped to frame this postcard view, taken *c.* 1912. Because of its proximity to downtown and its rural flavor, the Kenduskeag Stream in this vicinity has long been sought by couples and others who might appreciate the history of the area. The city has built a walking and jogging path from downtown past the Maxfield Dam property. There are also picnic spots for a lunch on a sunny day.

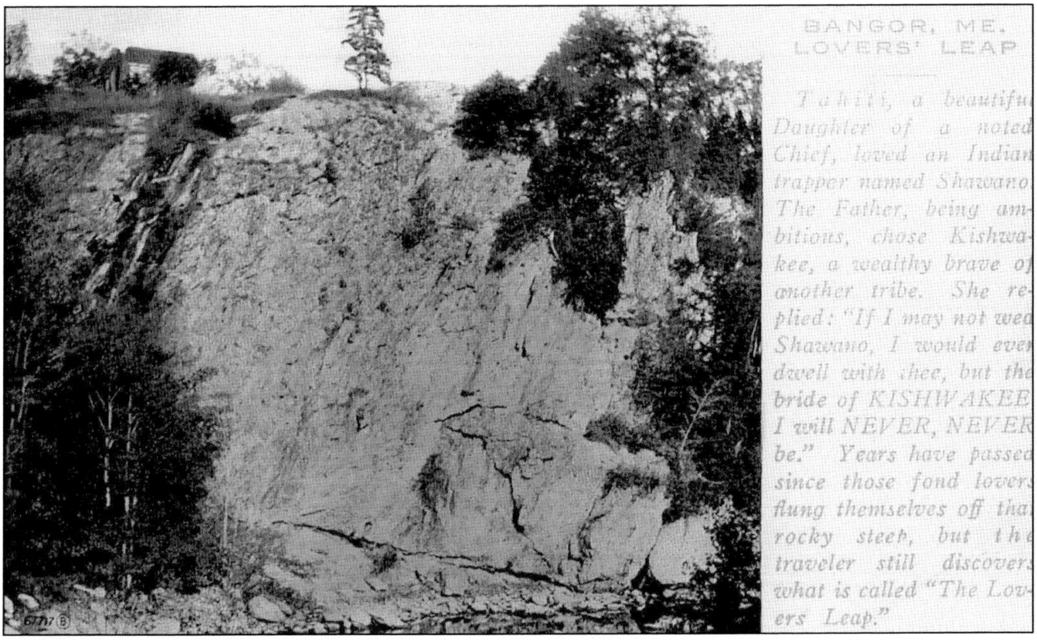

The legend of Lover's Leap is pure fiction, but romanticists ate it up in another era, even commemorating the story on a *c.* 1915 postcard. Tahiti and Shawano, star-crossed Indian lovers, joined hands and leapt to their death over this craggy streamside cliff when Tahiti's father shunned the romance. "They're not even Indian names!" scoffed historian James B. Vickery whenever the story arose.

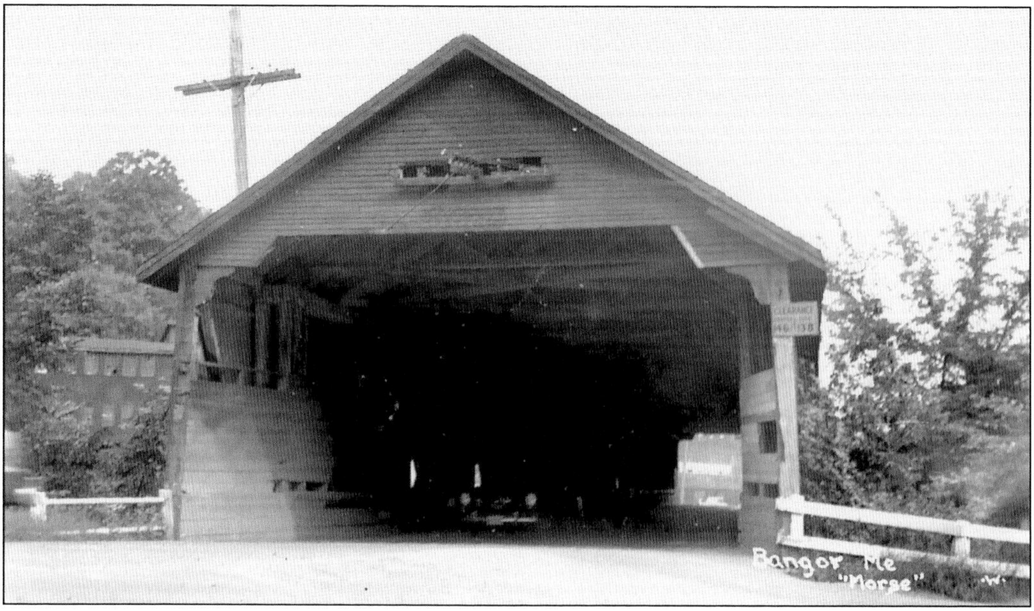

Just as the S. A. Maxfield tannery had its covered bridge spanning the Kenduskeag Stream, the Morse and Company lumber business had its own bridge as well. Older city residents may remember driving or walking through this two-span, 212-foot bridge that connected Harlow Street with Valley Avenue close to the Maxfield mill. In the 19th century, Maxfield millworkers drove herds of sheep to their slaughter through Morse's bridge, giving rise to the long forgotten nickname "the bridge of sighs."

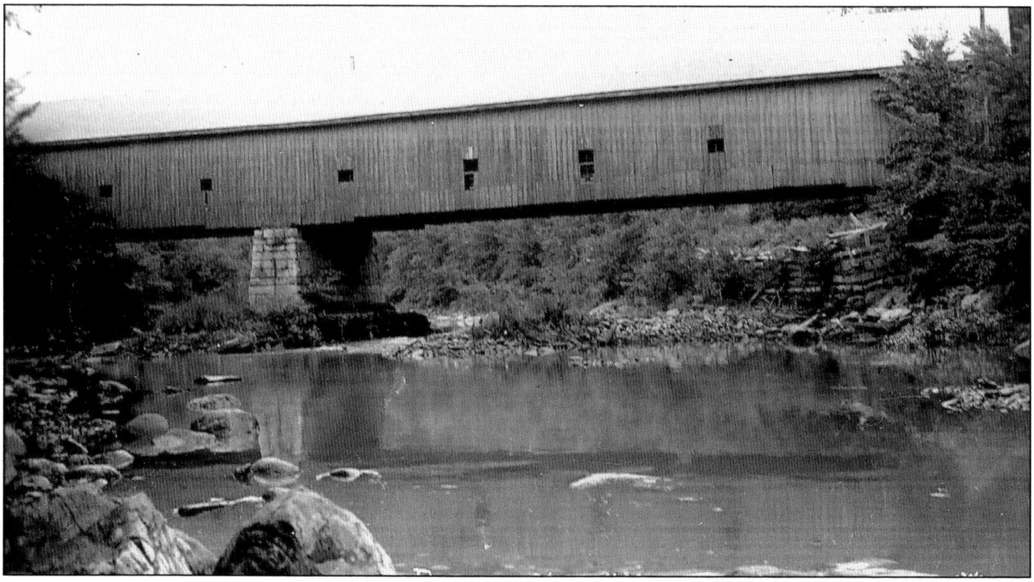

A side view from the 1940s shows the picturesque Morse's bridge. Built in 1884 near the millworks of Llewellyn J. Morse, this bridge served the city until 1961, when the Maine Department of Transportation oversaw its removal and the replacement of a modern steel bridge. A citywide preservation drive raised money to preserve the bridge, and it was eventually reassembled downstream behind buildings off Harlow Street. Its long life came to an end one night in 1983, when the structure was destroyed by fire.

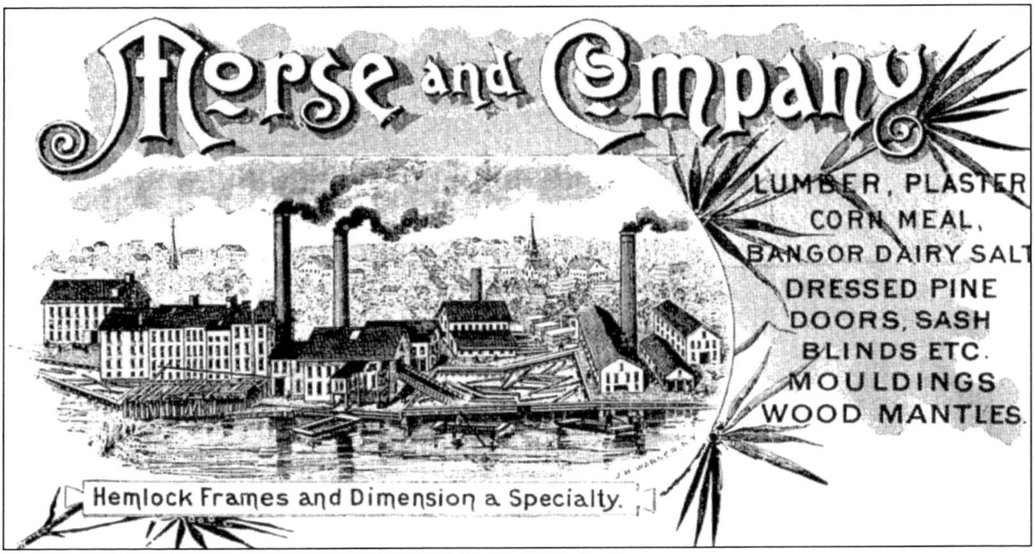

Workers at Morse and Company on the westerly end of Harlow Street used to say their mill buildings, totaling 48, stretched a mile along both sides of the Kenduskeag Stream. Old advertisements picturing its tall smokestacks and streamside activity dated to the years immediately following the mill's founding. Fancy wooden doors, sashes, molding, and other items were manufactured here until the late 1940s, when the business shut down.

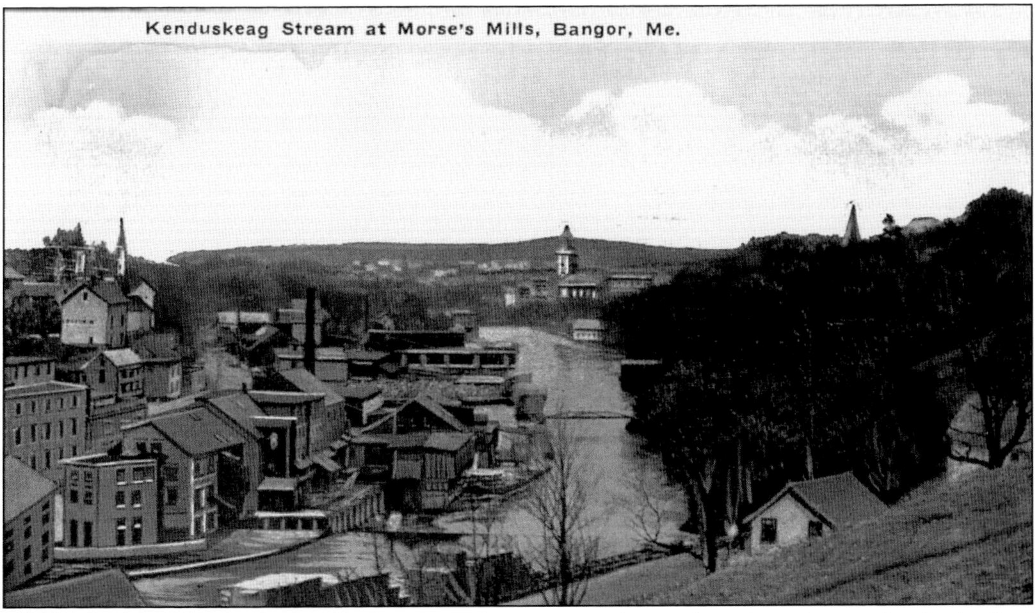

This hand-tinted postcard, postmarked April 26, 1937, shows the Morse's complex in its final years of full production. Taken from the steep hill on Nelson Street, the scene shows the tightly packed brick and wooden buildings that lined the stream. An easy walk from downtown, Morse and Company was known nationally for its quality workmanship and professional sales staff. Barely visible is one of only two surviving Morse buildings (left center). It is the two-story 1895 office and showroom building at 45 Harlow Street. In 2003, Jean Deighan, an investment adviser, lawyer, and historic preservationist, purchased and restored the unique two-story building and made it her business headquarters.

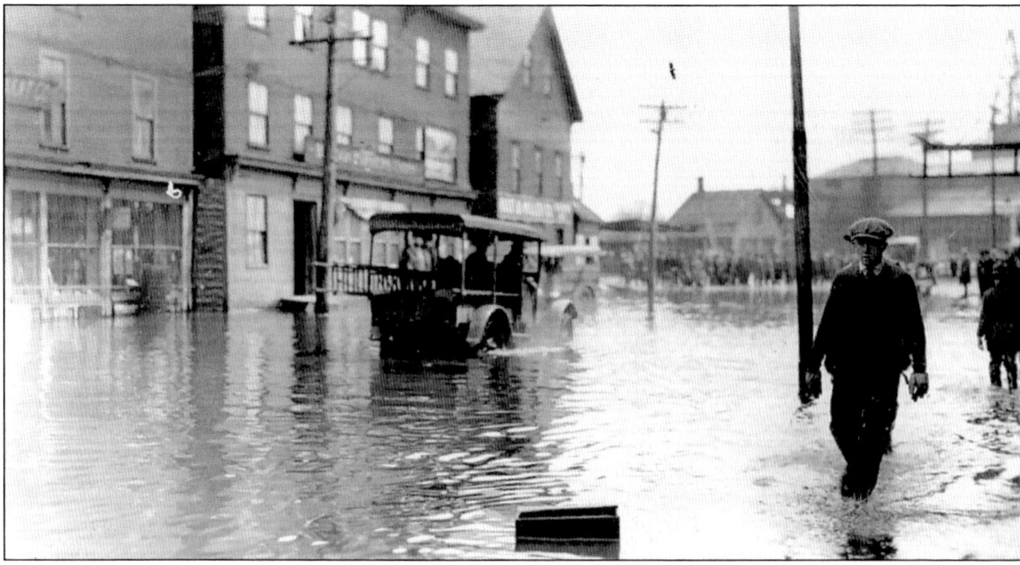

Kenduskeag Stream waters have not always been smooth and tranquil. This real-photo postcard pictures high water from spring flooding in 1923. A teenage boy slogs through the brackish water on lower Broad Street while an open truck maneuvers the disaster scene with water halfway up its hubcaps. The Penobscot River flooded that same year, as it had in 1846 and 1902. Blocks of ice made river and stream water frigid during March and April flooding, but in true Bangor fashion, merchants and shoppers got on with their lives as the waters receded.

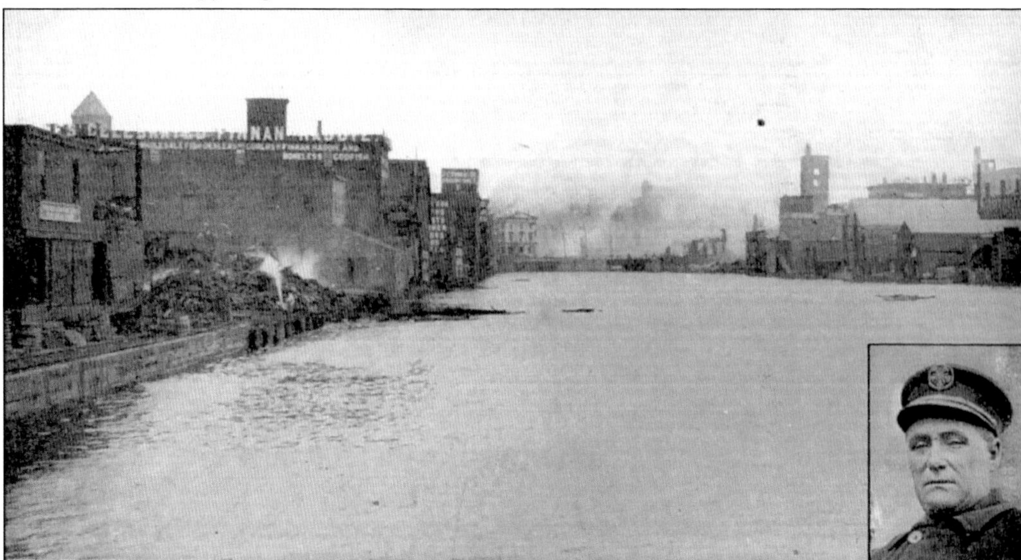

WHERE THE BANGOR FIRE STARTED AND JUMPED OVER KENDUSKEAG STREAM APRIL 30, 1911 Chief W. S. Mason

The stream was much wider in 1911 than it is today, owing to a 1960s-era parking plaza project that narrowed the stream with tons of concrete. Following the April 30 inferno, a postcard marked the fire's streamside origins on Broad Street (left) and commemorated the heroic efforts of Fire Chief William S. Mason, who supervised the firefighting efforts. On a calmer day, the stream might have stopped the flames from jumping onto the city's east side, but a stiff easterly breeze carried the embers onto Exchange Street (right).

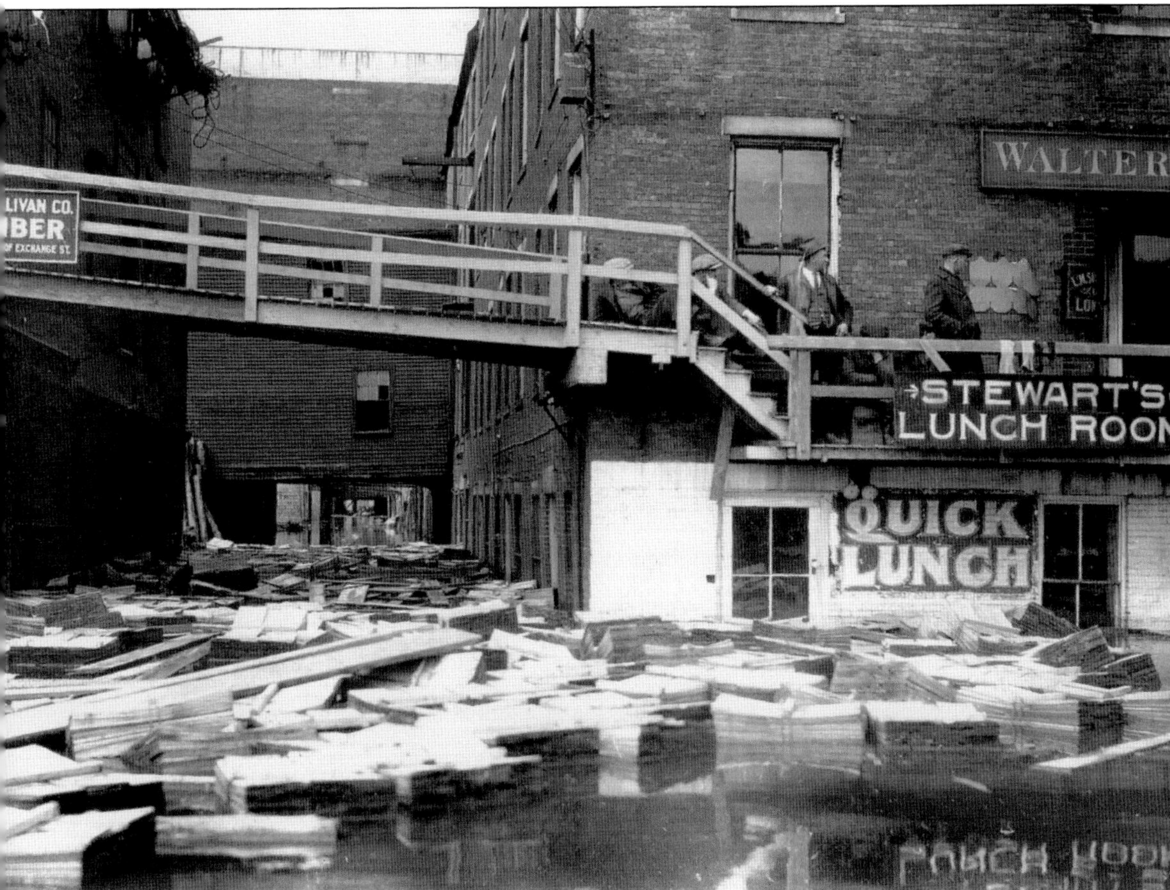

A view captures spring flooding from the 1923 Bangor disaster. As they had done in earlier years, and again during the 1936 disaster, the Penobscot River and Kenduskeag Stream showed their fury by submerging much of Broad, Washington, Exchange, and other downtown streets under several feet of water. No one was killed in any of these flood events, but the equivalent of millions of dollars in damage in today's currency was inflicted upon downtown merchants. This picture shows three especially devastated businesses: Lawrence M. Sullivan's lumber company, Walter Ross's steam towage business, and Stewart's Lunch Room, all located along the stream at 66 Exchange Street. Joe White's Submarine Lunch, located at the end of Exchange Street near Washington in the 1930s and 1940s, got its name because of its many bad experiences with flooding. The basement-level business is said to have finally closed down for good because of the water damage. The lower-level press room of the former *Bangor Daily News* building at 170 Exchange Street was also flooded on a regular basis, along with the basements of Friedman's furniture and other businesses lining the stream side of Exchange Street.

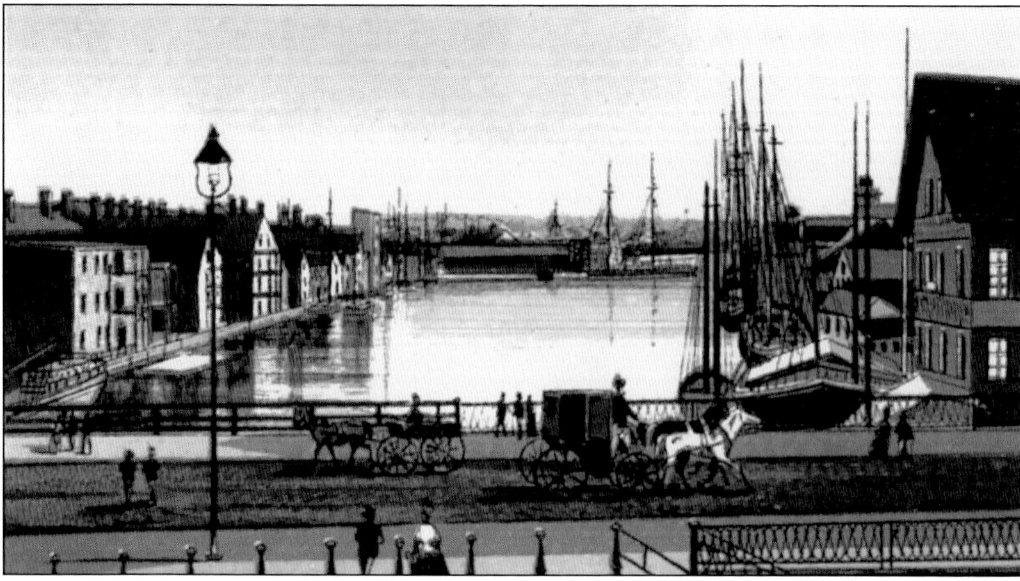

Can you envision sailing vessels traveling up the Kenduskeag as far as the State Street Bridge? This view, looking from the bridge downstream to the river, shows schooners that loaded and offloaded a variety of goods from streamside warehouses that lined the Broad and Exchange sides of the Kenduskeag. Look closely and you will spot a railroad covered bridge at the confluence of the river and stream, complete with its own draw span that allowed vessels to continue up the stream.

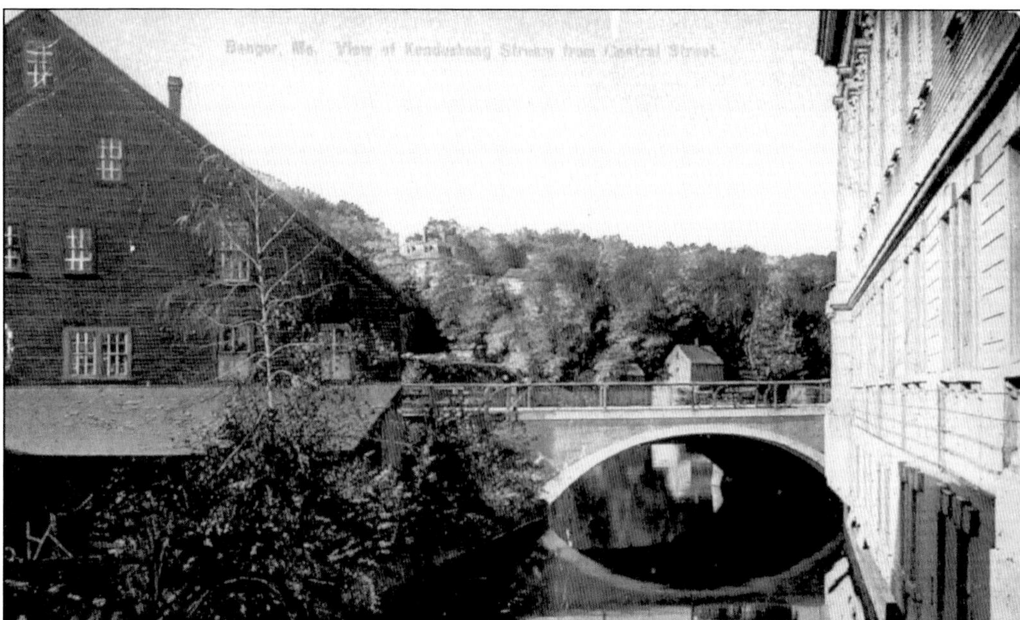

This 1911 view of the Franklin Street Bridge was postmarked April 12, 1911, just 18 days before the great fire changed this and other scenes forever. Taken from Central Street, the photograph shows the massive Norumbega Hall on the right and a large wooden warehouse on the left. Both were ravaged by the flames. The arched bridge gives an idea of the Venetian effect 19th-century architects and planners had in mind for Bangor.

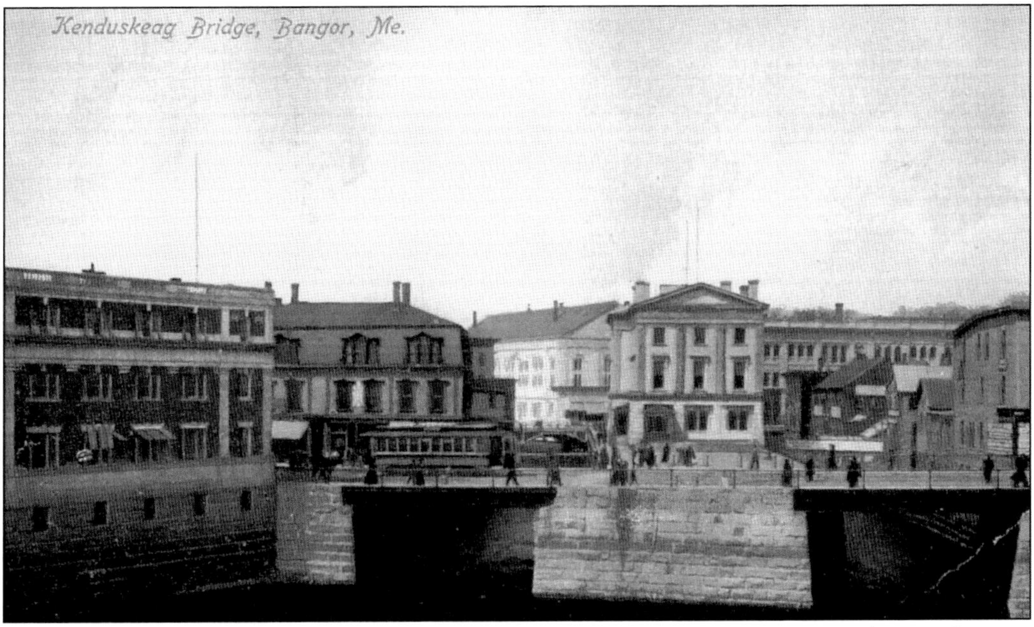

This unique view shows the State Street Bridge and surrounding buildings prior to the transforming April 30, 1911, fire. The old post office building in Kenduskeag Mall is the centerpiece, and behind it stands the grand old Norumbega Hall, where politicians, poets, and entertainers appeared. The former Merrill Bank building (left) is on Hammond Street. To the right is the row of businesses known as Kenduskeag Bridge. Pedestrians and a streetcar add movement to this early view, which was taken in black and white, then hand-colored and printed in Germany.

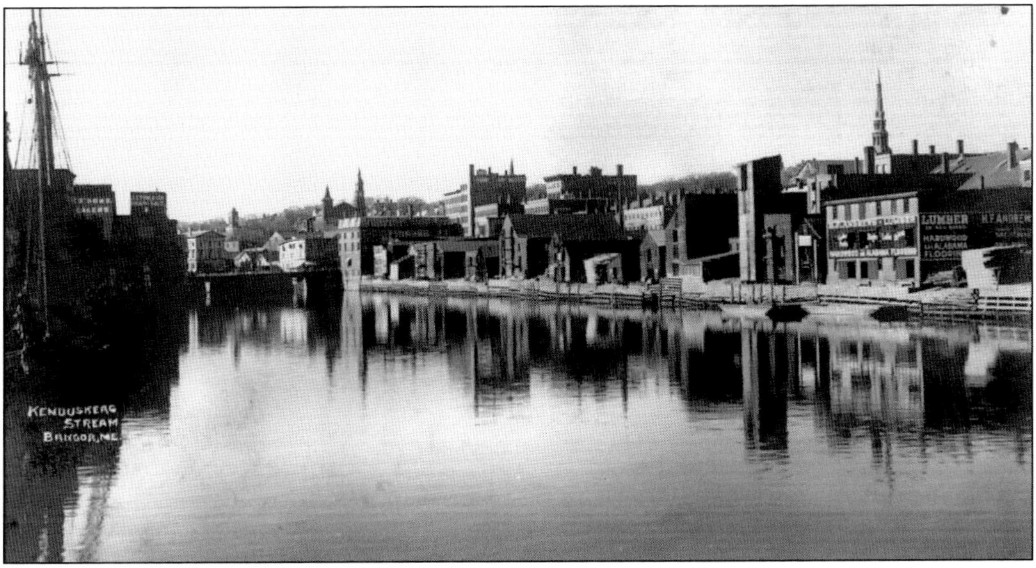

Postcard views such as this, showing Kenduskeag Stream *c.* 1909, are pure artistry. The photographer must have spent hours waiting for the right moment to open his shutter. The result is an unusual picture looking upstream toward the State Street Bridge. Notice the wooden cribwork along the Exchange Street side on the right, along with old wooden warehouses and businesses. A tall schooner is tied up to a dock at the left. This is the spectacle sailors had throughout the 19th and early 20th centuries as they sailed up the Kenduskeag for three city blocks.

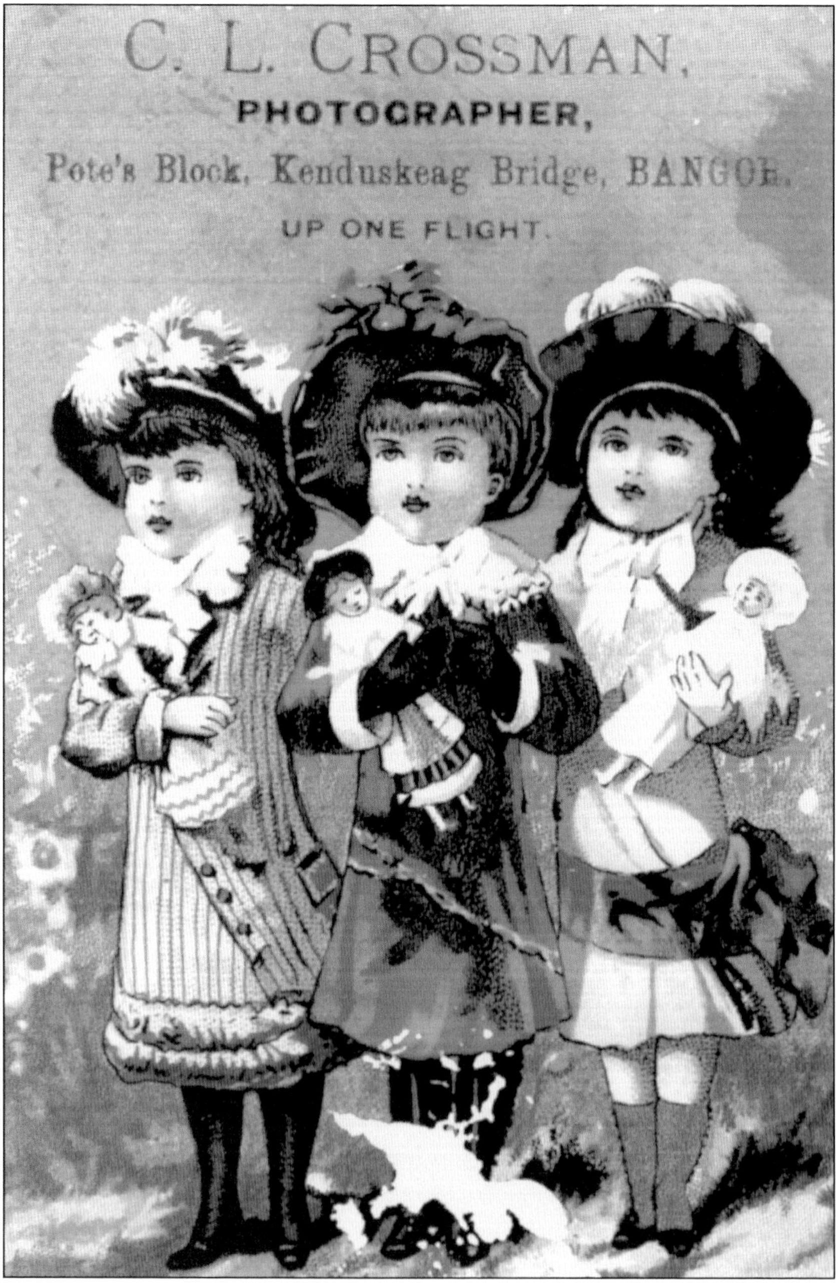

Charming color trade cards like this one advertised a myriad of downtown businesses in the late 19th and early 20th centuries. Some of the companies lined Kenduskeag Bridge, a district located on the easterly side of the Kenduskeag Stream off State Street that lost much of its old-time atmosphere following the great 1911 fire, when modern business blocks replaced little shops and studios. This *c.* 1888 card depicts three girls dressed to the nines and carrying dolls that advertised not a girls' clothing store but the upstairs photographic rooms of Charles L. Crossman, located in Pote's Block on Kenduskeag Bridge. The *Bangor Daily Whig & Courier* was based at the easterly end of Kenduskeag Bridge. Nearby was David Bugbee and Company, booksellers and stationers, and another photographer, named Charles L. Marston.

Six

Stout-Hearted Men and Women

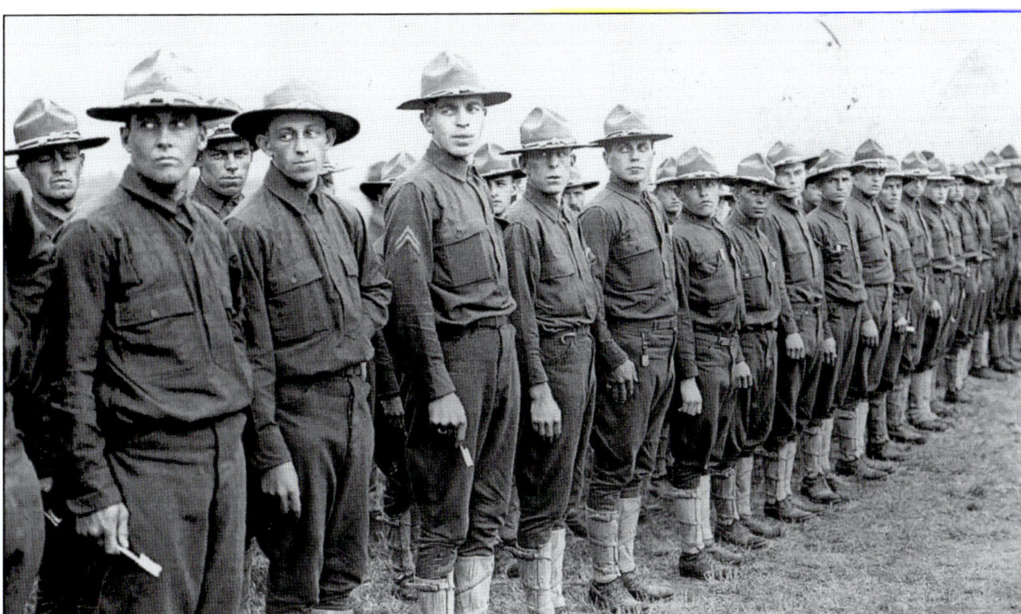

This real-photo postcard shows a unit of Maine army men in 1916 after a border war broke out between Mexico and the United States. Maine sent many soldiers to Texas to fight the forces of Pancho Villa, the Mexican leader who caused an international uproar when he and his men crossed into New Mexico and slaughtered some townspeople. Few men saw action, and most were returning back to the city's Union Station only months after departing. Note the summertime khaki uniforms, broad hats, and leggings. Many of these same men donned their uniforms again in 1917, this time to join in a shooting war with Germany.

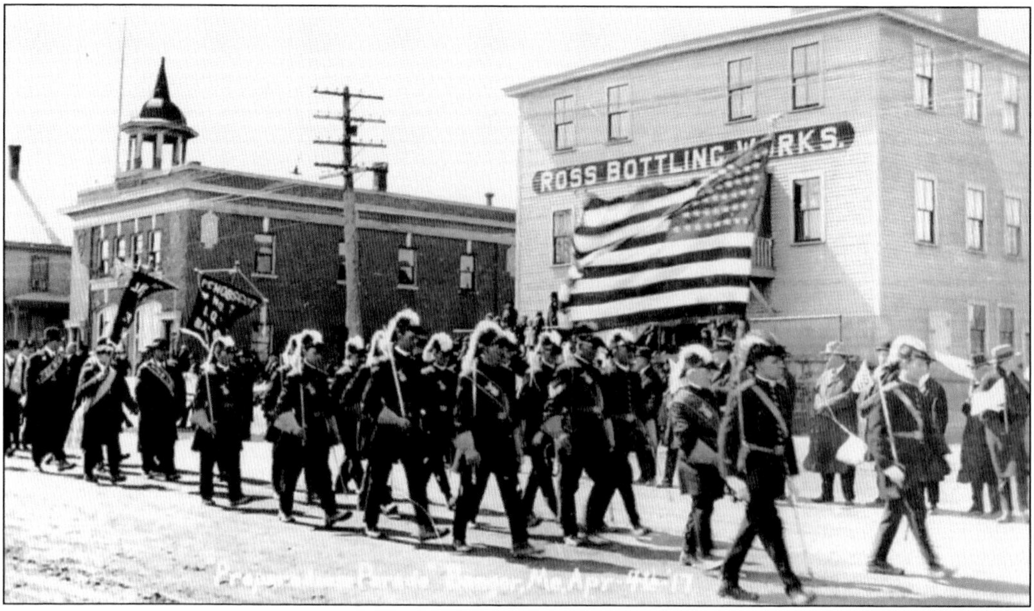

As the United States was drawn closer to war, cities across the nation held preparedness parades such as this one in Bangor on April 4, 1917. Their purpose was to demonstrate a level of readiness and patriotism not seen for many years. This scene, taken in front of the Ross Bottling Works at 359 Main Street, near the present Shaw's supermarket, shows what is assumed to be a contingent of Masons marching toward downtown. America entered the war on April 6. More joyous parades were held here on November 11, 1918, when "the war to end all wars" was finally over.

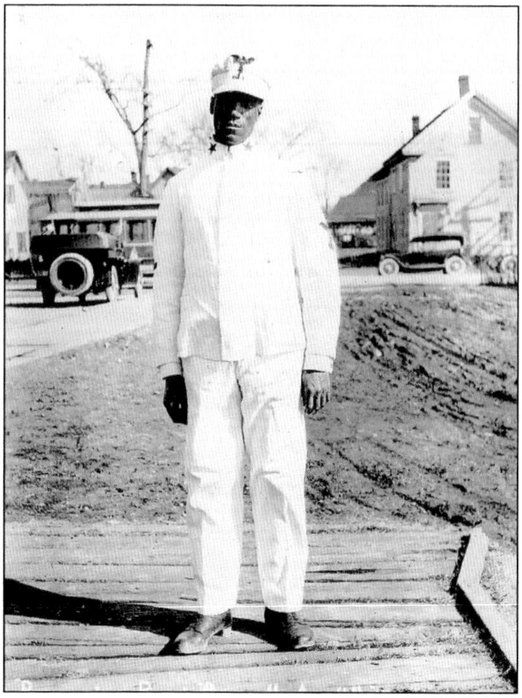

Another view taken at the 1917 preparedness parade pictures a serious-looking man dressed in a spotless white uniform. Since the U.S. Navy was not integrated at the time, one can assume he was steward on a ship docked in Bangor who joined in the celebration. Early automobiles and a trolley car are visible in the background, suggesting the picture was taken on Main Street or some other street accessible to the river. Other parade participants were local businessmen and University of Maine students. (BPL.)

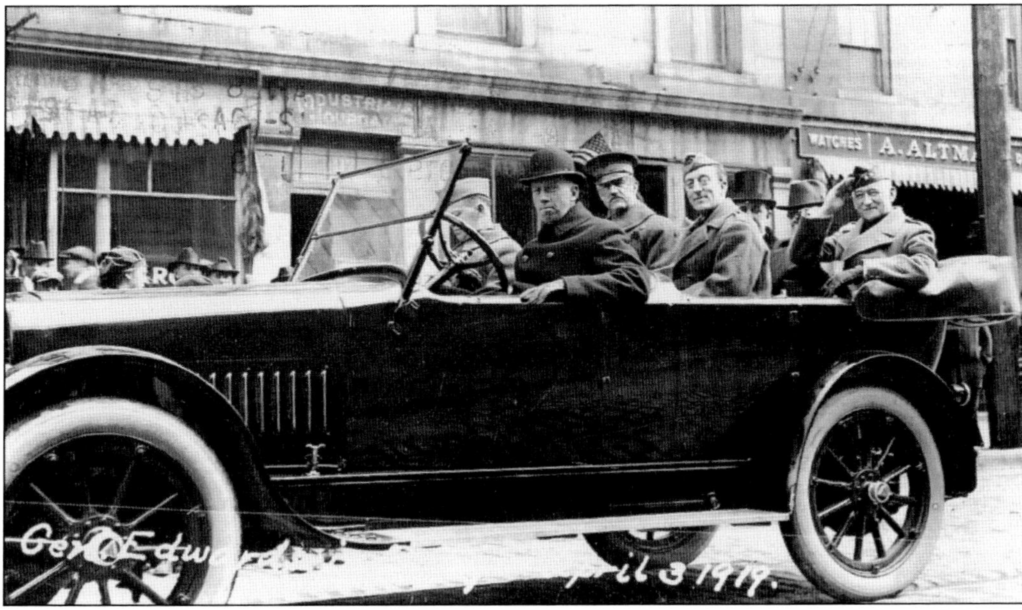

Patriotic celebrations continued well into 1919, long after the armistice ended the Great War the previous November. Sometimes, a general would show up and be paraded in open cars through downtown. This real-photo postcard view was mailed to Annie Washburn, of East Corinth, Maine, on April 8, a mere five days after the picture was taken. The scene is in front of the A. Altman jewelry store at 187 Exchange Street. The other six men in the automobile may be military brass and local civic leaders.

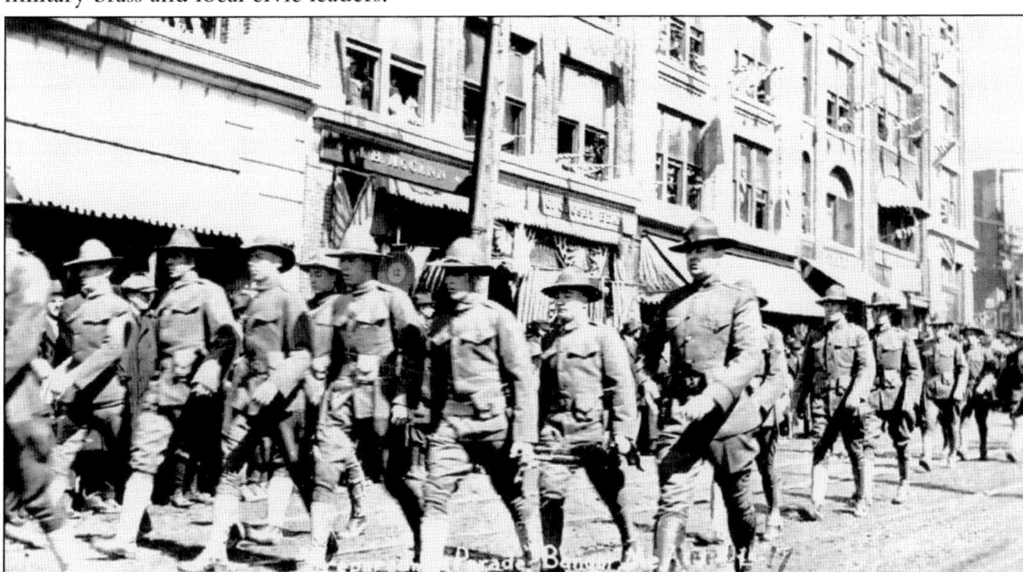

Yet another in a sequence of real-photo postcards shows some hail and hearty soldiers marching down State Street in 1917. Other views of the preparedness parade capture a trolley car on Main Street surrounded by a crowd of hundreds. These soldiers got their nicknames because of the large buttons on their uniforms that were said to resemble dumplings, or doughboys. World War I claimed 10 Bangor men who were killed in action, 9 who died of war wounds, and another 13 who succumbed to pneumonia. (BPL.)

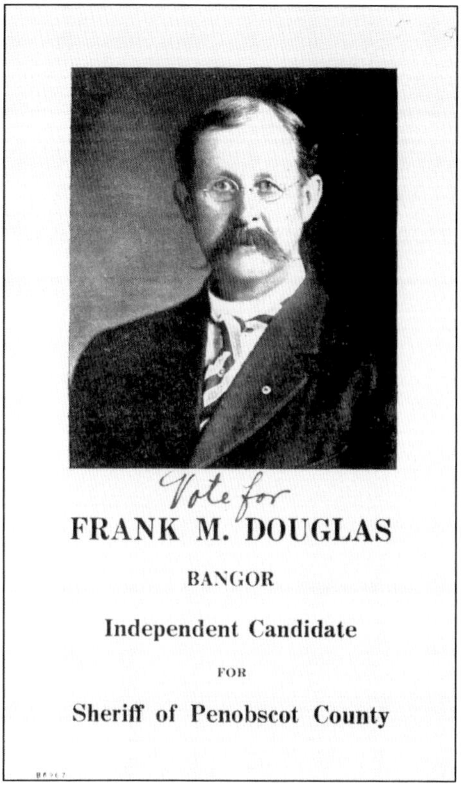

Independent candidates have been a part of the political landscape for generations. This stern-looking man, Frank M. Douglas, was an independent candidate for sheriff of Penobscot County. As advertised in a hand-out card—a pocket-sized stiff card handed out to voters on the street and door-to-door—Douglas looks up for the task. The handlebar mustache and wide-lapelled suit is reminiscent of the 1920s or before.

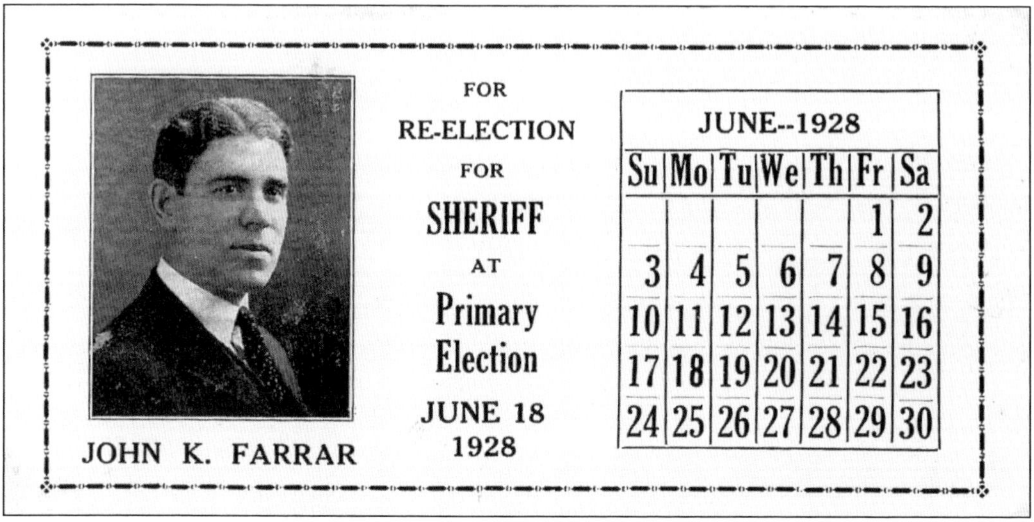

John K. Farrar was a well-known name around the Penobscot County Courthouse and jail in the years that he was the county sheriff. This calendar card, actually a blotter, was obviously intended to leave no doubt when voters could go to the polls and help elect Farrar sheriff: June 18, 1928. Farrar was sheriff for many years, notably in October 1937, when FBI agents shot two members of the notorious Brady Gang on Central Street. Farrar and other law enforcement personnel were pressed into service. That year, he appointed 40 deputies, as reported in a January 1 newspaper article.

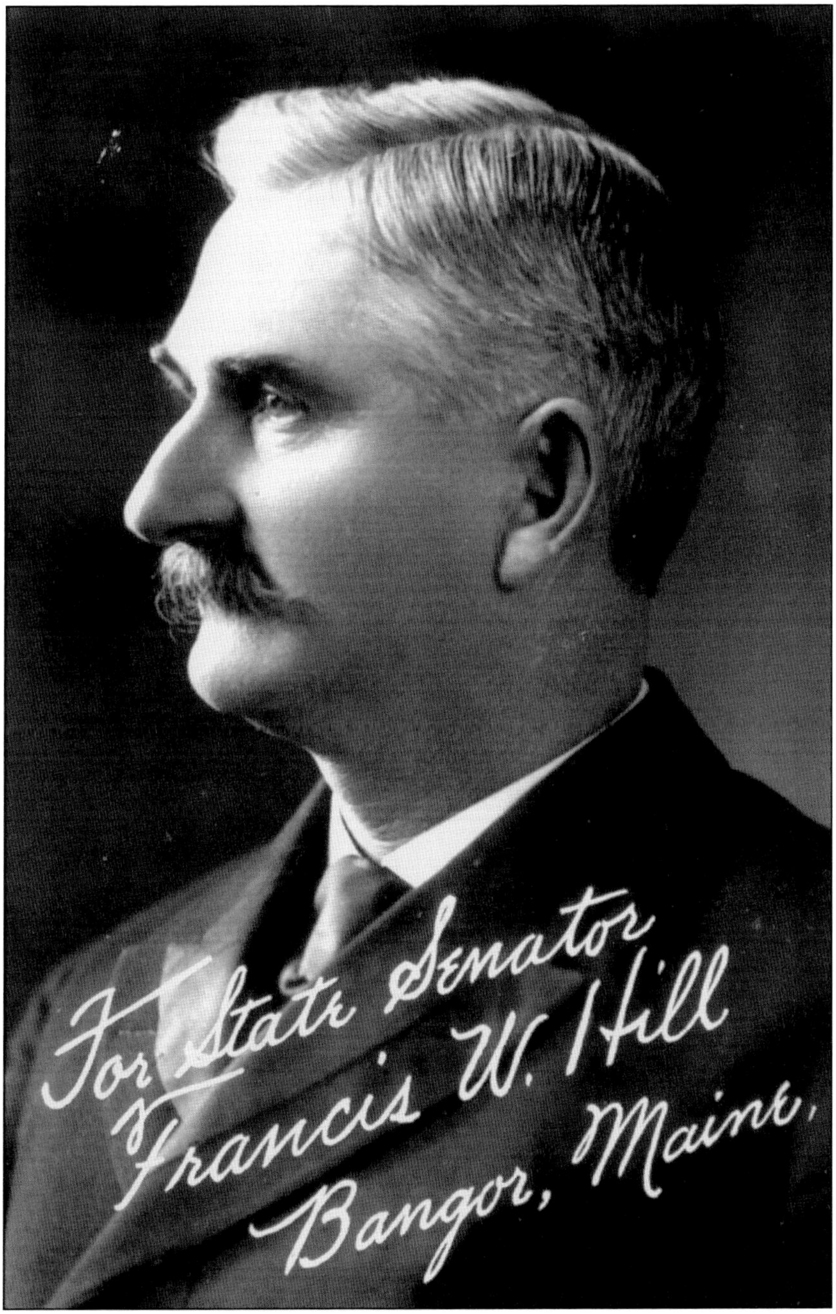

Is this the face of a stout-hearted man? Francis W. Hill, known as "Will" to his many friends, was born in Exeter, lived there for decades, and in 1920 moved to Bangor, where he was living when this undated political postcard was printed. His 1940 newspaper obituary is titled "Long busy and honorable life comes to the end / Francis W. Hill before the public for many years." It mentioned his election to the state legislature in 1901 and his election to the state senate in 1909, to which he was reelected in 1911. He was involved with the Exeter fair, eastern Maine's Bangor State Fair, and the board of registration of voters for the city of Bangor. He died at 64 Third Street on the city's west side, his home for many years.

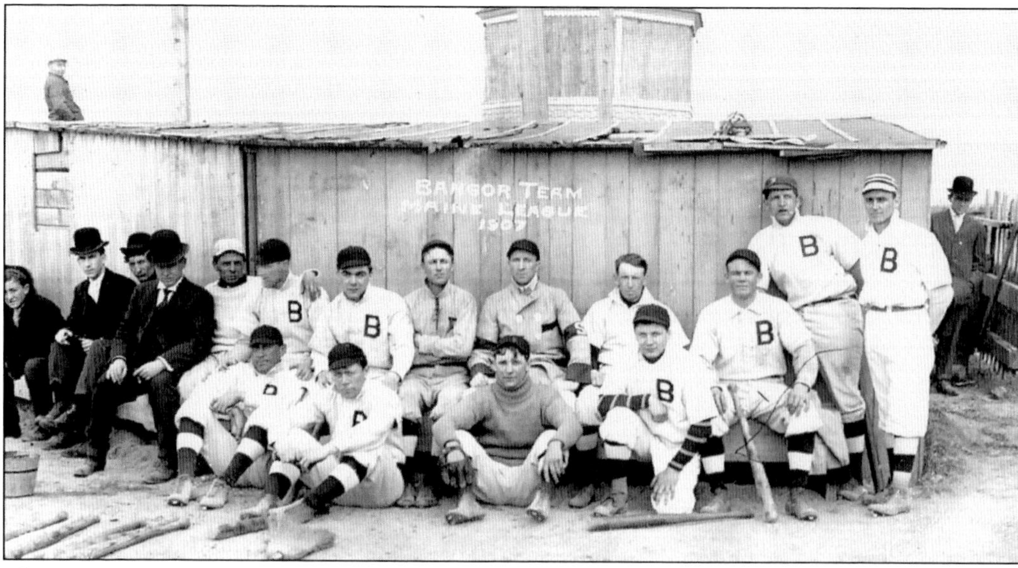

This impressive-looking Bangor baseball team played in the Maine league in 1907. The game was held at Maplewood Park, now called Bass Park. The May 24, 1907, edition of the ***Bangor Daily News*** reported that both Bangor and Augusta, the opposing team, would play in "nice, new spik and span uniforms." The paper listed only last names in those days. Mallay played shortstop, Donovan played second base, and McLellan played third base. In right field was an outstanding Penobscot Indian player, Lous Sockalexis, whos is pictured in the middle of the second row, fifth from the right.

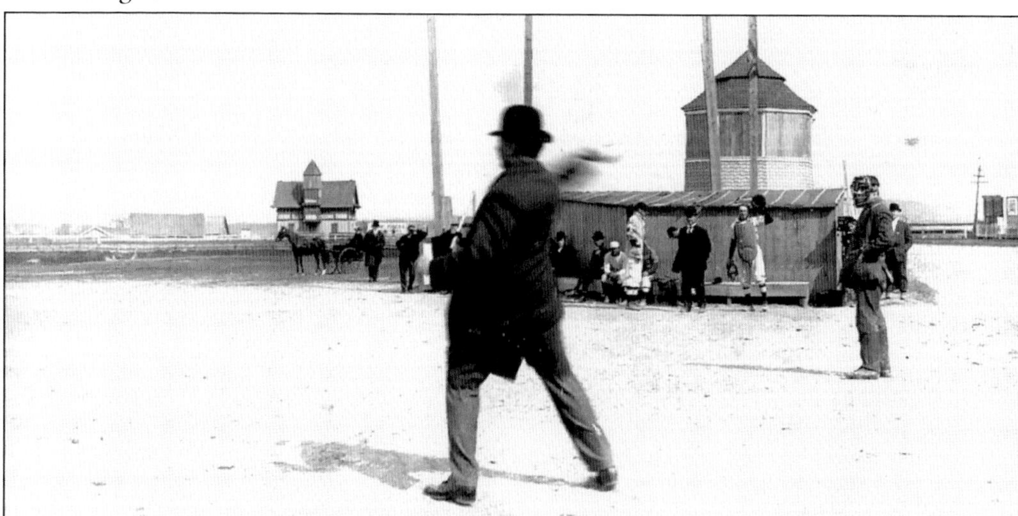

MAYOR WOODMAN OPENING THE MAINE LEAGUE AT BANGOR, MAY 24,'07

A rare real-photo action postcard shows Mayor John F. Woodman throwing out the first ball in the 1907 Maine league game in Bangor. A big new scoreboard was a highlight of the season. The cost of admission was 25¢. An extra dime would guarantee a seat in the wooden grandstand. Although baseball aficionados have proposed returning baseball to Bass Park, the city-owned area is now largely home to harness racing and the Bangor State Fair. The Bangor Lumberjacks, a semiprofessional baseball team based in the city, began playing in a new stadium at Husson College in the spring of 2004.

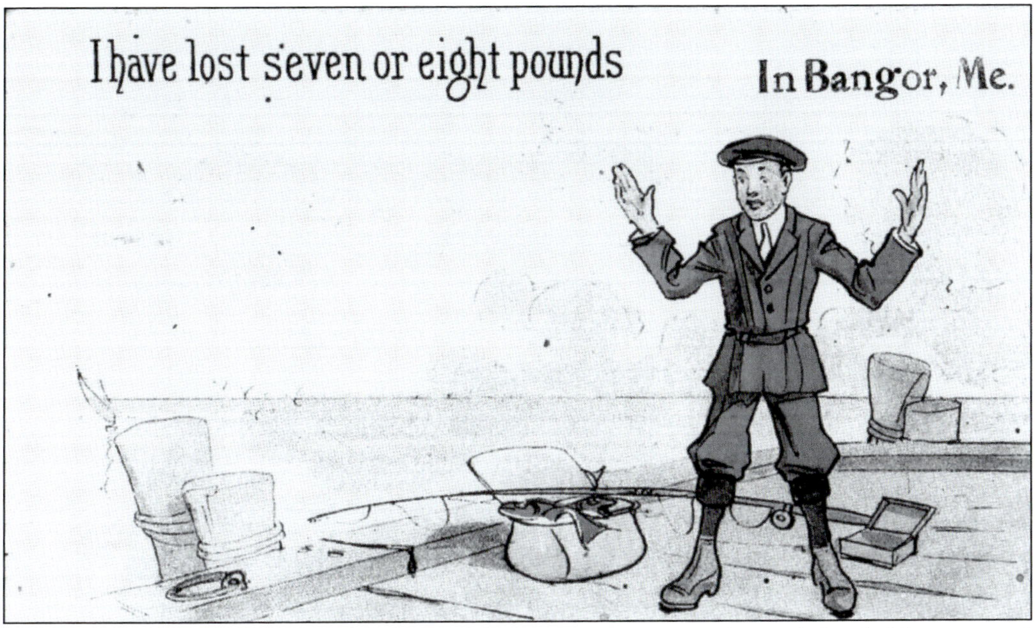

Standard novelty cards such as this, postmarked 1915, were popular with local fishermen and anyone who has tried to lose even a pound or two. "In Bangor, Me." was simply printed onto a mass-produced postcard to boost sales at downtown stores. Note the wooden dock on which the man stands with his fishing pole and tackle box. Is it too much of a stretch to imagine a man of his time fishing in suit and tie? At least the high boots look reasonable.

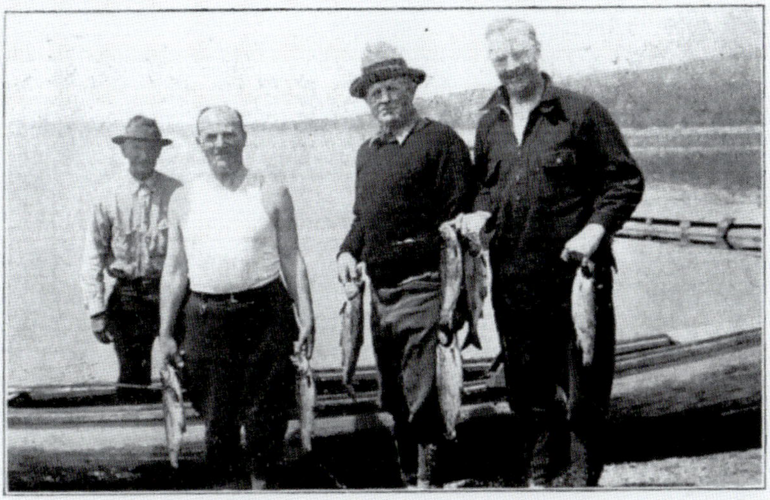

Three Successful Bangor Fishermen at Square Lake,
Charles P. Conners, Esq., Dr. James F. Cox, Dr. Allan Woodcock

Bangor lawyers and doctors have always worked hard and played hard. This undated limited-run postcard shows an attorney and his two physician friends playing hard following an especially productive fishing expedition. Doctors Allan Woodcock and James F. Cox were well known in Bangor, as well as Charles P. Conners, a lawyer and city solicitor. The location is Square Lake in Aroostook County, one of a chain of five lakes that includes Eagle and Long Lakes. The man on the far left is probably their guide or host.

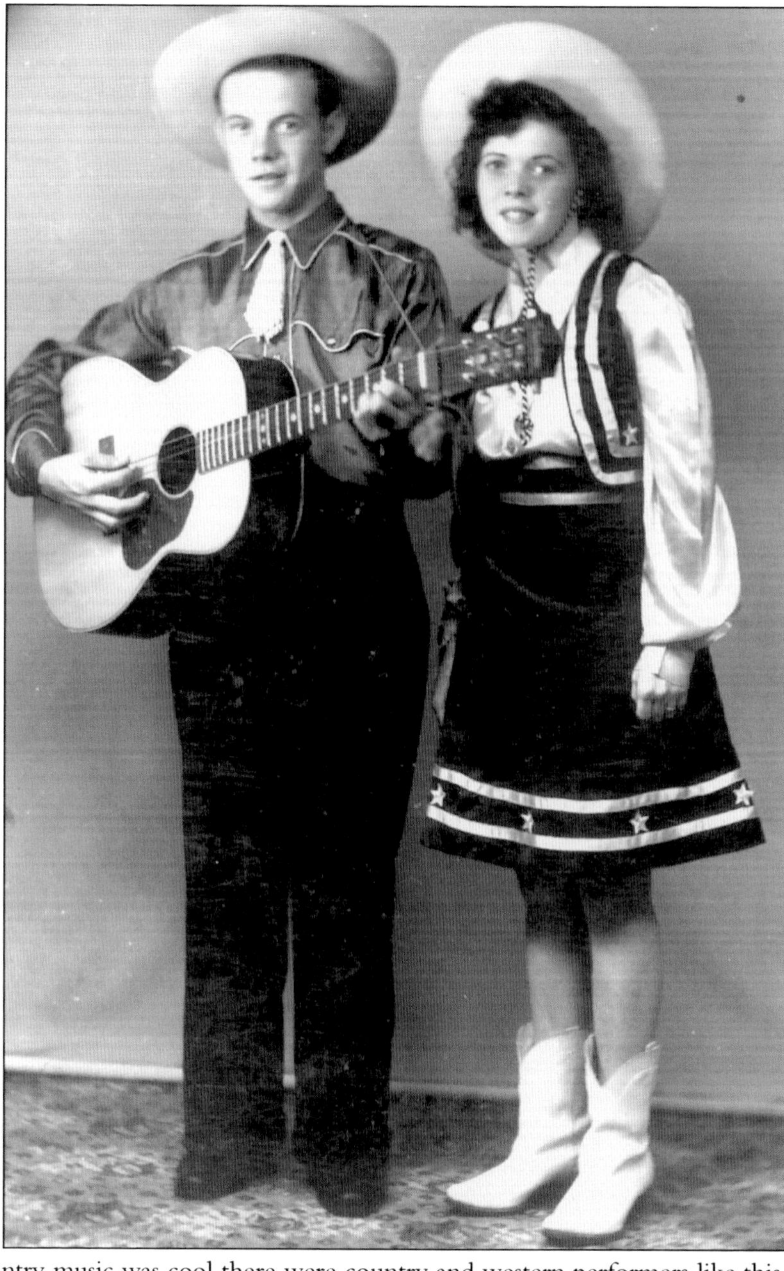

Before country music was cool there were country and western performers like this brother and sister act who performed on local radio programs in the 1940s and later. On the back of this postcard, postmarked in her hometown of Sangerville, Maine, on September 23, 1943, the duo's mother wrote a note to her cousin, Hattie Duran, of East Corinth. It reads, "Dear Hattie, This is a picture of Frances and Dana. They are going on the radio soon, W.L.B.Z. They are with 'Pick and Lib Mountaineers.' Doris Thomas." Dana "Shorty" Thomas gained regional fame in the 1960s with his own television show in Maine. He and his sister were pure country, right down to her white boots and his fancy shirt and kerchief. Shorty Thomas died in 1999 at age 73. Unfortunately, his and other performers' radio and TV performances were not recorded, as it was before the days of tape recorders and VCRs.

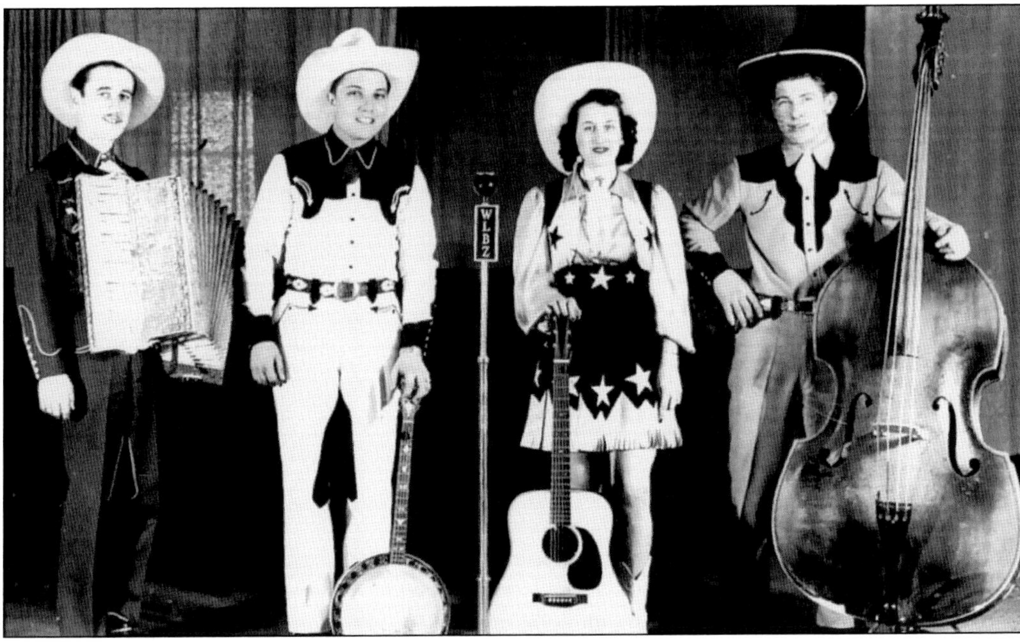

Ray Little and his band were another act popular with audiences who tuned into WLBZ radio each week to hear them sing and play their instruments. This Radio Cowboy Show consisted of musicians who played the accordion, banjo, guitar, and string bass. Typical of live appearances at dance halls at Auto Rest Park in Carmel and the Bar L Ranch in Newport, the band crowded around one microphone in the radio studio and played their hearts out.

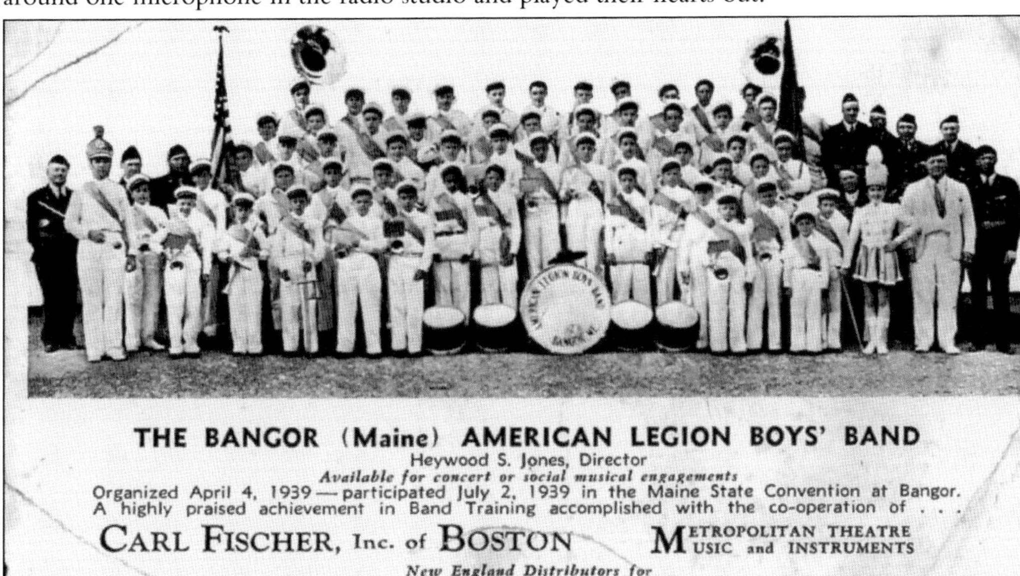

These future men comprised the acclaimed American Legion Boys' Band based in Bangor. This postcard, mailed to anyone interested in booking the band for "concert or social musical engagements," notes that the group was organized on April 4, 1939. The following July it participated in the Maine State Convention at Bangor, quite an achievement for a relatively inexperienced unit. Band director Heywood S. Jones, dressed in a white uniform, second from the right, wrote the fight songs for Bangor and Brewer High Schools.

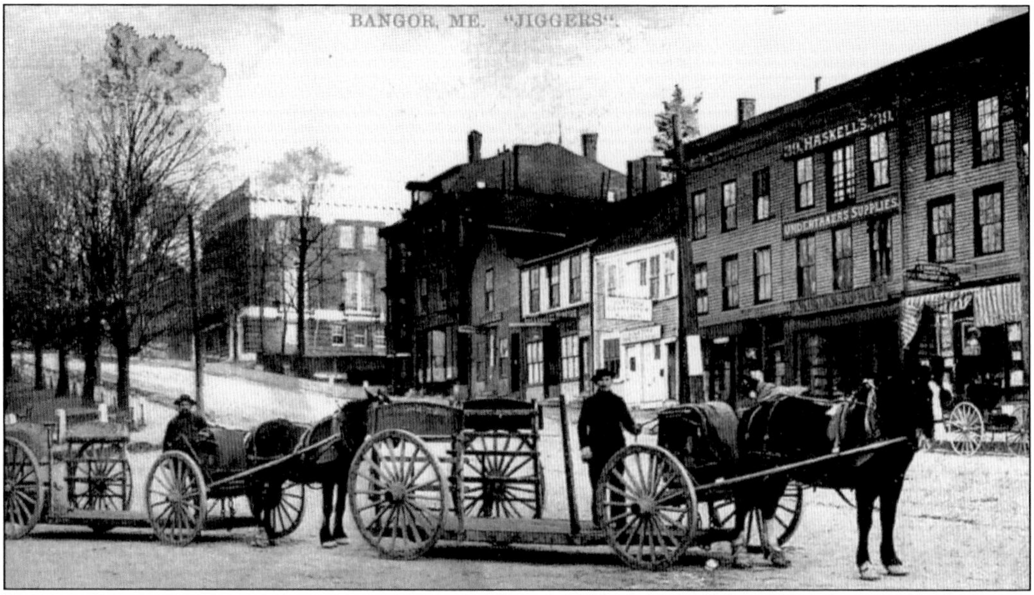

Long, low wooden wagons called jiggers were common sights around town well into the 1920s, and possibly after that. They were invented and produced in Bangor and soon gained favor because of their convenience. No longer did farmers and merchants have to hoist heavy barrels full of potatoes, fish, salt pork, and other items high onto a wagon. The jiggers were just inches off the ground. This view was taken at East Market Square, with Park Street and the Tarratine Club forming a backdrop.

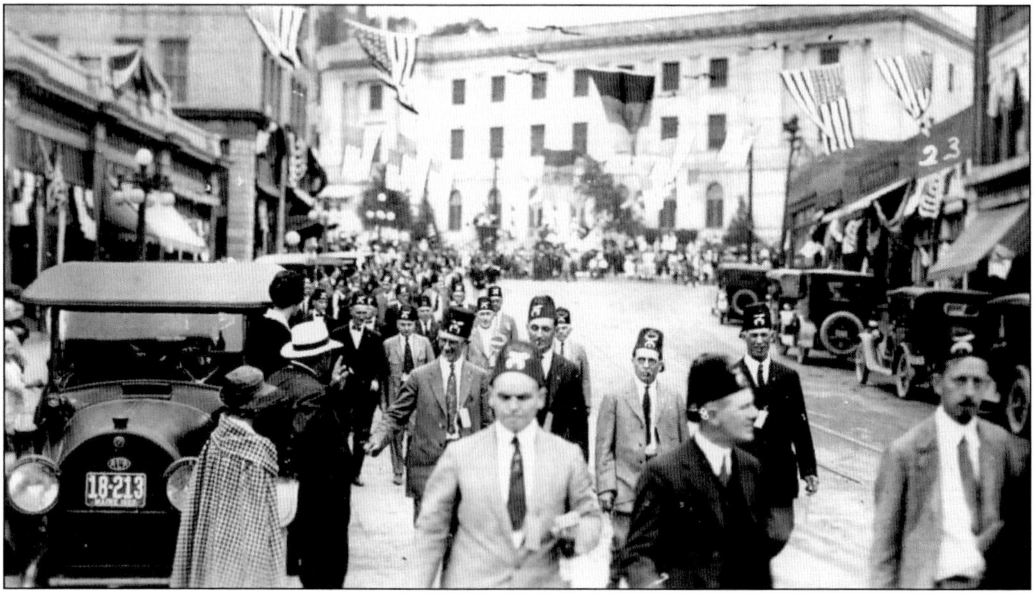

Anah Temple Shriners in Bangor date back to January 16, 1921, when the temple received its dispensation. On June 15, 1922, it received its all-important charter, which allowed it to hold ceremonies and build a temple. This real-photo postcard was taken sometime in the 1920s on Central Street, probably during a ceremonial for the benefit of new members. The annual event began with the donning of the Anah fez on each new member. Also, some of the men are wearing Shrine ribbons.

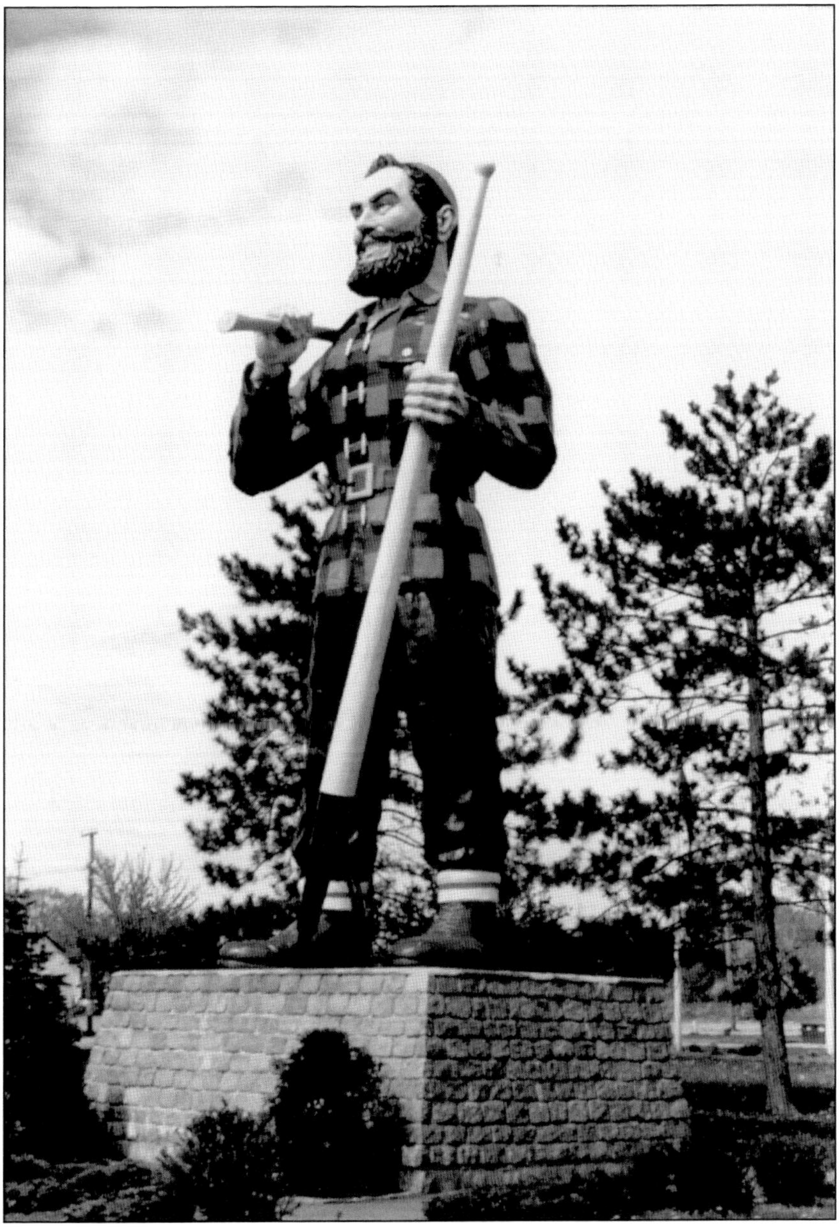

Here he is—the biggest, toughest, stout-hearted man of them all. Along with Minnesota and the Pacific Northwest, Bangor lays claim to Paul Bunyan, a mythical lumberjack who looms large in people's imaginations nearly two centuries after he is said to have lived. Normand Martin, a commercial artist, created the 37-foot-high statue at Bass Park on Main Street to commemorate the city's 125th birthday celebration in 1959. A wooden frame was covered with fiberglass, then hand-painted in red, white, green, and black to re-create the look of a man of his time. He is holding an ax in his right hand and a cantdog, used to drive logs downriver, in is left hand. Critics argue that the statue lacks artistic value and is historically inappropriate. The real Paul Bunyan, they say, would have worn a woolen union suit as underwear, not a round-neck T-shirt as the statue depicts. Most Bangoreans, however, appreciate the statue for what it is: a proud symbol of Bangor's lumbering heritage. (Brian Swartz photograph.)

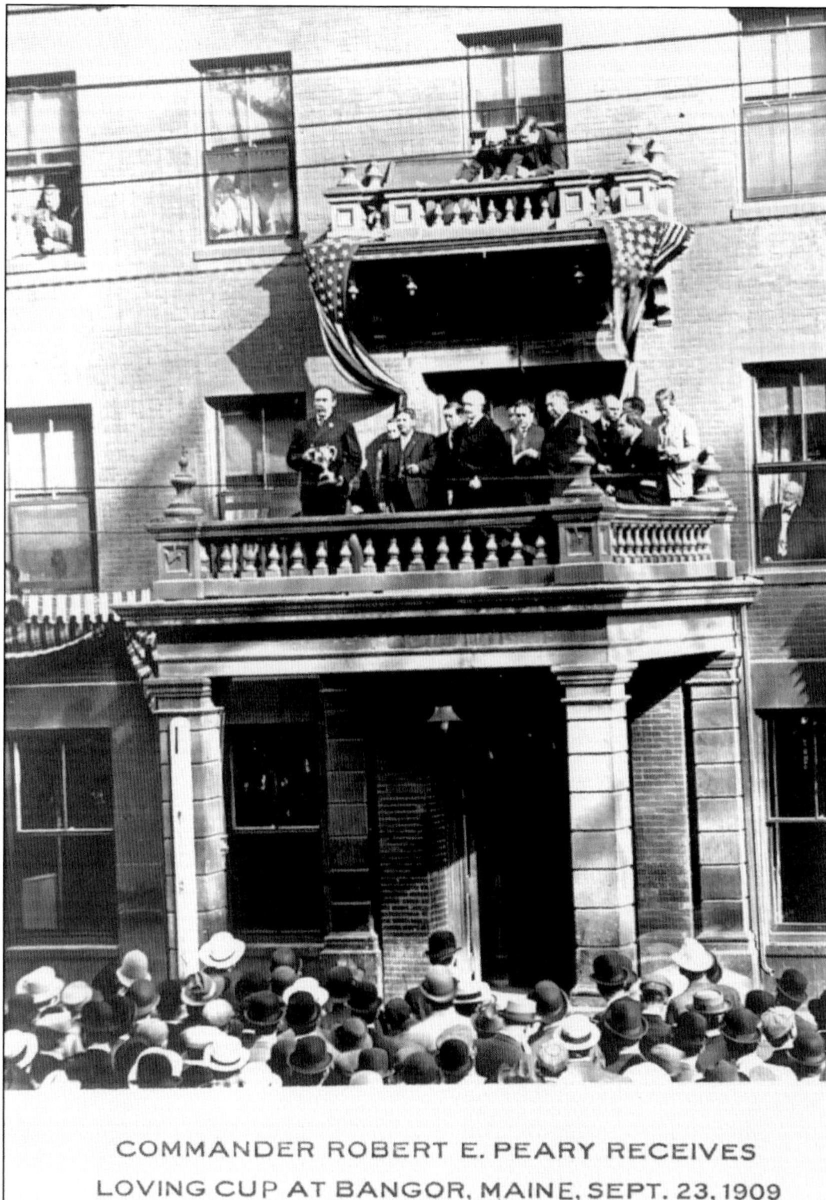

Arctic explorer Robert E. Peary made history in 1909 by what most historians agree was his discovery of the North Pole, where he raised the American flag. Peary's ties to Maine included the boat in which he traveled north, the *Roosevelt,* built at a Verona Island shipyard 20 miles downriver from Bangor. It was fitting that Peary made his first public appearance in the United States at the Bangor House, where he was photographed on September 23, 1909. Local newspapers had a field day describing his first shave on American soil, accomplished in private inside the hotel. He is pictured on a black-and-white postcard holding a silver loving cup from the Main Street jewelry store of W. C. Bryant, presented by Mayor John F. Woodman. Such postcard views are eagerly sought by collectors locally and nationwide.

Seven

A Stroll through Downtown

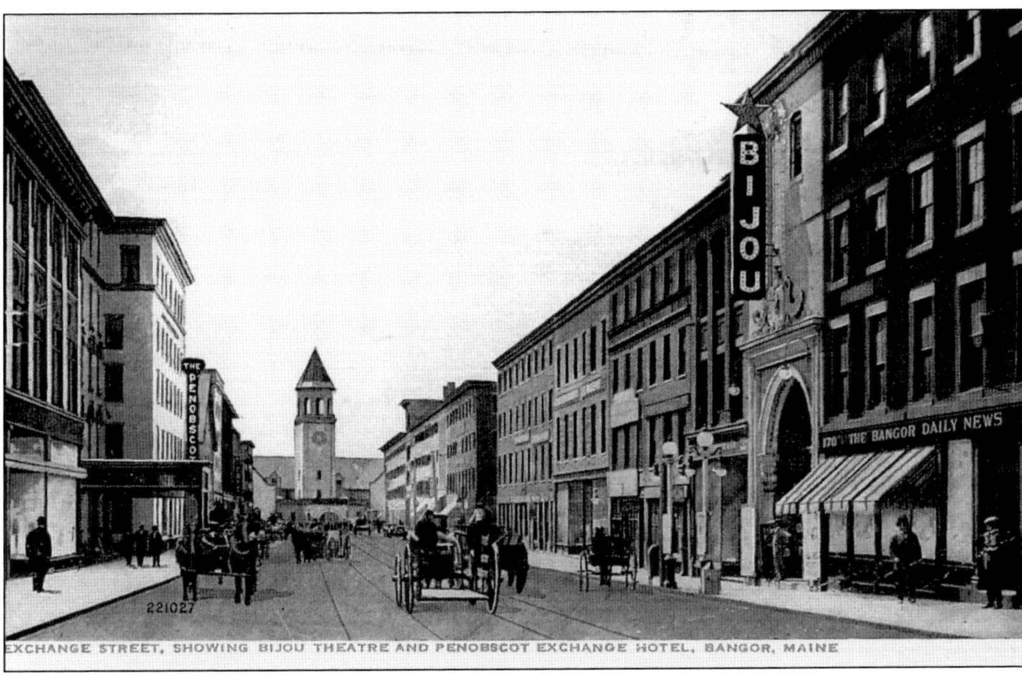

Exchange Street in the 1920s, when this postcard view was made, offered something for everyone. The three-block district stretched from State Street to Washington Street, with Union Station centered perfectly at the end. The Bijou Theater offered vaudeville acts and two-reelers. Next door, at 170 Exchange, were the offices of the *Bangor Daily News*. Across the street was the Penobscot Exchange Hotel, and between the hotel and the river was a string of barrooms, the most notable of which was the Silver Dollar. Nothing in this picture exists today since the street has been transformed into a banking mecca.

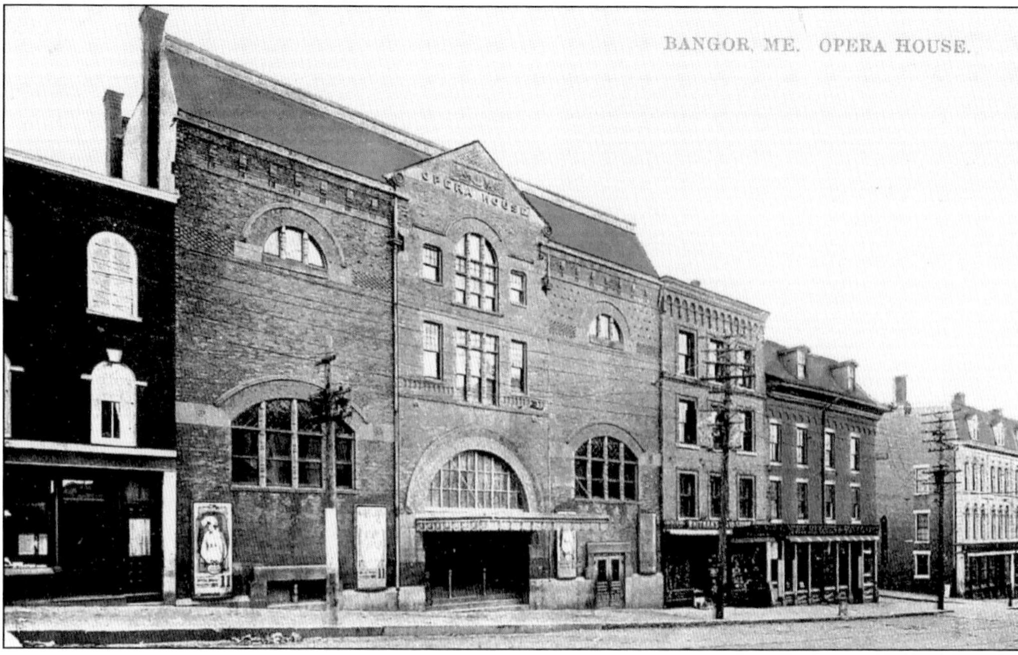

Many Bangor-area residents can recall Saturday afternoons filled with romance and laughter inside the new opera house, which is now home to the Penobscot Theatre Company on Main Street. But few if any can remember its predecessor, the first opera house, built on the same site in 1882 and financed by a group of theater aficionados who believed Bangor needed a theater of its own. Actors Ethel Barrymore and Edwin Booth and boxer-turned-entertainer John L. Sullivan performed there. The old opera house was destroyed by a fire in 1914 that claimed the lives of two firefighters (see pages 94 and 95).

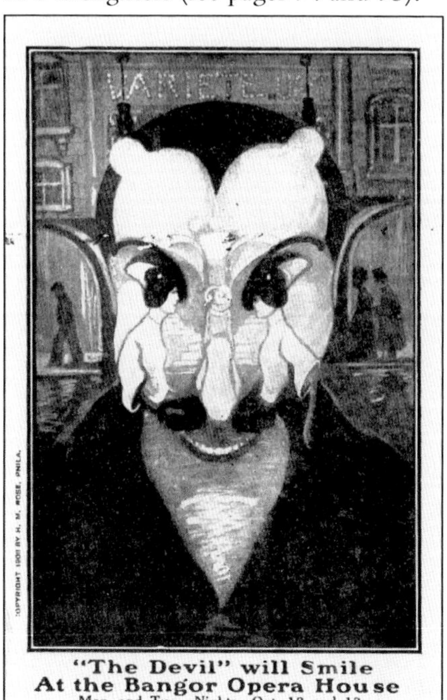

Oddball postcards like this one, dating from the early 20th century, were given and mailed to patrons of the old Bangor Opera House. It promotes a satirical comedy titled *The Devil,* touted as "the Sensational Success of Two Continents." Frank Molnar wrote the play, which was being promoted by a man named Henry W. Savage. The card's backside lists the "distinguished cast" of men and women. Look closely at the front of the card and you might discover dark and shadowy figures inside the Devil's eyes and beside his ears.

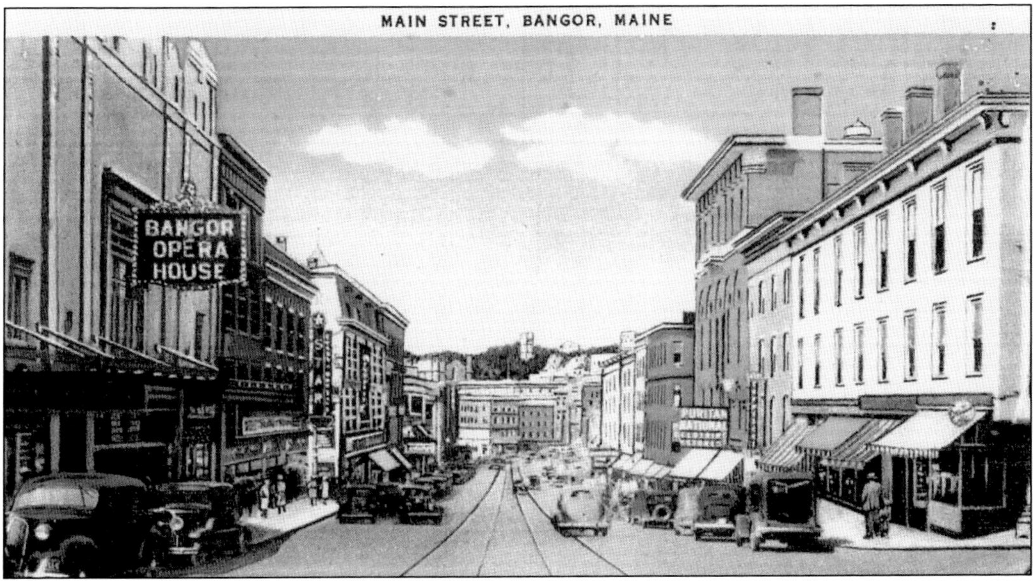

In this view looking down Main Street in the 1930s, the old opera house has been replaced by the modern, new one, complete with a sparkly sign and sidewalk canopy to attract moviegoers to such classics as *Gone with the Wind* and *Wuthering Heights*. The Star Store in an adjacent block at 115–125 Main Street sold women's clothing. John Skoufis, a Greek immigrant, ran a bar and grill in the long, light-colored building across the street. Also on Main Street were the Commodore Hotel and Puritan National clothing store, at 124 Main Street.

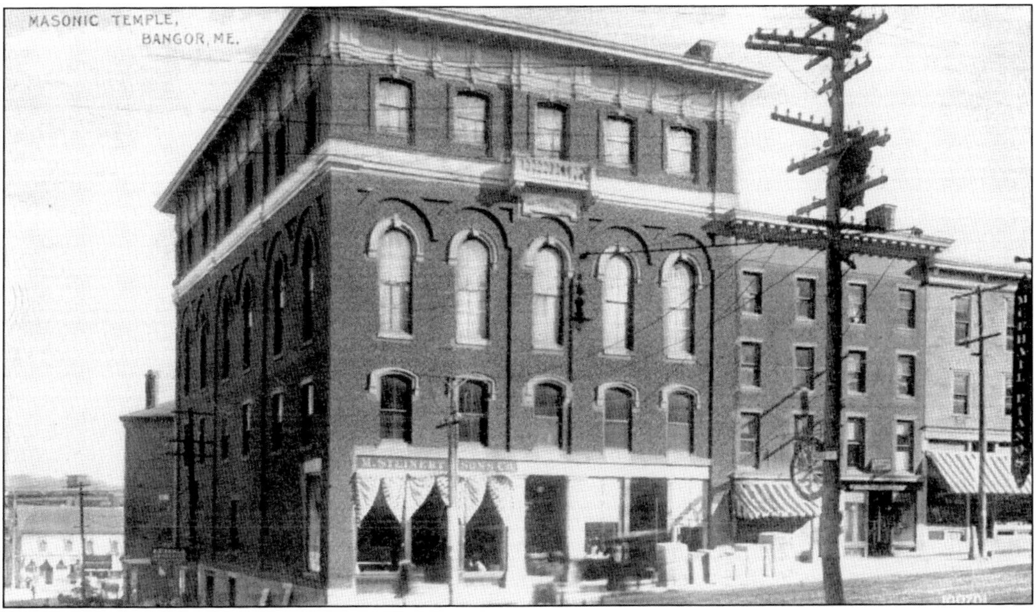

Sadly, this lovely building, which dated from the late 1860s, is only a memory. On the bitter-cold night of January 15, 2004, the Masonic Block at Main and Water Streets caught fire and was totally destroyed. Lost in the temple were priceless Masonic relics, including silver from Paul Revere's Boston foundry, a library, paintings, and a pipe organ. Also burned was the Yankee Shoe Repair around the corner on Water Street, a learning center for dyslexic children, and a gallery. The brick block was razed, leaving a vacant corner for the first time in about 135 years.

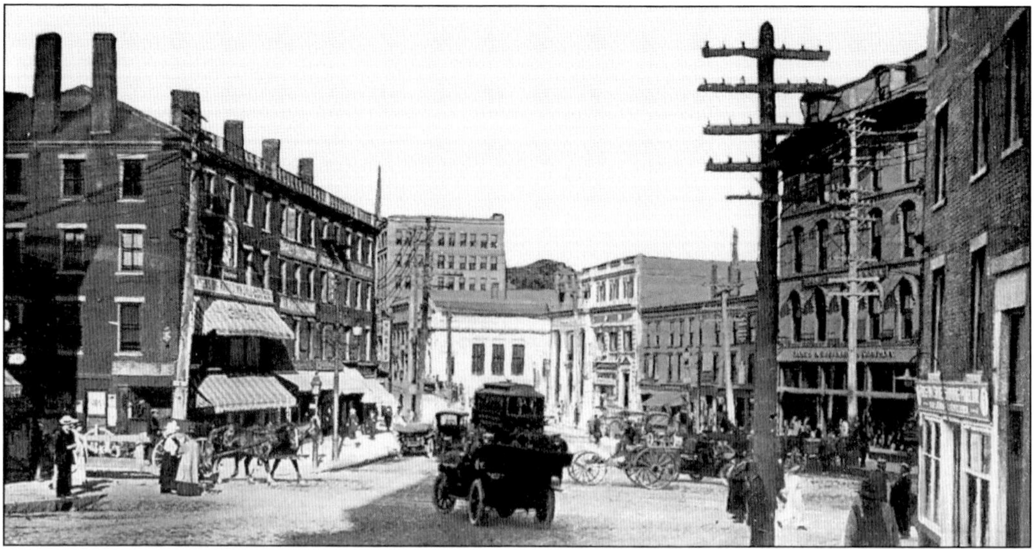

This view shows three modes of transportation in the heart of downtown at the intersection of Central, Hammond, and Main Streets. An open touring car is in the middle of the picture, behind that is a Bangor trolley car, and elsewhere in the view are horses and wagons. The building on the left is the Smith Block, part of which dates from the 1830s. Across from the Smith Block is the high Wheelwright and Clark Block, a downtown gem since its construction in 1859. The card at first appears to be an early one, but the automobile and the Exchange Building and Bangor Savings Bank in the distance, both built after the 1911 Bangor fire, suggest the view was taken *c.* 1920, setting it apart from the first local picture postcards, published just after 1900.

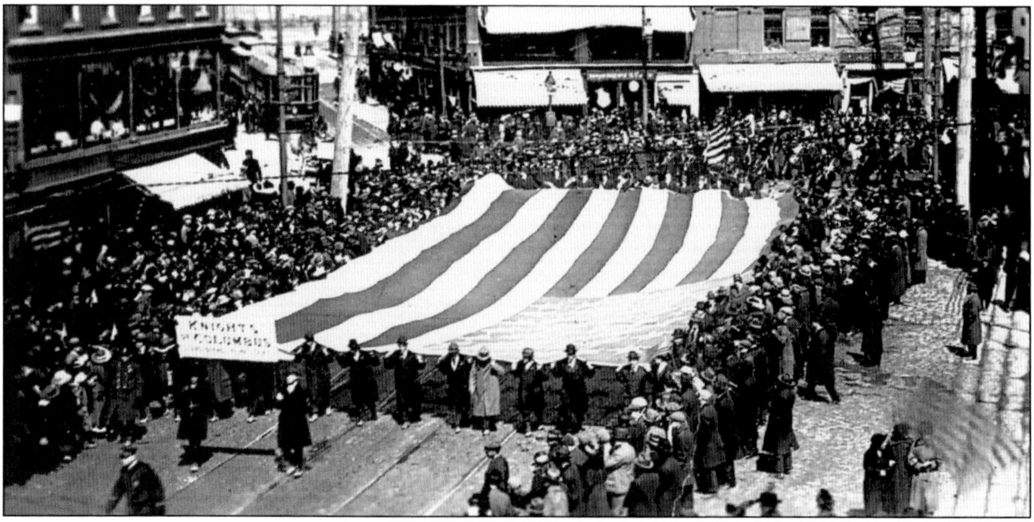

World War I saw several patriotic observances downtown. This one shows members of the Knights of Columbus carrying a mammoth American flag up Main Street, perhaps at the end of the Great War on November 11, 1918. Other postcards show what is probably the same flag being carried by sailors on May 22, 1919. Note the cobbled streets and streetcar tracks in this picture. Also, a streetcar in the background on Central Street waits for the foot traffic to clear before proceeding onto Main Street. The present whereabouts of the big flag are unknown, but it was most likely lost or destroyed. (BPL.)

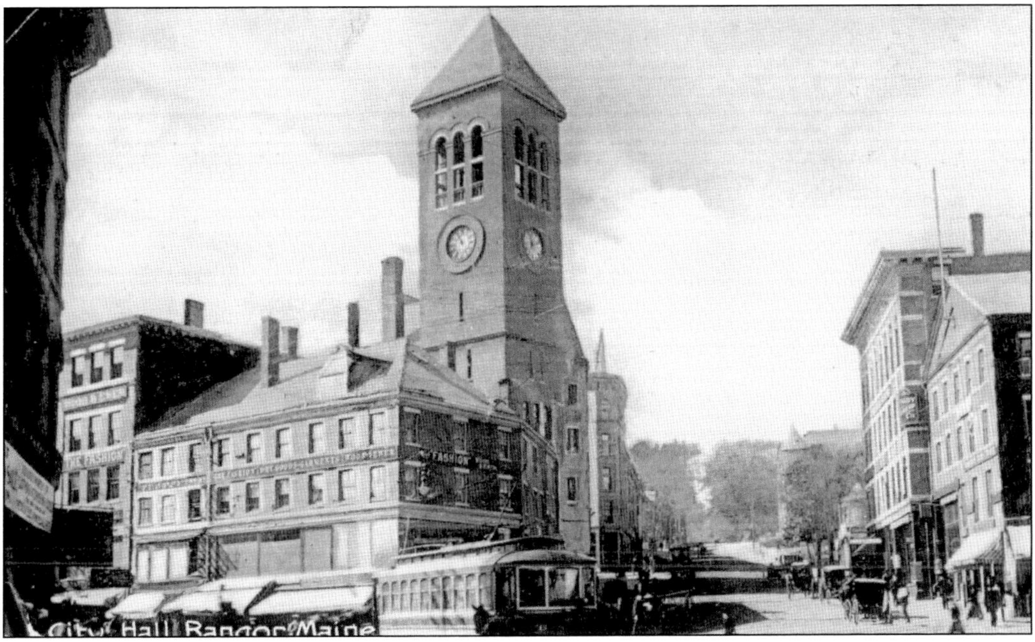

Can you envision a bustling downtown scene like this today? Imagine peering out the window of a streetcar and seeing horses, buggies, and cobbled streets. Towering above it all is the brick city hall building. The message on the back of the card, postmarked December 23, 1909, speaks of a Christmas reception at city hall. The sender wrote, "Had a lovely time." The 19th-century Bass Block at Hammond and Central Streets, razed in 1947 and replaced by the W. T. Grant building, is on the far right. (MHPC.)

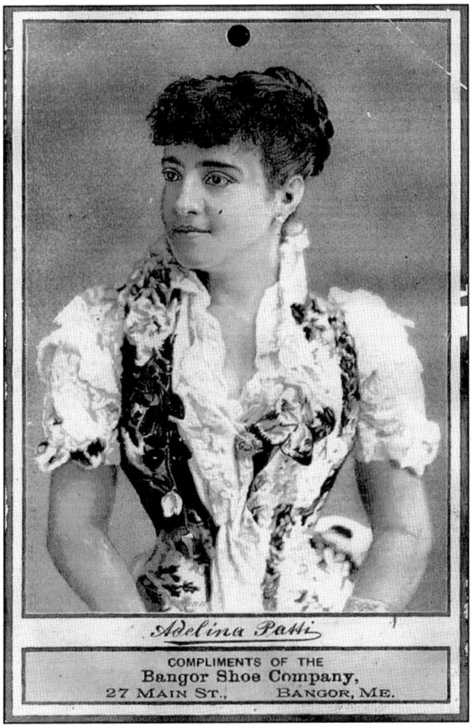

Once, there were many shoe stores downtown, and enterprising businessmen like the owners of the Bangor Shoe Company at 27 Main Street went to great lengths to draw in customers. This *c.* 1887 advertising card is a stock item, meaning the company simply printed its name on a purchased card for its customers. The Italian beauty on the card was Adelina Patti. In the 20th century, the Standard Shoe Company, founded by Cyrus Schiro, was located for many years at 48 Main Street.

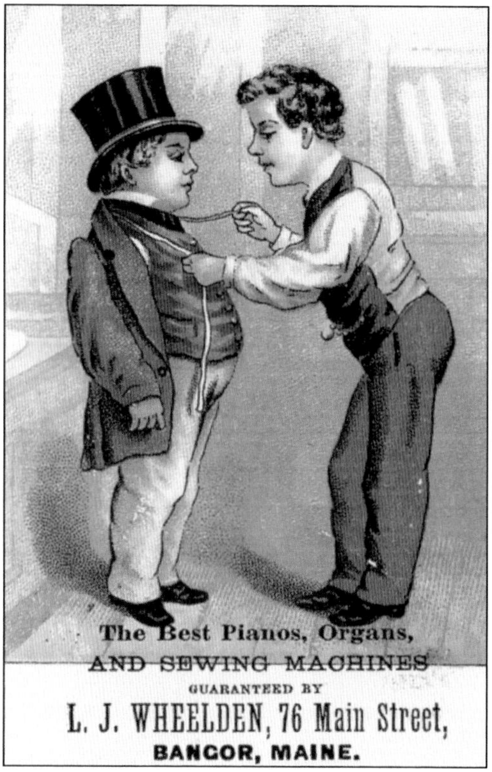

Pianos, organs, and sewing machines may seem like an odd combination, but in 1880s Bangor, when this trade card was given out, anything was possible. The L. J. Wheelden Company, located at 76 Main Street, issued an advertising card that spoke more of tape measures and fashion than musical instruments. In addition to selling Steinways and other pianos, Wheelden tuned, repaired, packed, and moved his merchandise. The Andrews Music House, also on Main Street, was a similar business that lasted well into the 20th century, except Andrews avoided sewing machines.

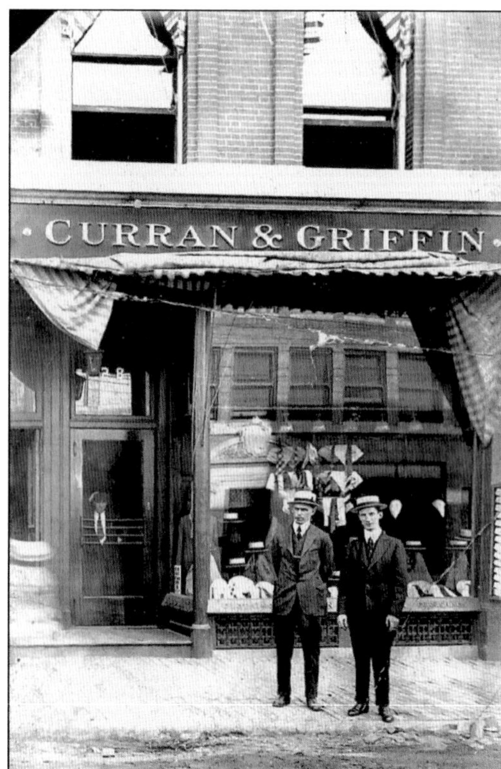

Would you buy a new dress suit from these men? No doubt you would, after you heard about their high-quality men's clothing store at 28 Central Street, and later, in the 1920s, at 38 Main Street. William A. Curran and Joseph Griffin sold clothing and furnishings to a devoted clientele. The two are impeccably dressed in tailored suits and straw hats called boaters. Unlike today, downtown in their time had many men's and women's clothing stores. The owner was always in the store, often with a tape measure hung from this neck, ready to be of assistance.

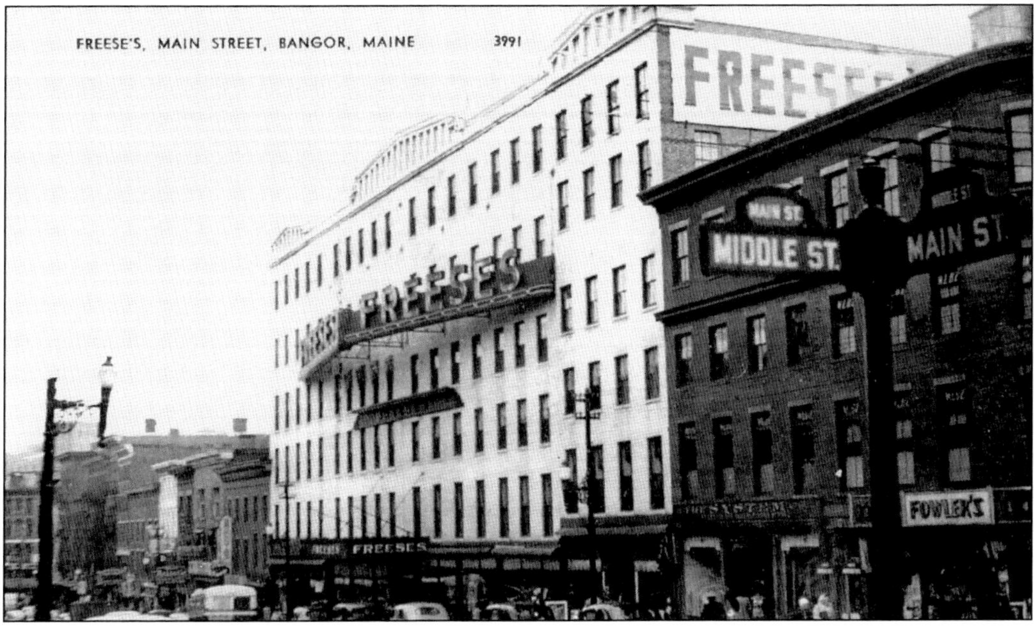

You had not seen downtown unless you visited Freese's Department Store, a Main Street attraction since its founding in September 1892. Local entrepreneur A. Langdon Freese started with a 19- by 60-foot store with one window facing Main Street. Originally selling suits and coats, he branched out over the years, expanding his line to include wedding gowns, Boy Scout uniforms, and fresh-roasted nuts. He also acquired adjacent property beside his storefront and behind it on Pickering Square. Feeling the pressure of consumer tastes and shopping centers' competition, the store, dubbed "Fifth Avenue in Maine," closed in 1985. Today, the building houses the Maine Discovery Museum and apartments for the elderly and disabled.

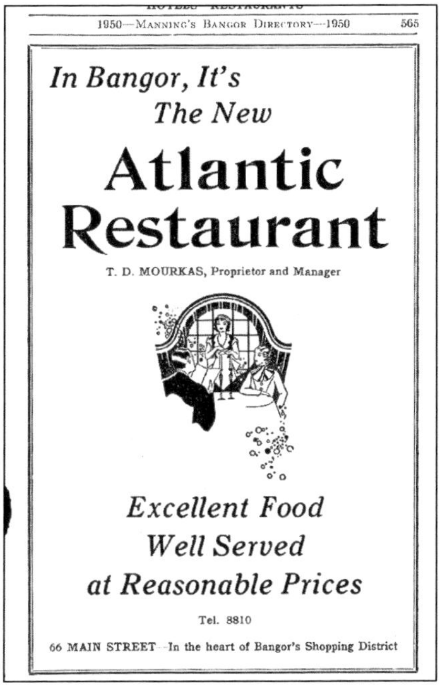
1950—Manning's Bangor Directory—1950 565

In Bangor, It's The New

Atlantic Restaurant

T. D. MOURKAS, Proprietor and Manager

Excellent Food Well Served at Reasonable Prices

Tel. 8810

66 MAIN STREET—In the heart of Bangor's Shopping District

The New Atlantic Restaurant served hot meals at reasonable prices for many years at 66 Main Street. Like downtown's clothing stores, its restaurants were noted for their owner always being on the premises, tending to the customers' every need. Thomas D. Mourkas was the New Atlantic's proprietor and manager for decades. Located next to Brountas Restaurant and just a few doors down from Freese's Department Store, Mourkas's eatery truly was in the heart of downtown.

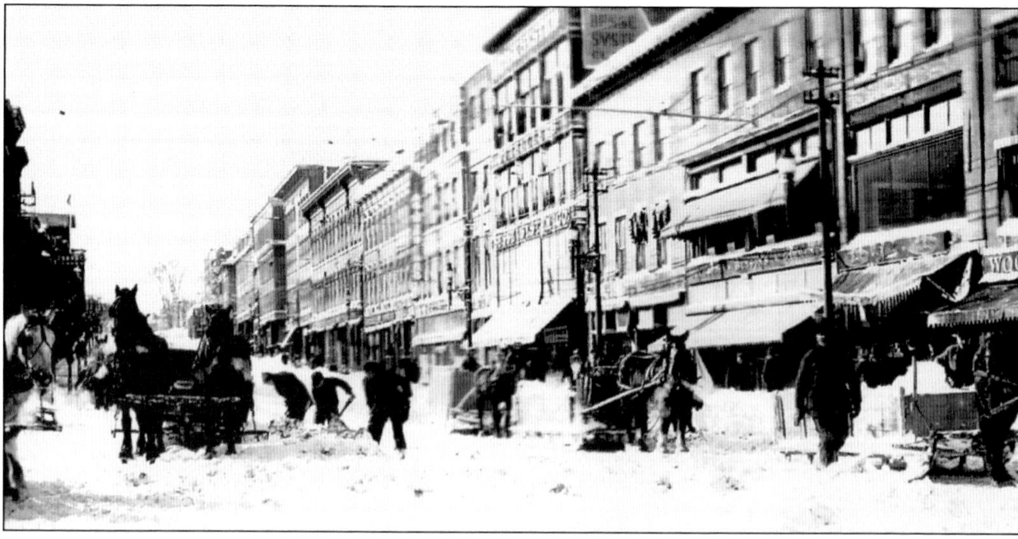

Wintertime photography must have been a lot of trouble in the days of wet plates and heavy cameras. Few postcard views such as this one, the only winter view in this book, are known to exist. Taken sometime in the 1920s, it pictures men and teams of horses clearing deep snow from Main Street. This was in the days before motorized city snowplows and salt and sanding crews. Some of the brick buildings in the background have been replaced by more modern blocks.

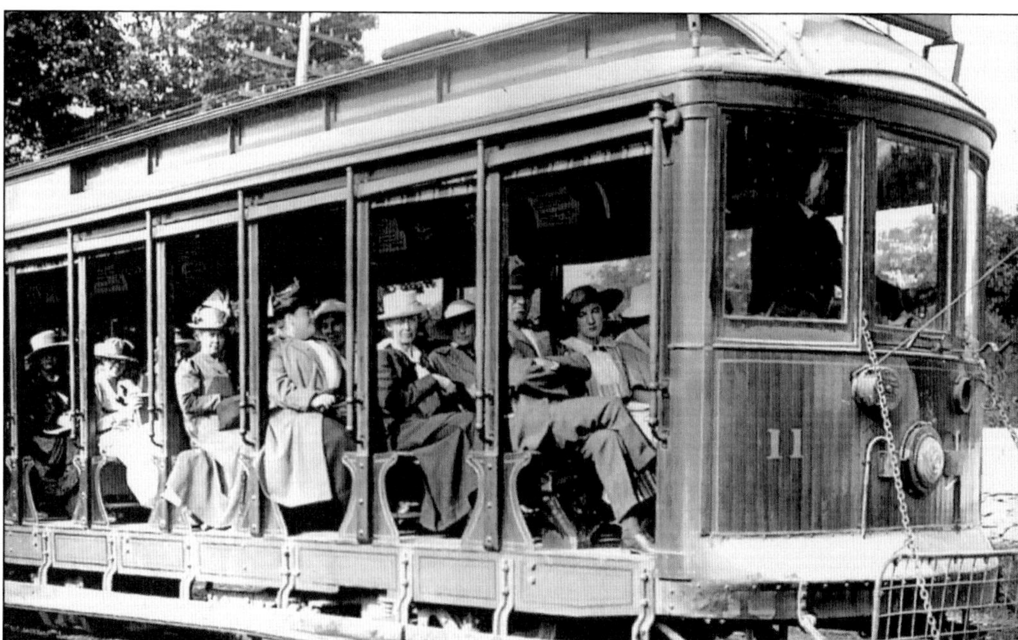

Bangor's street railway system was established in 1888 and ran until 1945. It proved especially useful during World War II, when its aging cars and conductors were pressed into service during a time of scarce rubber and gasoline for buses and cars. This early view shows car No. 11 making its Hampden run. Other routes operated by the Bangor Railway and Electric Company extended to Old Town, Brewer, and Charleston. Open-air trolleys were popular in the summer, allowing women like those shown here to show off their colorful, flowing dresses.

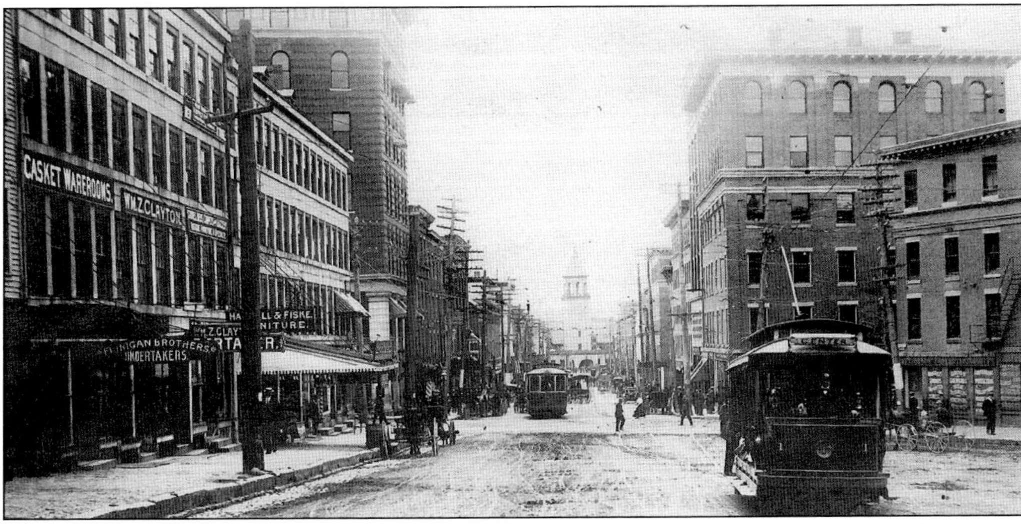

For a nominal fare, locals could ride the Bangor trolleys for hours, switching from the downtown route to other cars that took them farther from downtown. This view shows a streetcar approaching the photographer at East Market Square on Harlow Street, while another car is in the distance on Exchange Street. All of the buildings in this picture were destroyed by the 1911 fire. The long block on Park Street (left) was nicknamed "undertakers' row" because of the abundance of casket dealers located there. (BMCH.)

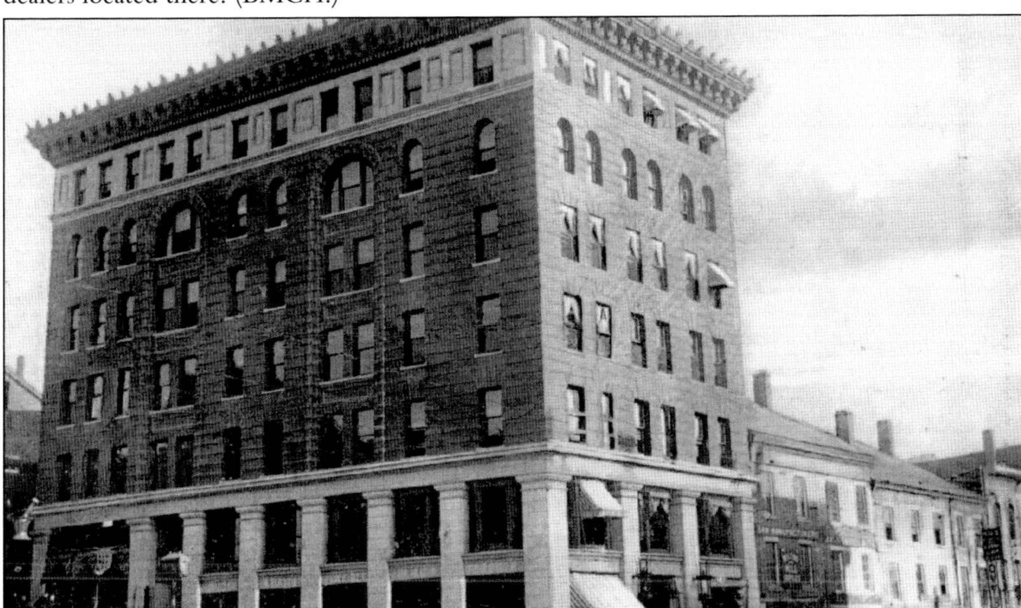

The impressive Morse-Oliver Building graced the corner of Exchange and State Streets until one memorable day in 1911, when it was left a pile of rubble by the great Bangor fire. Deborah Thompson, the city's architectural historian, said the city avoided building this high in post-fire planning, so this postcard view shows what the city was and probably never will be again. The seven-story office building was named for the two men who financed it: Lewellyn J. Morse and Hiram Oliver. John Scribner, one of two people to die in the 1911 disaster, perished in the rubble of this building. (MHPC.)

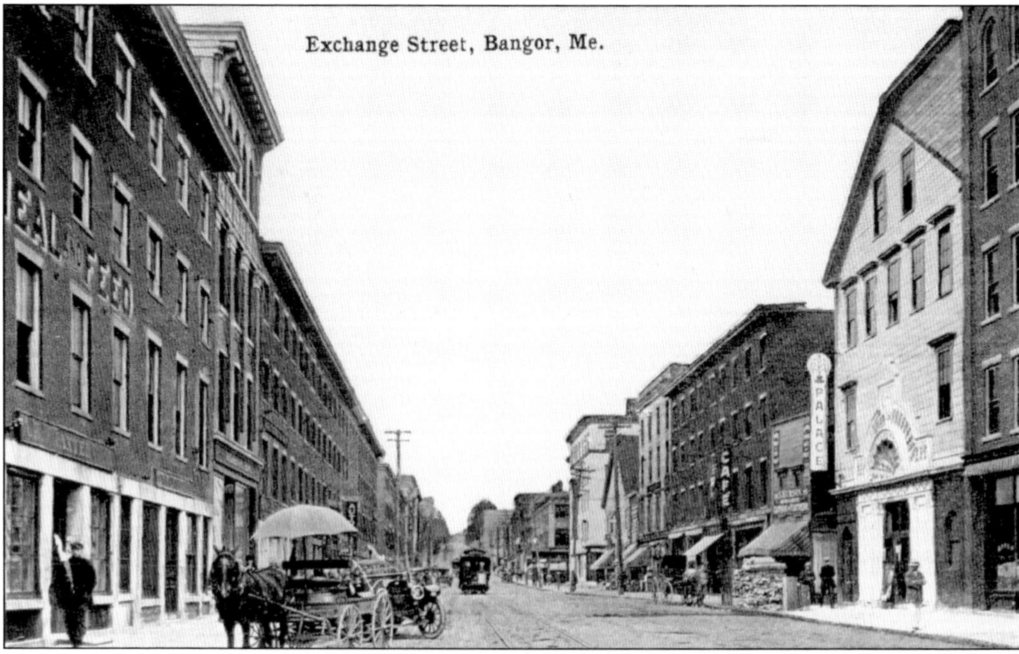

Since no building standing today on this lower part of Exchange Street was built before the 1970s, this view is probably unfamiliar. Most postcard views of this area look down Exchange Street toward the railroad station, so a view looking in the opposite direction, toward downtown, is hard to find. The light-colored block on the right, with the fancy arch over the doorway, was the Palace Theater, where early movies nicknamed "flickers" were shown for a nickel. (MHPC.)

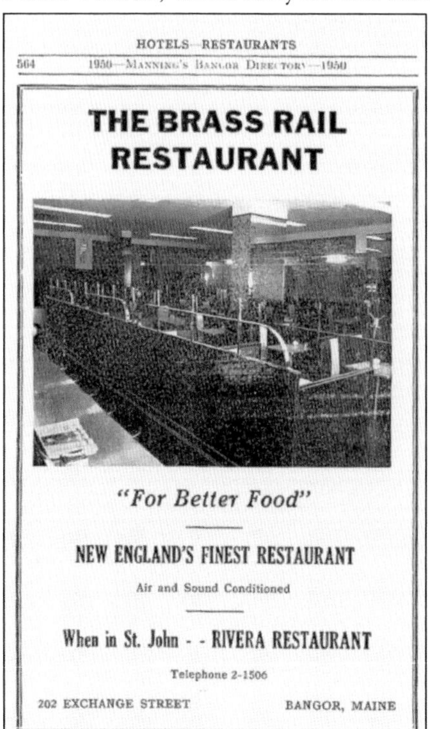

The Brass Rail Restaurant, owned by Louis Stavron and Max Kominsky at different times in its long history, was a fixture at 202 Exchange Street for decades. Today, it would sound strange to advertise your eatery as being "air and sound conditioned," but in 1950, the date of this advertisement, the phrase was an attention grabber. Named for an actual brass rail located close to the floor of this fine restaurant, the place served steaks and seafood to satisfied diners. Heavyweight boxer Jack Dempsey dined here during a tour of eastern Maine. Most of the diners, however, were everyday folks who liked its convenience and cozy atmosphere.

Telephone 3631

PEKIN RESTAURANT

W. J. JONES, Manager

Mandarin and American Style

BUSINESS MEN'S LUNCH

Special Attention Given to Parties and Banquets

24 POST OFFICE SQUARE

BANGOR MAINE

A strange, exotic restaurant on Harlow Street (at 24 Post Office Square) opened in 1924. Founded by Wong Hee and Wong J. Jones, the Pekin served Mandarin and American-style businessmen's lunches. Later, Charles W. and W. Frederick Wong carried on the Asian dining experience at the Oriental Restaurant, located at 209 Exchange Street. These pioneers in local exotic cuisine probably could not have imagined a time when Bangor had an abundance of Chinese restaurants, as well as those serving Thai, Japanese, and Vietnamese cuisine.

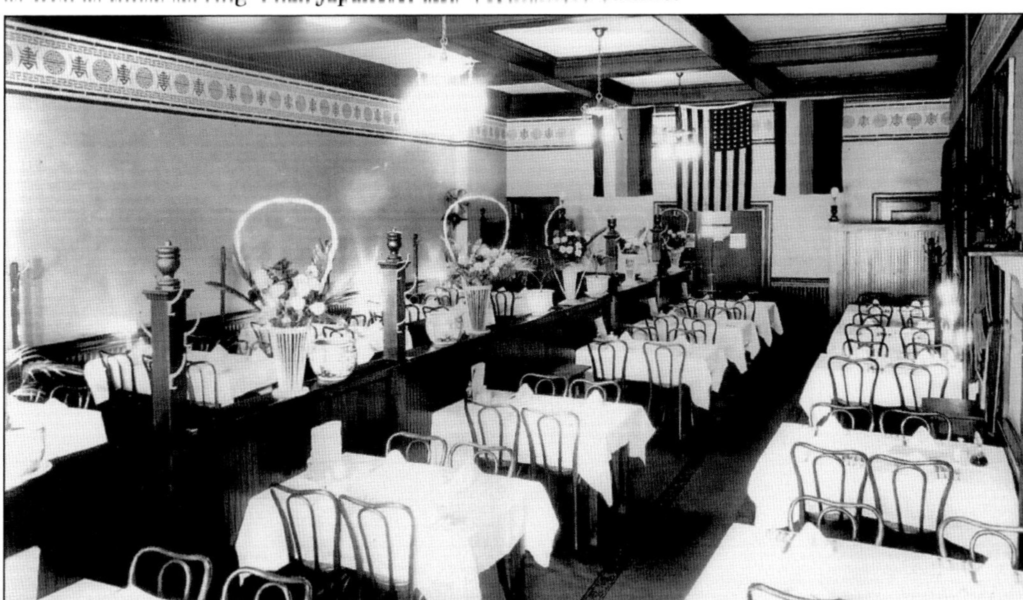

A rare interior view of the Pekin Restaurant, dating from the 1920s, shows an immaculate setting with white linen tablecloths and baskets of fresh-cut gladiolas. Chinese flags hang from either side of the American flag, a poignant study in patriotism from Asian immigrants. Most Bangor residents had never tasted Asian cuisine before the Pekin opened its doors. The small restaurant's decor included a border of Asian designs near the ceiling. This picture was taken by Frank L. Franklin, a local photographer whose remarkable pictures have been preserved by his daughter, Betty Shibles, of Orrington.

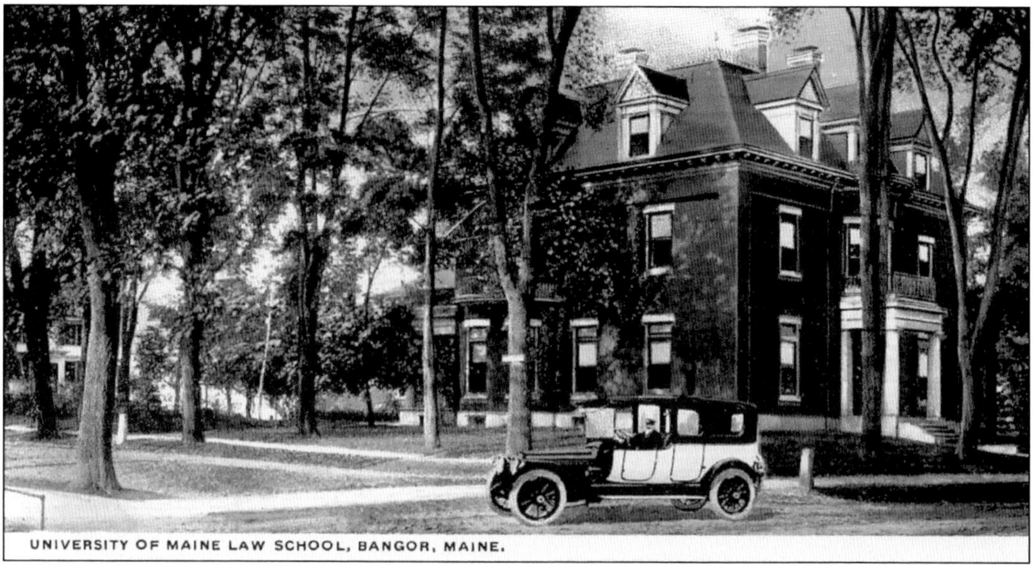

Union Street's Isaac Farrar mansion had been transformed into the University of Maine Law School when this postcard was circulated in 1918. After the school moved south to Portland, the former brick residence was sold to the Northern Conservatory of Music, which named the mansion the Symphony House. In the beginning, however, it was the private residence of timber tycoon Farrar and his family, who desired an opulent home located near downtown with which to impress their fellow Bangoreans. The Merrill family and others later owned the mansion, which was expanded in the late 19th century. Margo Cobb chronicles the building's history in the book *If the Walls Could Talk.*

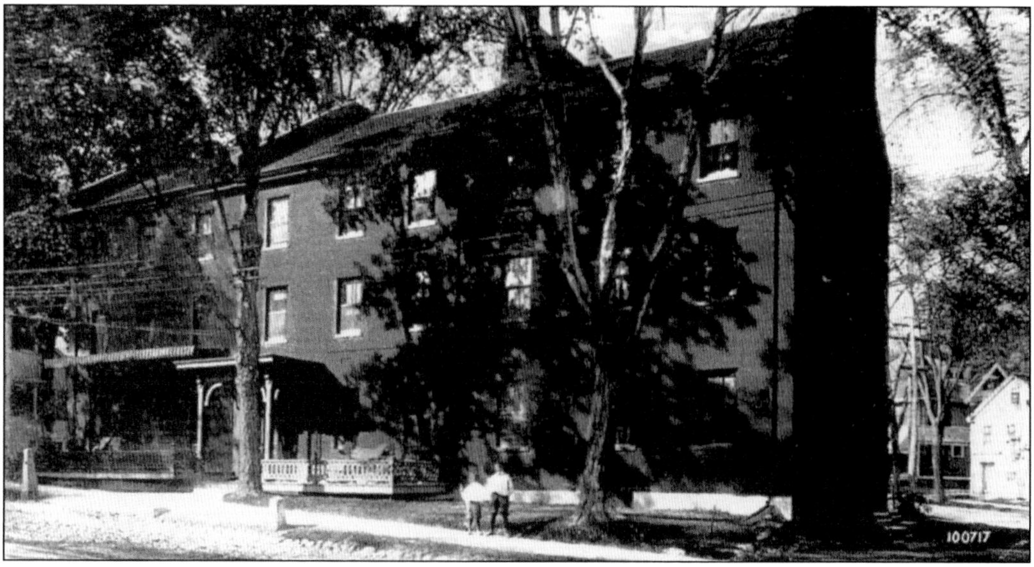

The Lowder apartment building on Hammond Street is a survivor. The red-brick landmark has been home to generations of tenants since its construction in 1834. Named for Samuel Lowder, who lived next door, the building is still a popular residence because of its convenient location and fine apartments. Located close to downtown, the Lowder has outlasted many other brick blocks of a similar age that have succumbed to the wrecking ball. Corner blocks are especially prone to developers of filling stations and convenience stores.

Eight

Great Bangor Fires

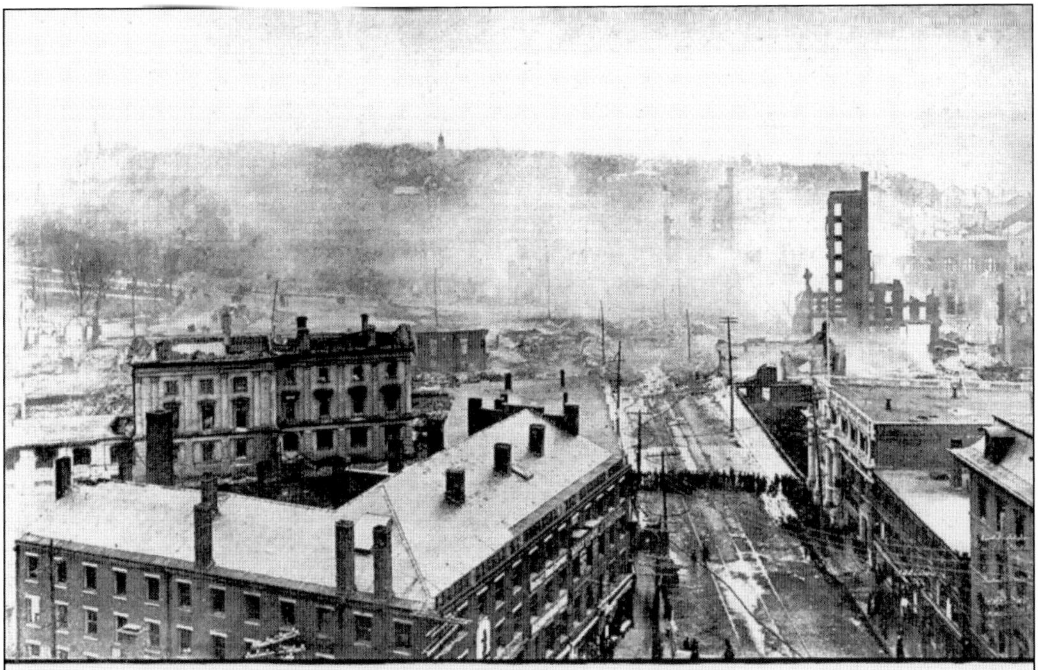

The Burnt district from the Tower of City Hall.

The inferno of April 30, 1911, remains the single most transforming event in Bangor history. On that Sunday afternoon, a $3 million wall of flame ravaged the city's downtown, leaving in its path scenes such as this at lower Hammond and State Streets. The view, captured from the city hall clock tower, also pictures a row of men standing on Kenduskeag Bridge, perhaps forming a bucket brigade, or maybe they are just a string of horrified spectators.

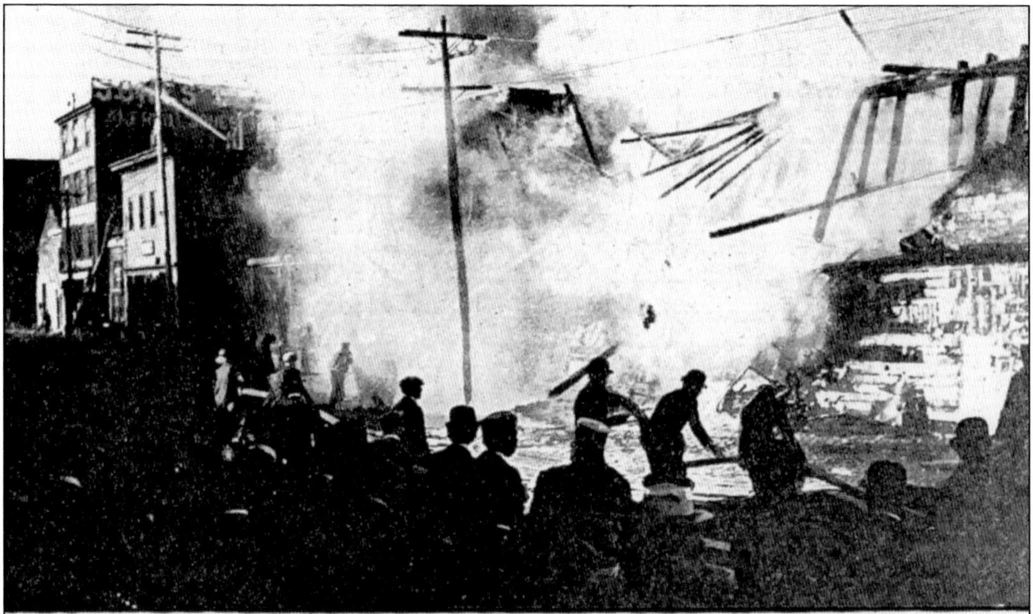

Start of Fire on Broad Street, West side of Kenduskeag Stream.

This dramatic view shows the actual start of the fire shortly after 4:00 p.m. on April 30. Men carelessly smoking in J. Frank Green's hay shed on Broad Street are believed to have ignited the inferno, but its origins will probably always remain a mystery. Since horses and wagons still outnumbered automobiles in 1911 Bangor, dry hay and other combustibles were commonly stored in downtown sheds and warehouses.

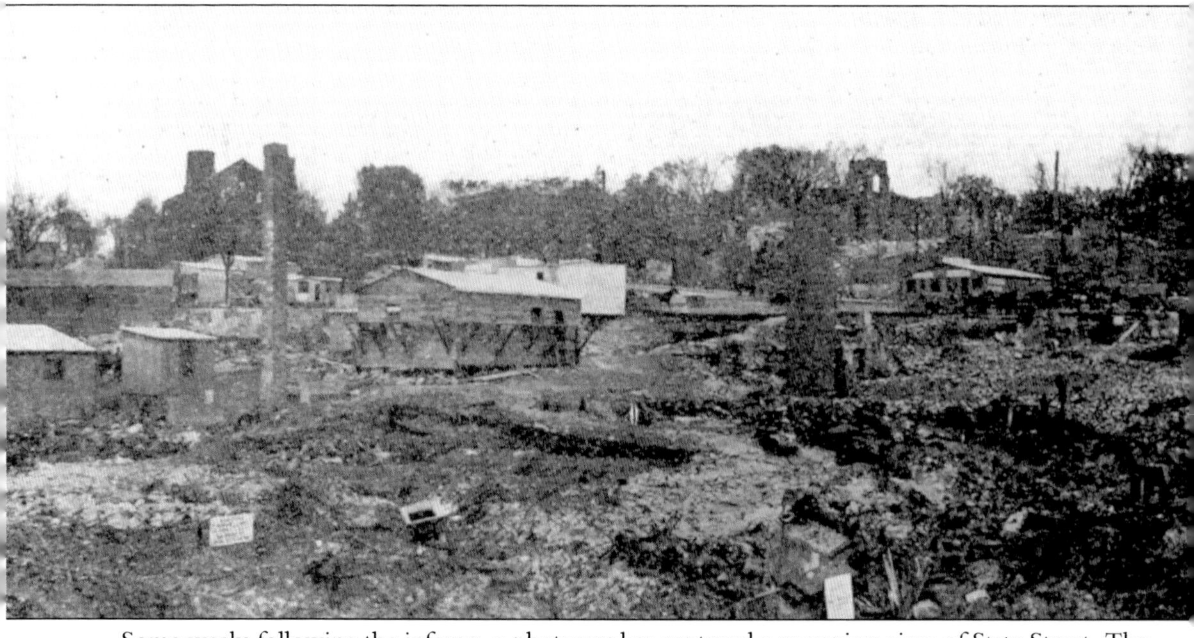

Some weeks following the inferno, a photographer captured a sweeping view of State Street. The shell of the Morse-Oliver Building at Exchange and State Streets (see page 93) is on the far right. The outlines of the burned First Universalist Church (far left) and Central Congregational Church (left of the center) were also recorded on film. Temporary buildings put up along Harlow Street,

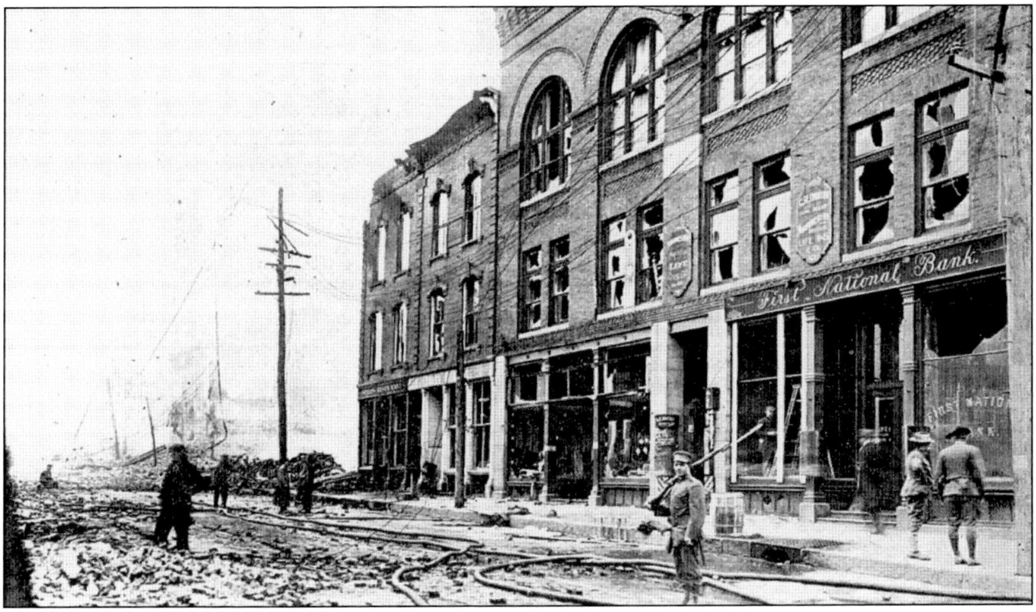

National Guardsmen such as this man, clutching a long rifle while standing in front of the First National Bank on Exchange Street, were pressed into service after the fire. Local newspaper accounts downplayed the extent of the looting, perhaps to keep morale up. In reality, it may have been a bigger problem than many realized. The street rubble in this photograph, and the tangle of fire hoses, can only begin to convey the hazards pedestrians such as the couple at the far right encountered. Crowds of the curious filtered into the city for weeks to survey the fire damage.

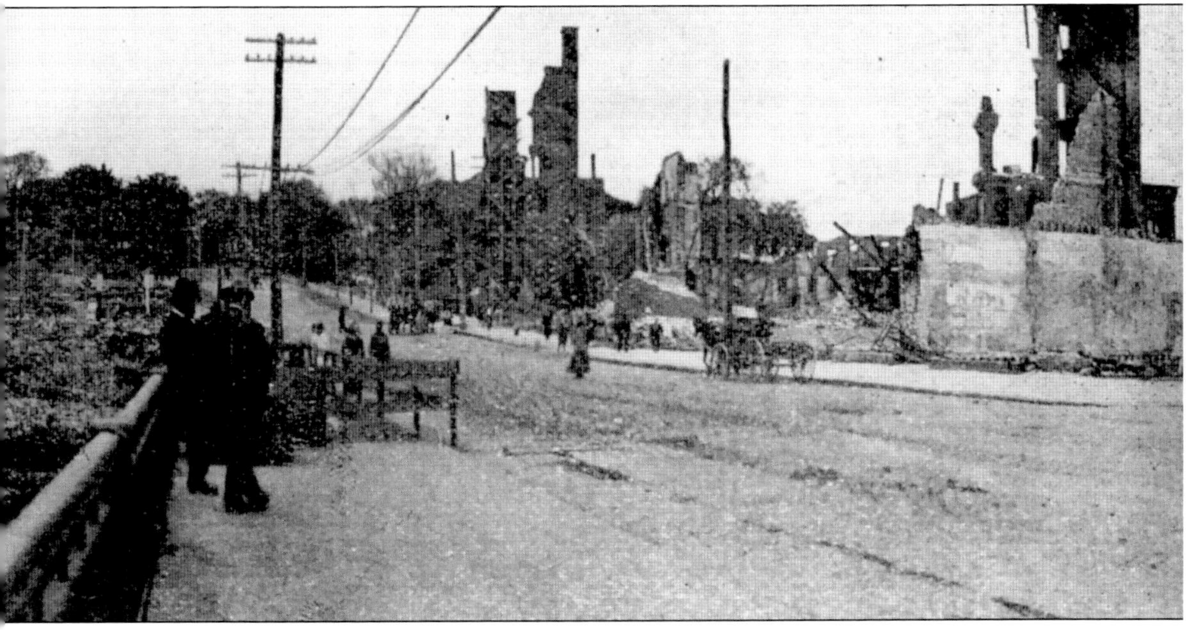

in addition to other spots downtown, helped stunned businessmen and residents to regroup and plan their next moves. Many property owners were heavily insured and built bigger and better buildings. Small grocers and entrepreneurs were not so fortunate. A rundown of businesses in the 1912 city directory reveals many names missing from the previous year's roster.

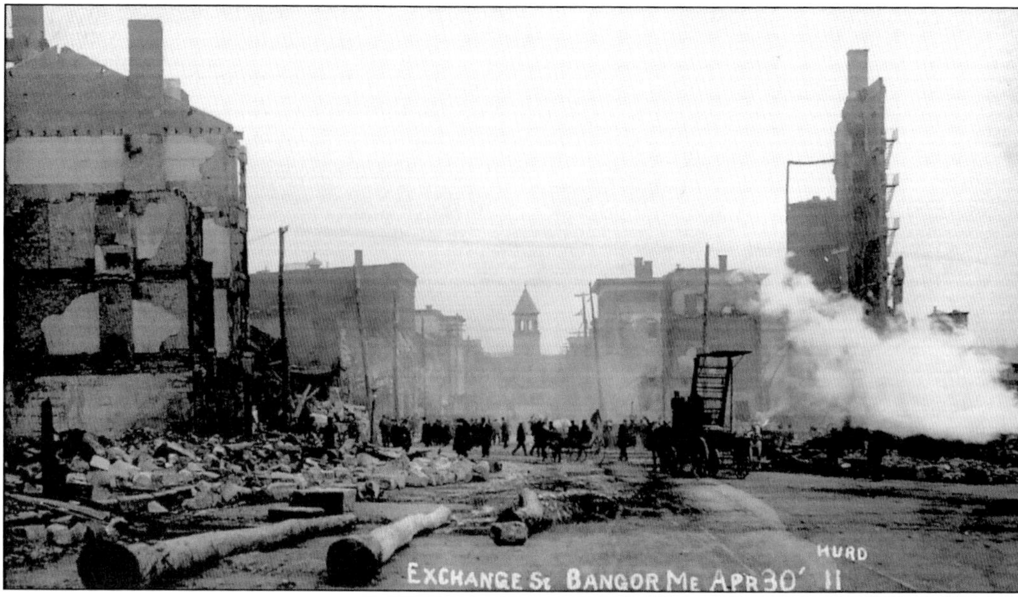

Telephone polls resemble giant matchsticks on Exchange Street following the 1911 disaster. When the flames jumped the Kenduskeag Stream, they consumed some Exchange Street blocks while leaving much of the lower street, heading toward the river, untouched. Union Station's bell tower stands like a silent sentinel visible through the haze in the distance. The landmark escaped the fire's fury.

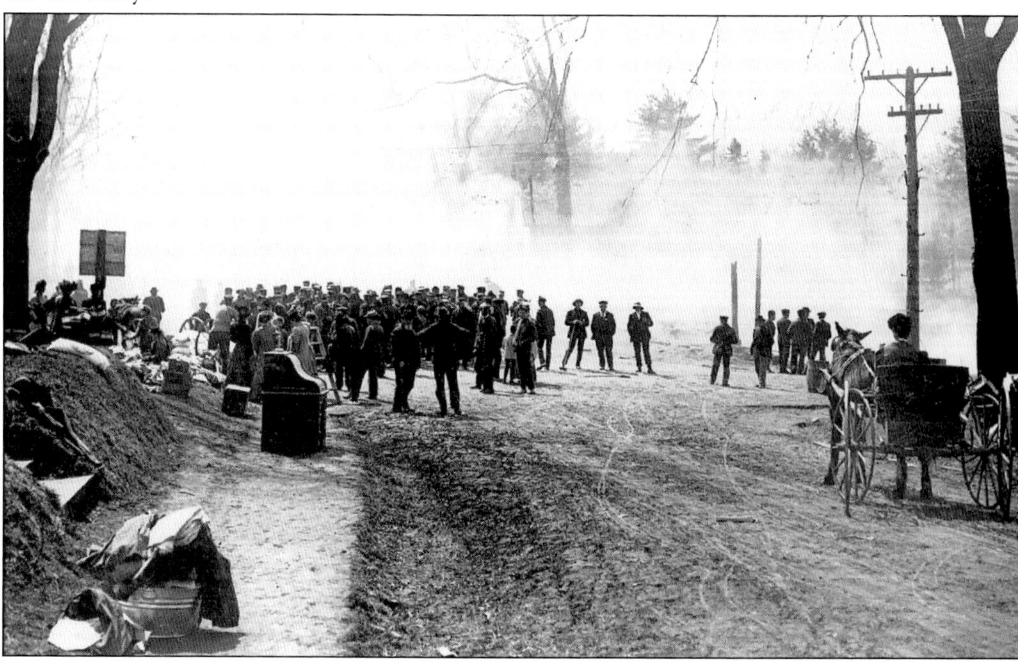

Many stories, some true, some apocryphal, made the rounds in the months following the great Bangor fire. One concerned a certain woman on Broadway who removed the furniture from her home and stacked it in her front yard. She watched in horror as the flames consumed the furniture but not her home. Many heirlooms were lost in the fire, along with family pets and a reputed 2,000 trees. This picture shows a roll-top wooden desk and other items placed by the roadside.

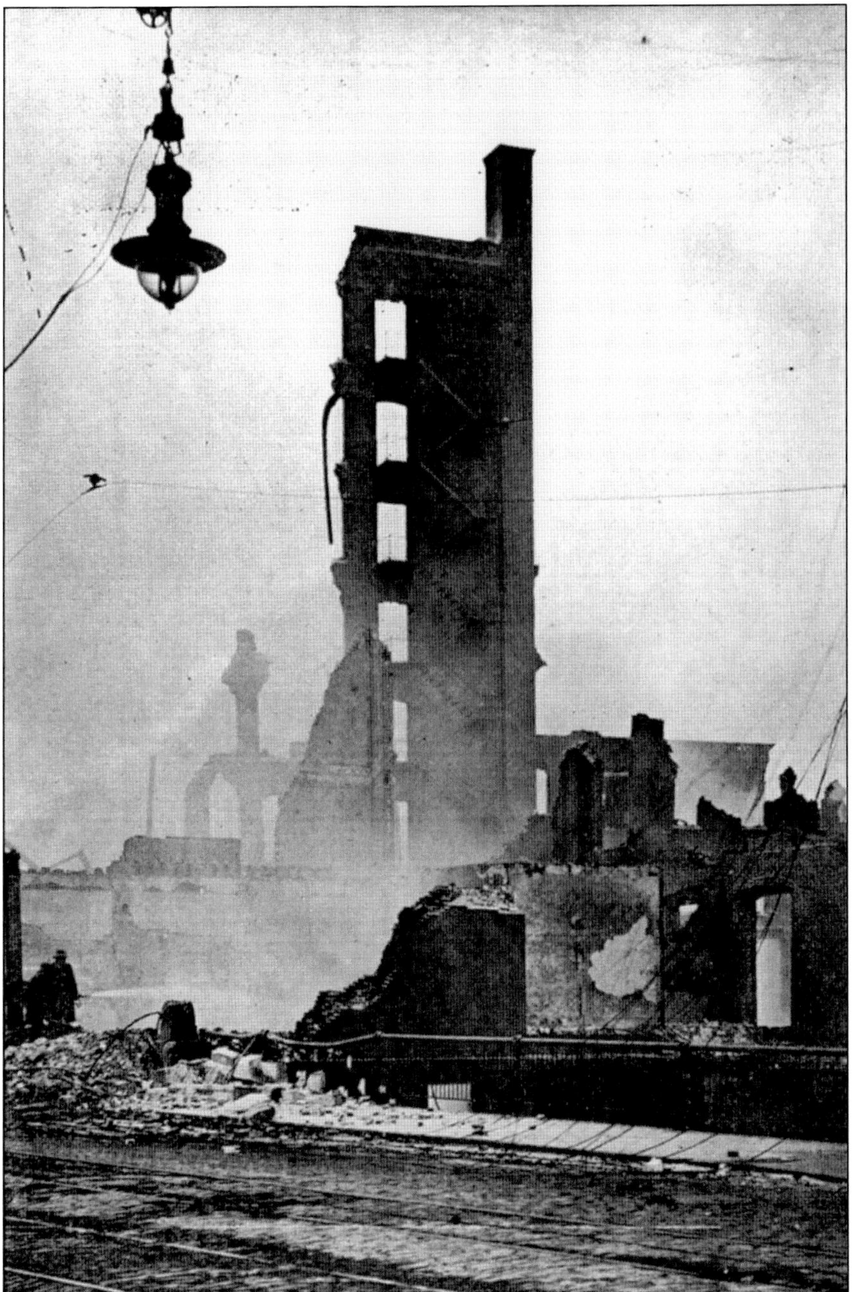
Ruins of the Morse-Oliver Block.

The seven-story Morse-Oliver Building at Exchange and State Streets was in the line of fire on April 30, 1911. Only this shell remained. John Scribner, an elderly shoemaker from Brewer, died here when falling rubble trapped him. George Abbott, a 41-year-old volunteer firefighter also from Brewer, became the fire's second casualty later that night, when he was buried under superheated bricks when a chimney collapsed on Penobscot Street. As tragic as those losses were, most felt it miraculous that more lives were not lost in the disaster.

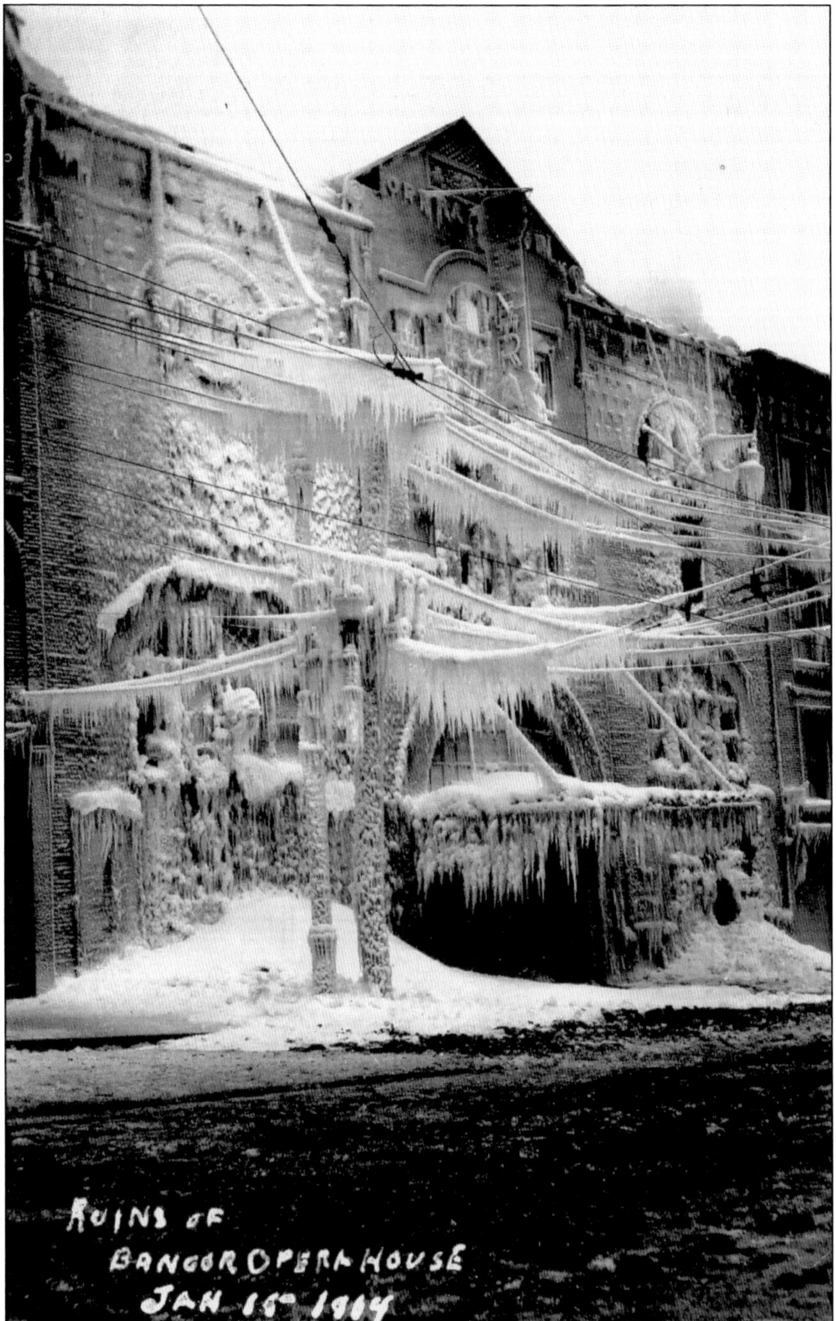

Only a handful of firemen have died in Bangor's long history. Two of them perished one extremely cold night on January 15, 1914, when the old Bangor Opera House caught fire. The inferno started in the basement boilers and then moved rapidly up the stairs, which acted like oxygen-sucking funnels. Flammable paint on scenery located behind the theater's stage added to the fire's intensity. The next day, and in the days following, photographers such as John C. Thayer captured the theater coated in ice. The rubble was eventually removed, and not until 1920 was the present opera house building constructed on the site.

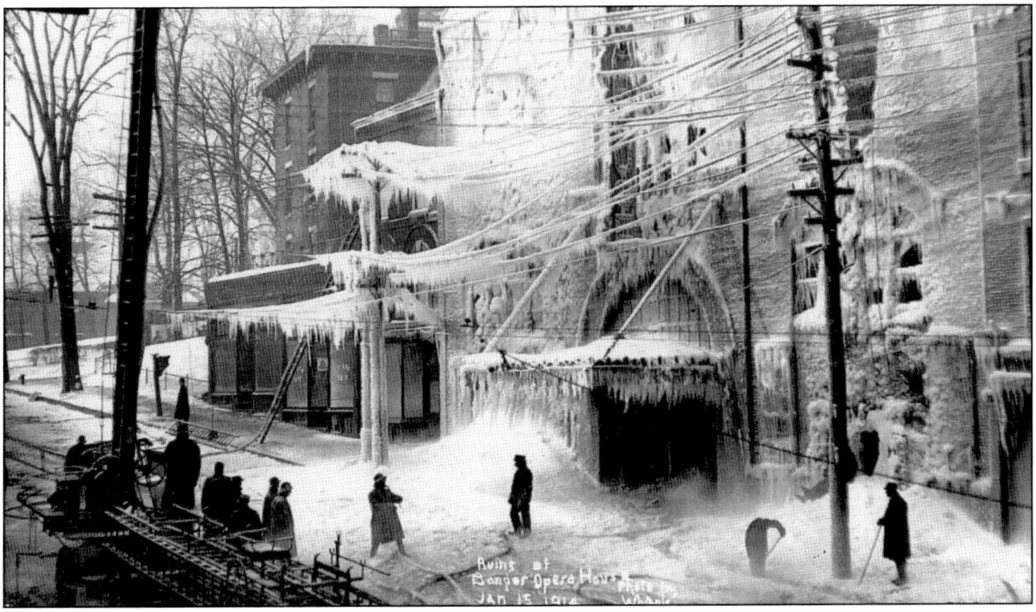

This postcard view of the 1914 opera house ruins was auctioned on eBay following the January 15, 2004, fire directly across Main Street that destroyed the 135-year-old Masonic building. The twist of fate—two downtown wintertime fires spaced exactly 90 years apart—was not lost on firefighting experts like Paul E. Tower, nor on the Masons or anyone else with an interest in fate. The one difference between the two fires is that no one died, or was even injured, in the 2004 devastation. Tower pointed out the new state-of-the-art aerial ladder truck in this picture used to fight the opera house fire.

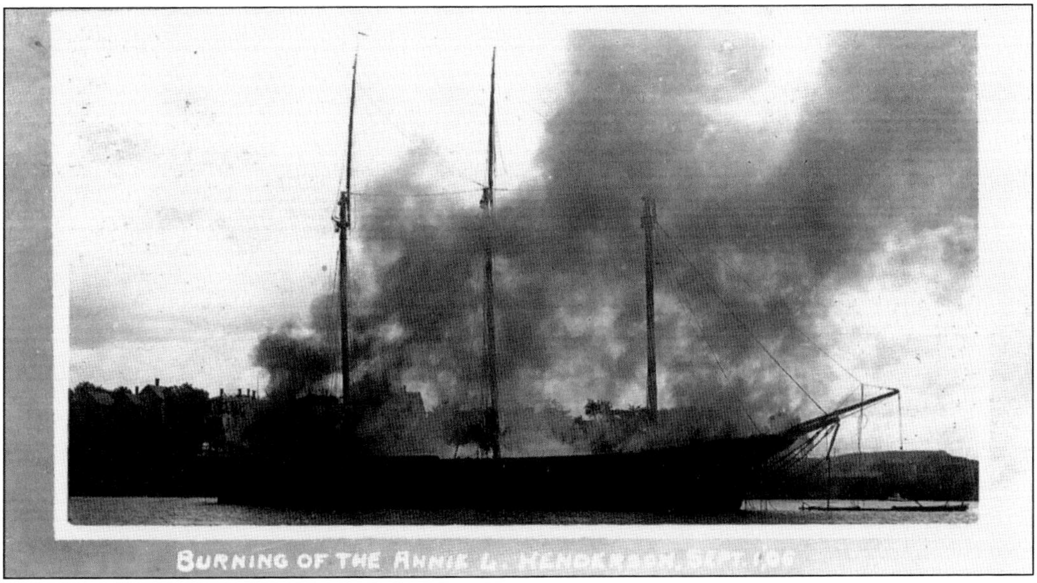

One of the more dramatic real-photo postcards ever taken in Bangor shows the burning of the *Annie L. Henderson* in the Penobscot River. On September 1, 1906, the schooner's sails and rigging were ignited by a nearby coal fire while it was tied up to a wharf. A stiff wind carried the schooner across to the Brewer shore, and it was then towed to the middle of the Penobscot, where the fire smoldered throughout the day and night.

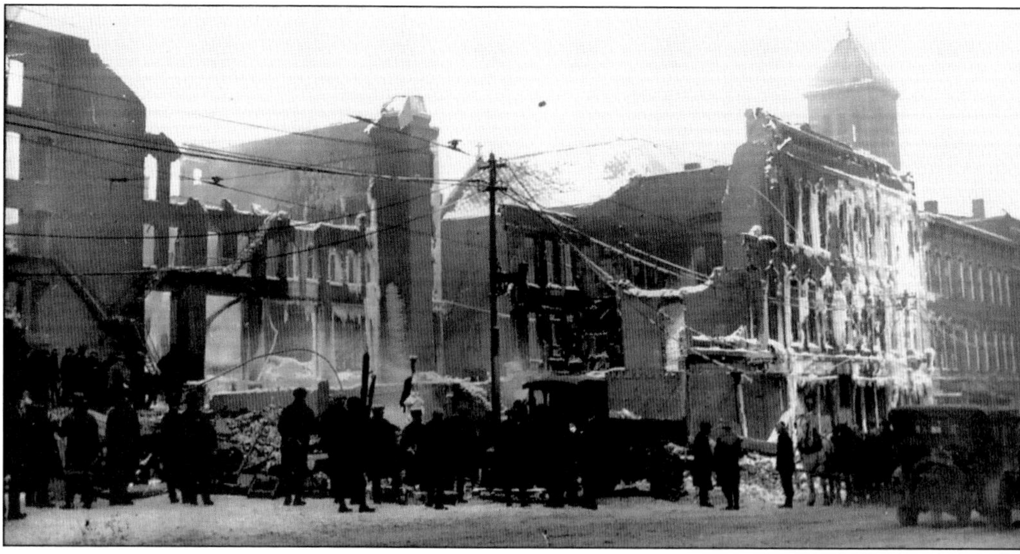

The 1911 Bangor fire was still burned into people's minds on February 10, 1927, when a furious fire consumed the Hatch Block on Main Street. What the earlier inferno had failed to do—jump onto Main Street—the 1927 blaze was able to do. Unlike in the1911 fire, which was fought using horse-drawn apparatus, motorized vehicles were used to battle the furious 1927 inferno. This real-photo postcard shows men and vehicles on Main Street, with the charred, ice-covered remains of the block behind them.

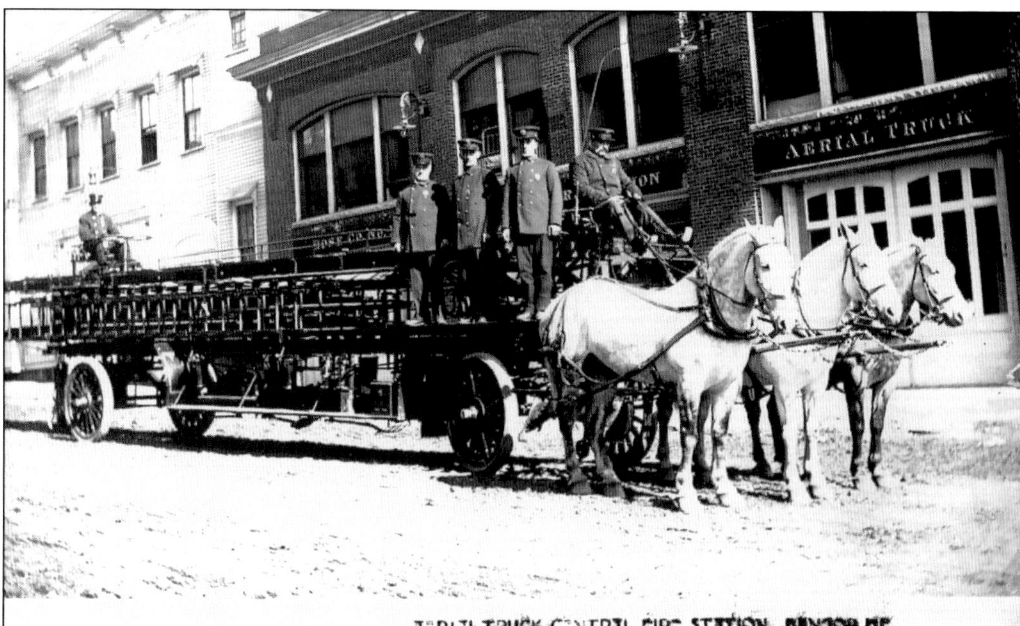

Paul E. Tower, a firefighting historian who oversees the Hose 5 Fire Museum at 247 State Street in Bangor, had no trouble identifying this great old view. "It's a Tiller hook and ladder truck," he said. "The fireman driving the truck steered three white horses." The picture was taken on lower Union Street in front of the old Union Station. To the station's left is the Olympia Theater, which kept firefighters busy when it burned for hours in 1963. By then, needless to say, firemen had more modern apparatus than the one pictured here.

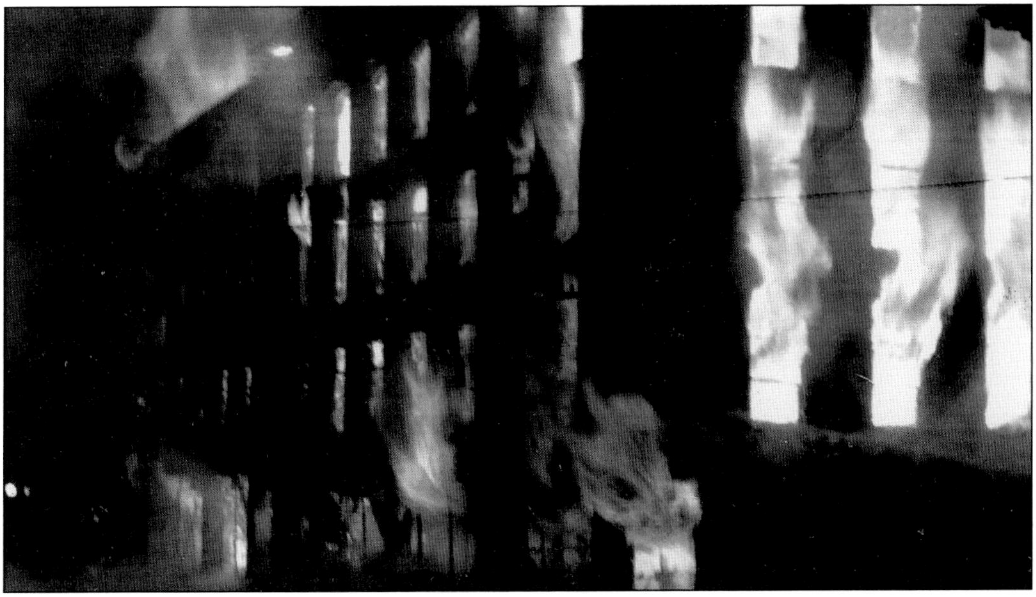

A rare postcard view of the 1927 fire in progress conveys a sense of the flames' destruction. Following the disaster, the entire block, stretching from Main Street back to Columbia Street, was razed and replaced by a more modern Coe Block that survives today. This and other images of the Coe fire are often misidentified in articles and antique shows as depicting the 1911 fire, but close inspection shows a different street than that ravaged in 1911. Another way to distinguish between the two is the time of year. Hanging icicles visible in the 1927 disaster would not be evident in the 1911 inferno, which occurred on April 30.

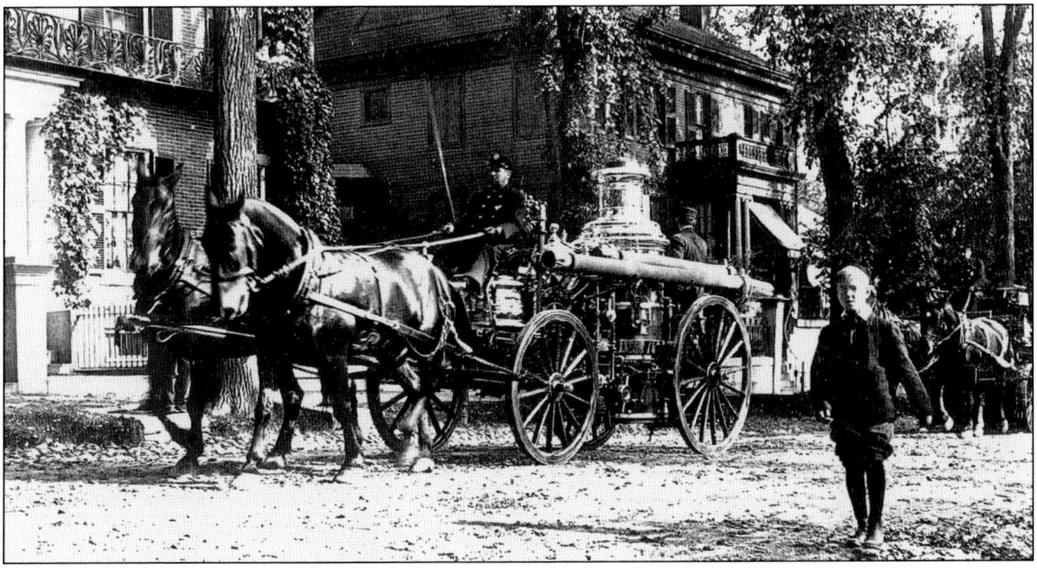

This much reproduced picture shows a scene on Broadway, near Penobscot Street, probably during a parade. A firefighter has his hands full driving a boiler truck hauled by two horses along the city's dirt streets. The boy on the right shows a child's fascination with parades and all things relating to fires and firefighting. The photograph, made available by Northeast Reprographics, is remarkable because it shows a relic from another time that was used to fight the great 1911 Bangor fire.

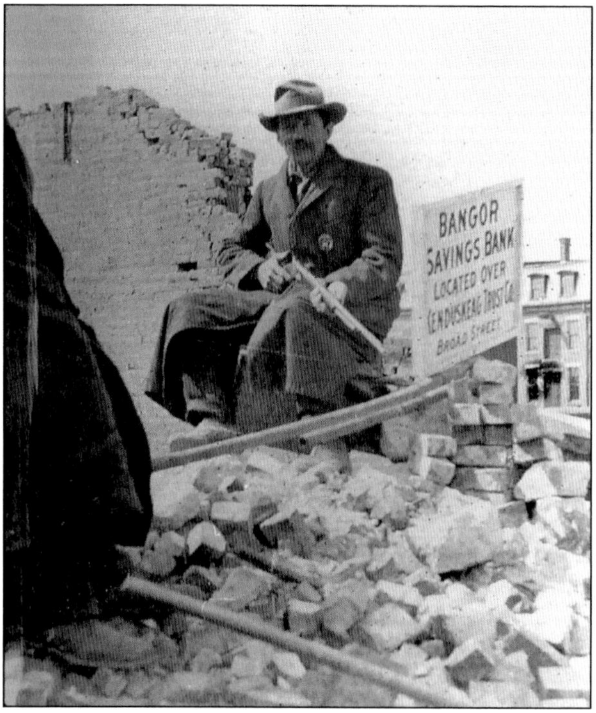

Banks hired armed marshals to stand, or sit, guard over their exposed vaults following the 1911 inferno. After the Bangor Savings Bank, located on State Street, was destroyed in the fire, the bank temporarily relocated over the Kenduskeag Trust Company on Broad Street. The bank rebuilt a granite bank on the same site where its main office is still based. Dean Lunt writes of the fire and other decisive events in a 150-year history of the bank titled *Here for Generations: The Story of a Maine Bank and Its City*, published in 2002. (BDN.)

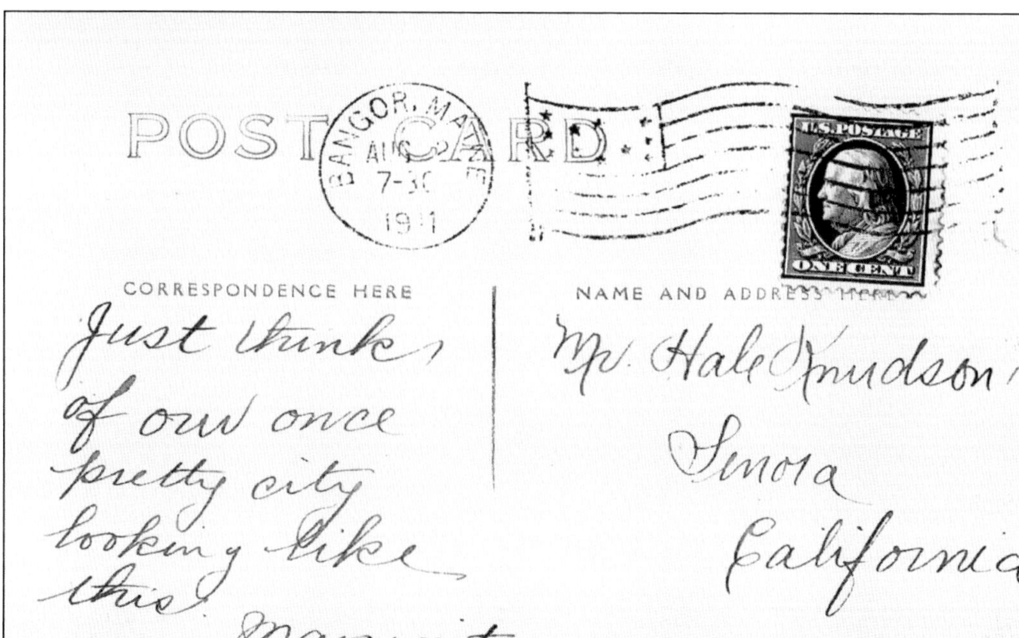
POST CARD
BANGOR, MAINE AUG 7-30 1911
CORRESPONDENCE HERE
Just think of our once pretty city looking like this. Marguerite
NAME AND ADDRESS HERE
Mr. Hale Knudson, Senora California

Sometimes simply turning a postcard over tells more about an event than the picture on the other side. A local woman named Marguerite poured out her thoughts in 10 words to Hale Knudson of Senora, California, in this card, postmarked July 30, 1911, three months to the day after the great fire. She wrote, "Just think of our once pretty city looking like this." The card's photograph side shows a scene of devastation on Franklin Street, where a brick fire wall stopped the flames from crossing onto Hammond and Main Streets.

Nine

Steeples and Stars of David

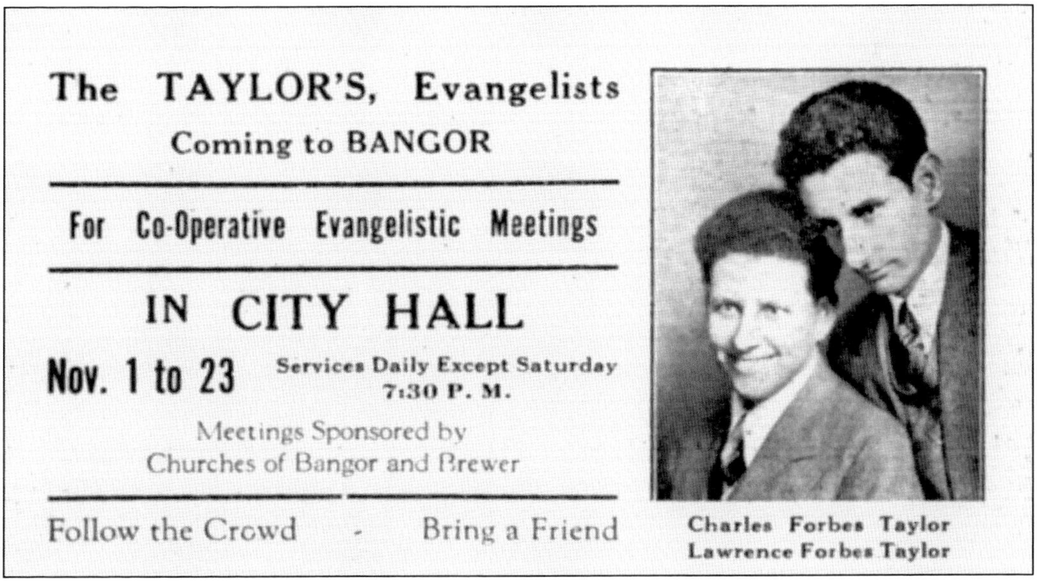

Churches in Bangor and Brewer sponsored evangelistic meetings conducted by the Taylors in the old city hall auditorium, as advertised in this undated postcard. The card's reverse side quotes a pastor in Worcester, Massachusetts, as saying of Charlie Taylor, "He is easily America's leading evangelist. He is Scriptural and sane, brainy and eloquent. People in crowds listen to him in amazement. His youth draws them and then his maturity holds them."

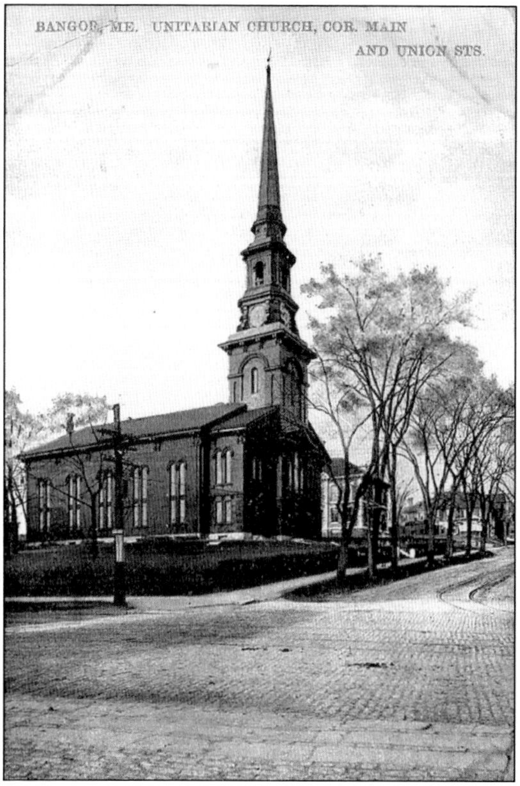

Although it is no longer a church, the spire of the Unitarian church building at Union and Main Streets will always reach skyward in true church fashion. Independent Congregationalists, also known as Unitarians, built this church in 1853 after a fire destroyed an earlier church on Main Street. Church families purchased pews to help pay for the cost of construction. Vice Pres. Hannibal Hamlin worshiped here, and among those who spoke in the building was former First Lady Eleanor Roosevelt. The building lives on a cultural center called the Old Brick Church.

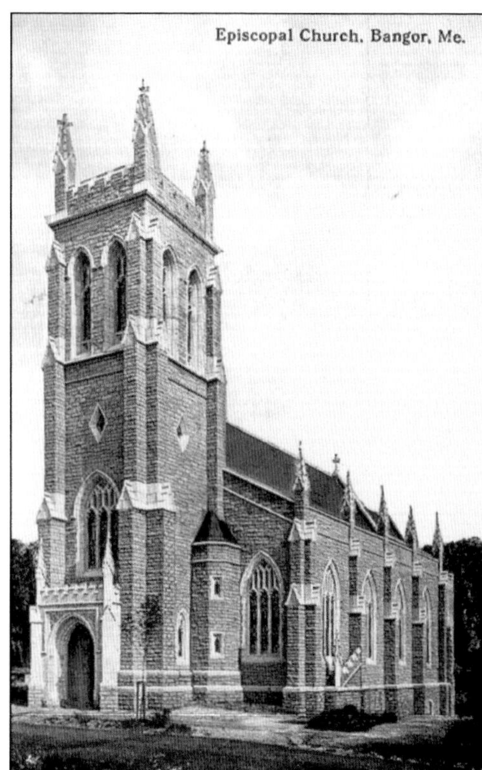

The stone St. John's Episcopal Church at 234 French Street replaced an 1839 church located at the same site and designed by the famous architect Richard Upjohn. It burned in the 1911 Bangor fire. The present church is of Gothic design and contains just two items saved from the old building: a brass lectern and marble baptismal font. After the building's dedication in 1918, the *Bangor Daily Commercial* reported, "Never has the stately Episcopal ritual been more effectively presented than at the reopening of St. John's Church."

St. John's Catholic Church and rectory still stand on York Street overlooking the Penobscot River. The brick church was built in 1856 near the site of a log cabin built by Bangor's first white settler, Jacob Buswell, who moved here in 1769. Its first pastor was Fr. John Bapst, a Swiss-born Jesuit priest who returned to Bangor after being tarred and feathered by hostile residents of Ellsworth. The church was originally intended to serve all of east side Bangor. Despite modern renovations, its interior, with its ancient E&GG Hook organ and stained glass, continues to inspire.

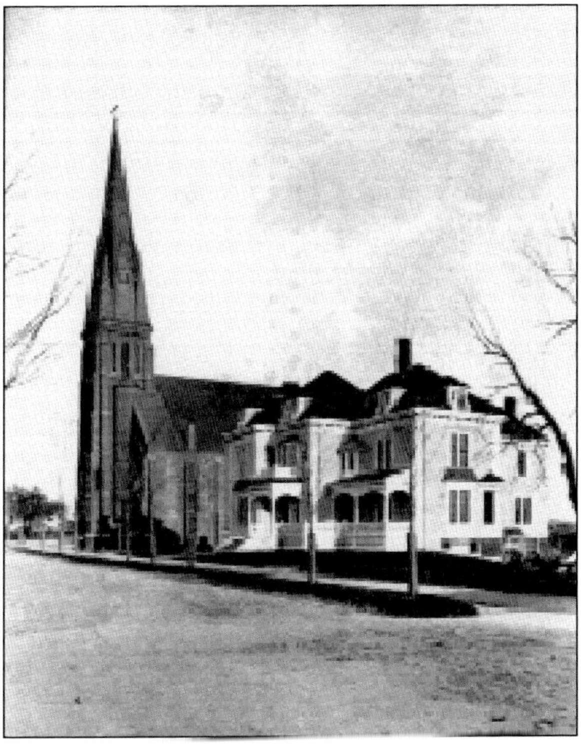

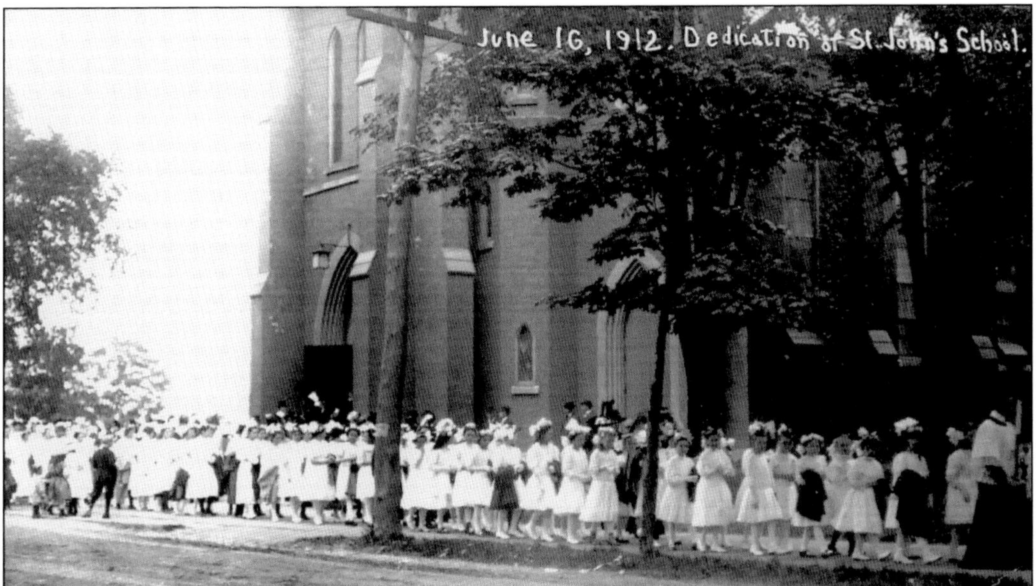

A real-photo postcard shows a rare scene of children in their Sunday best walking from St. John's Catholic Church to the dedication of St. John's School on State Street. The date was June 16, 1912, and it must have been a major event in the history of not only the church, but the parochial school community. Other postcards in this series (see page 39) show Knights of Columbus, altar boys, a bishop, priests, and nuns lining the walkway outside of the brick church. It was a bright, sunny day and one of high ceremony for the east side Catholics.

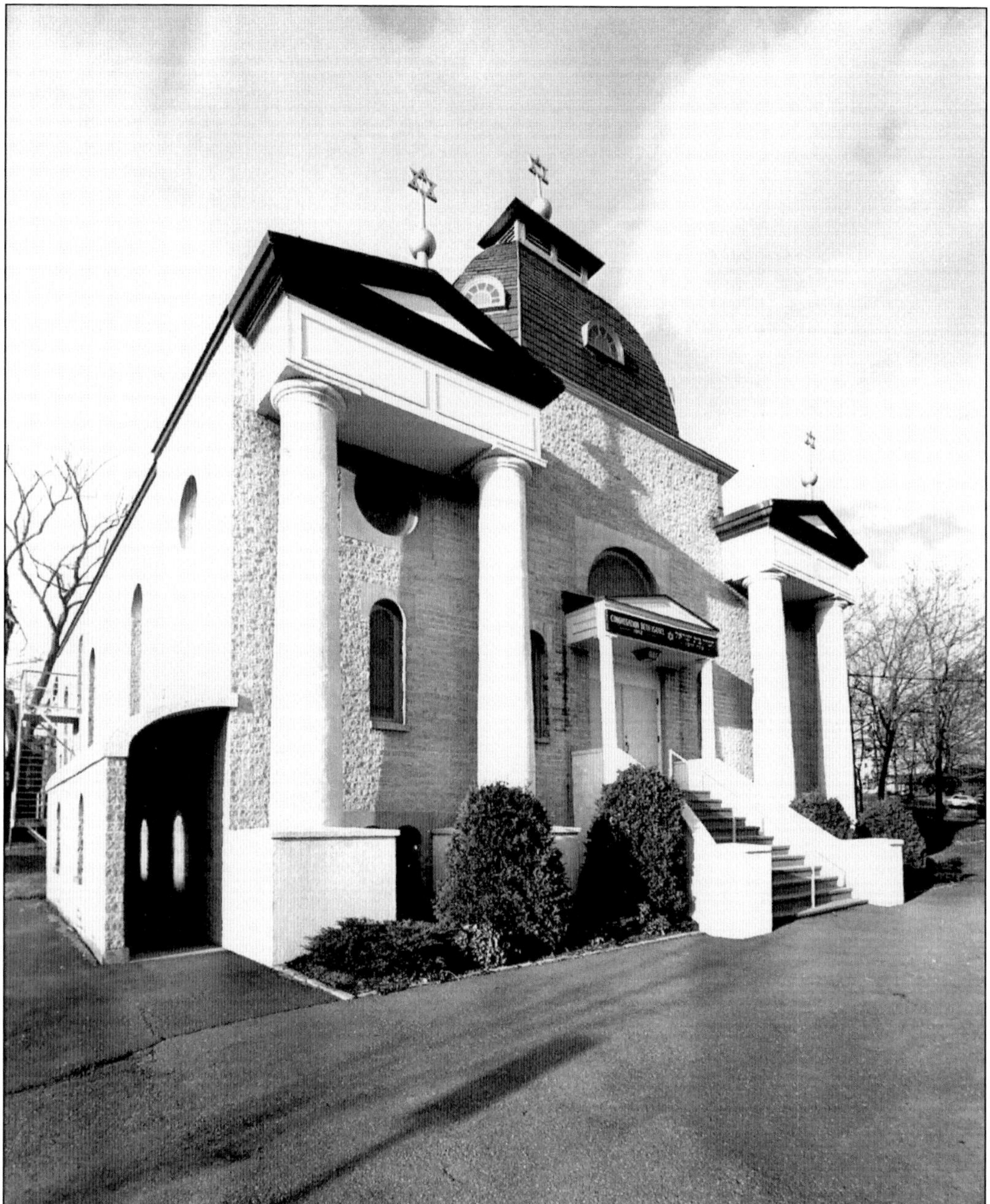

Congregation Beth Israel, the oldest congregation in Maine, dedicated this building in 1913. The congregation had met in other places in Bangor before that. Even prior to the great fire of 1911, which destroyed its Center Street synagogue, conservative members had been planning to build closer to Jewish neighborhoods in the area of York and Hancock Streets. Generations of Jews have worshiped here at 144 York Street. The synagogue was expanded in 1991 with the addition of the Helen and Sidney Epstein Conference Room. Beth Israel's three Stars of David are visible from some distance, which must have been the intention of its designers. (BDN.)

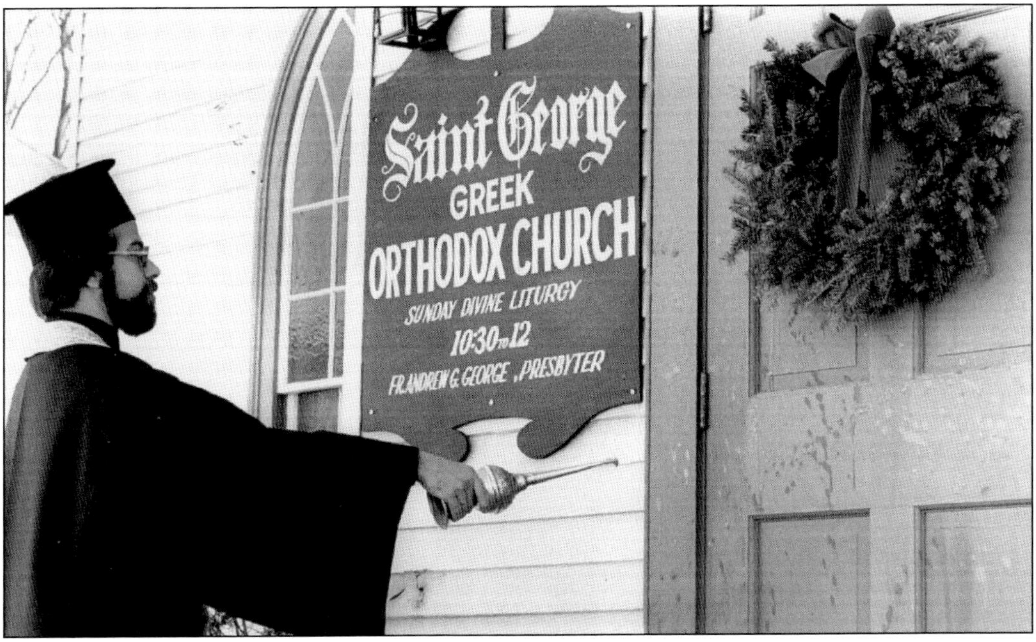

The St. George Greek Orthodox Church at 90 Sanford Street is one of Bangor's best-kept secrets. Tucked away on the west side of town, away from the downtown hustle and bustle, St. George is a quiet treasure. The Eastern Orthodox Society of St. George incorporated in Bangor in 1926 and held its first services in this church in 1930. Fr. Andrew G. George was presbyter in 1978, when the *Bangor Daily News* published a picture of him outside the church. (BDN.)

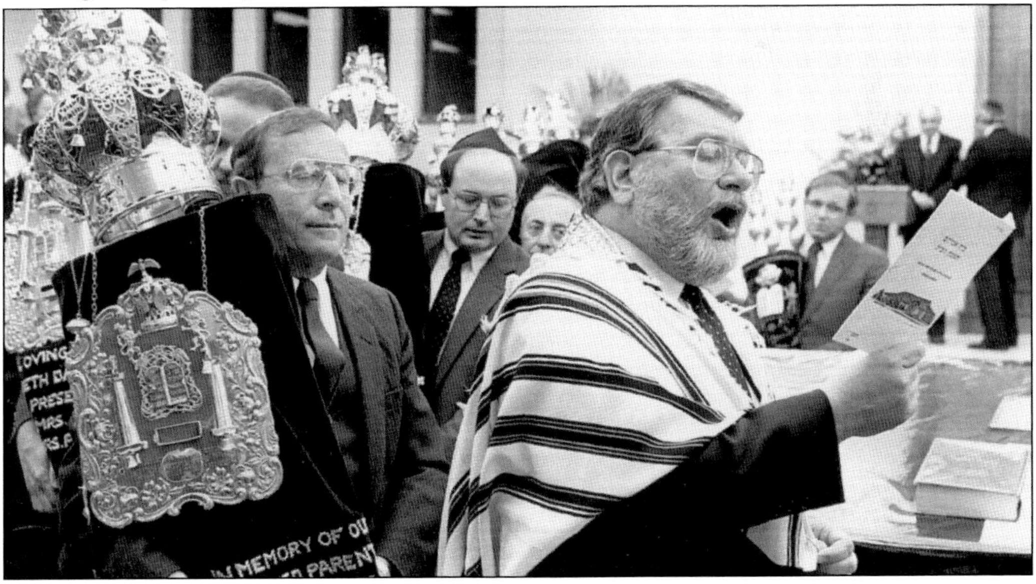

After a 1984 fire destroyed the Orthodox Beth Abraham Synagogue across York Street from Beth Israel, congregation members dedicated a new building on December 15, 1985, the final day of Hanukkah, the Festival of Lights, or Rededication. A *Bangor Daily News* photograph captures the solemn ceremony, a marked difference from an earlier front-page picture showing Rabbi Henry J. Isaacs leaving the burning synagogue dressed in a fireman's hat, cradling a silver crown that adorned the top of the holy Torah. (BDN.)

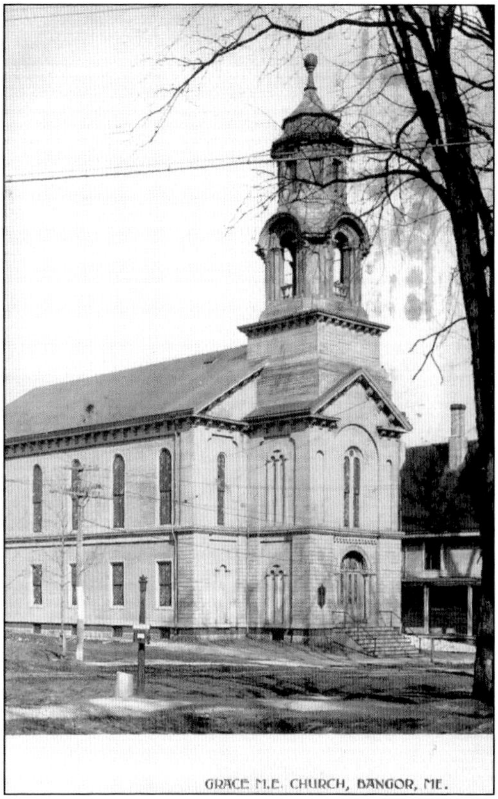

Grace Methodist Church, located at Union and Clinton Streets, serves worshipers on the city's west side. Its members have worshiped in this church building since purchasing the lot in 1853 and dedicating the building a year later. Originally, it had a taller spire than it does today. This postcard view shows a truncated steeple, and today it is even shorter. Apparently it presented maintenance headaches. The church first known as Union Street Church was designed by Harvey Graves, an architect who designed and remodeled other churches in Bangor.

This lovely old brick church once sat at the corner of Pine and Somerset Streets. Built in 1836 and destroyed by fire in 1978, the First Methodist, or Pine Street Methodist, Church was designed by Bangor's preeminent architect of the 1830s, Charles G. Bryant. Because its upstairs sanctuary contained theater-style seats, not pews, some people nicknamed it the Methodist Opera House. A large pipe organ filled Sunday morning worship services with heavenly sounds. Parishioners sold the building and built a new First United Methodist Church that was dedicated on outer Essex Street in 1962.

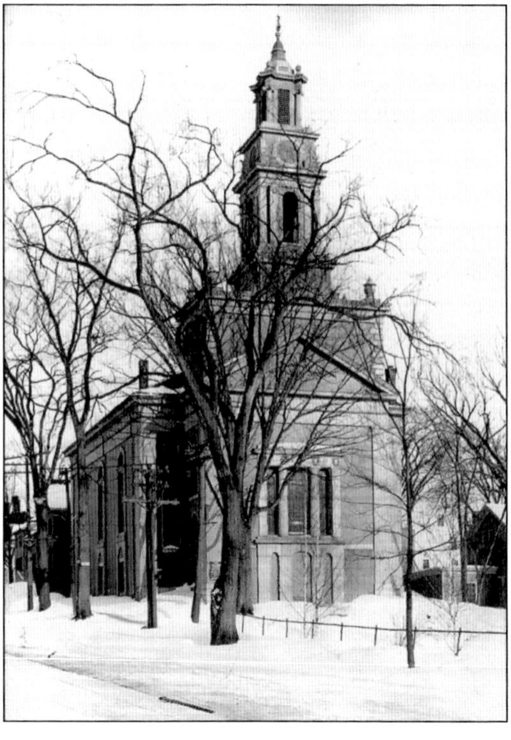

Since its dedication in 1873, the First Universalist Church on the Park Street hill has overlooked downtown. Ashley A. Smith, the longtime minister, became pastor shortly before the great fire, which gutted and then toppled its two towers and destroyed its sanctuary. Smith was the man of the hour in the weeks and months following the disaster, supervising the church's restoration. The Dorothy Memorial was later added to accommodate church activities.

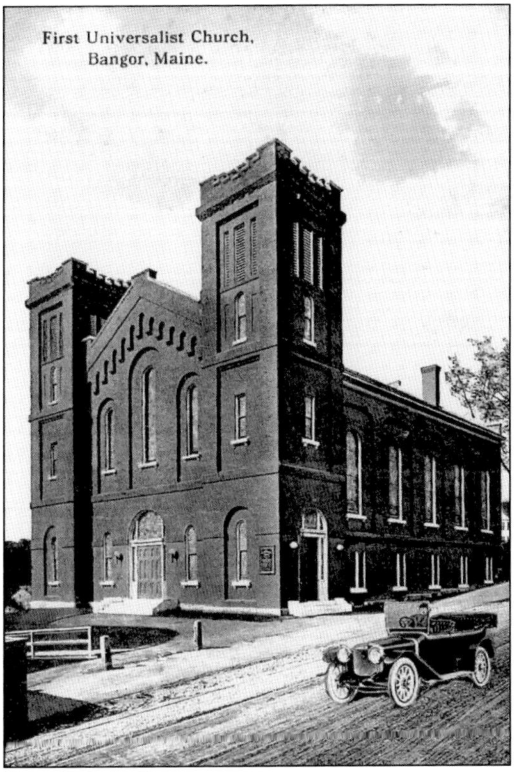

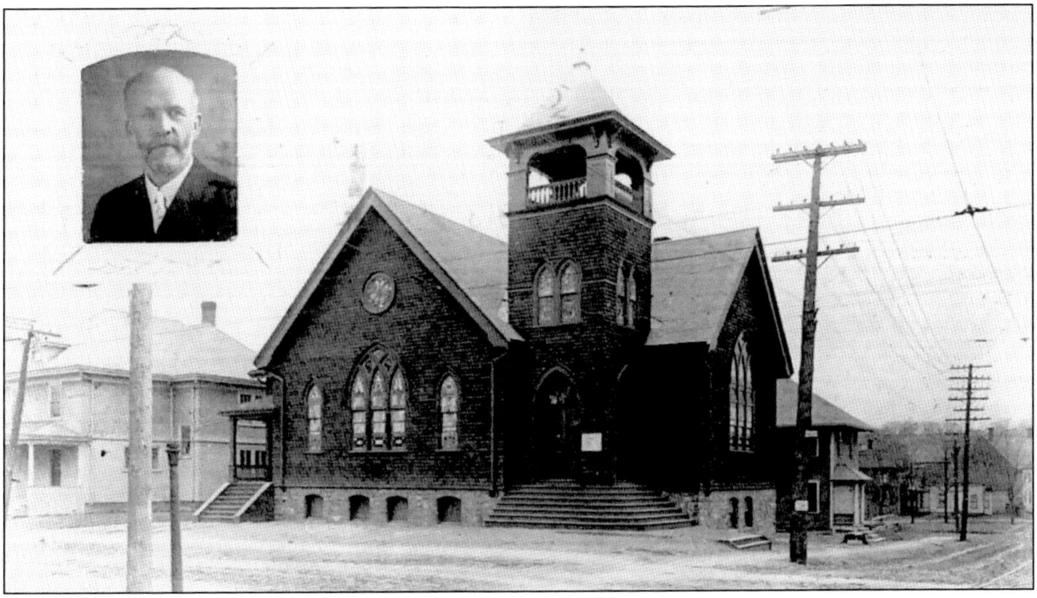

Most residents know this building at 96 Center Street as the location of the Bangor Floral Company, which purchased the property several years ago. Earlier generations attended church services here when it was the Advent Christian Church. It was built after the 1911 fire, when its 1886 predecessor, of similar design and on the same site, was destroyed. Deborah Thompson writes that the main auditorium was designed to seat 300. A Sunday school room was also on the main floor. In the basement were three classrooms, a banquet room, a kitchen, and a boiler room.

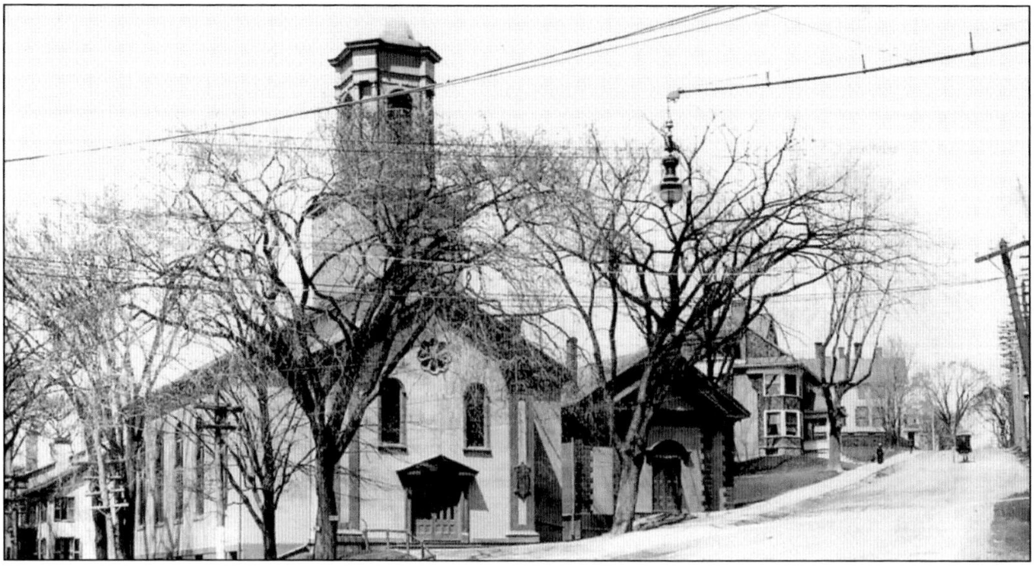

The First Baptist Church and adjacent chapel were in the line of fire on April 30, 1911. The corner of Harlow and Center Streets was ravaged by the advancing flames, and the landmarks could not be saved. The church was dedicated in 1828 and the chapel in 1851. The city's Baptists organized in 1818 and first met at a hall on Broad Street. The 1991 Bangor history *Woodsmen and Whigs* mentions the frequent church baptisms in the often icy Kenduskeag Stream, the first two taking place in 1817.

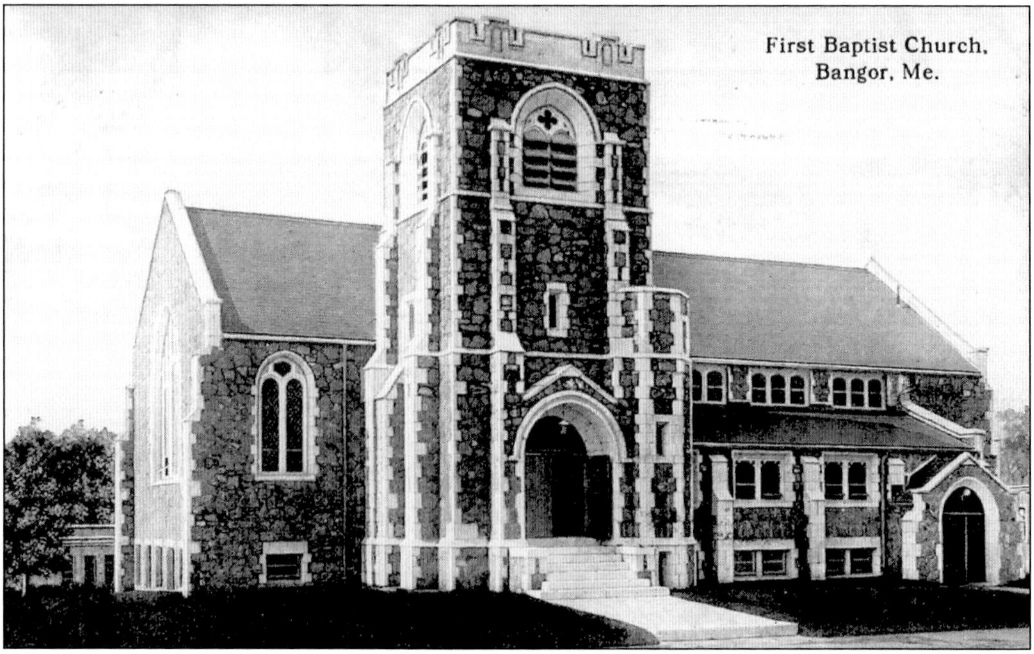

Following the 1911 fire, the First Baptists built this smaller church up over the Center Street hill from its former burned location. It was built in 1912 and designed by the Boston architect George F. Newton. The church is largely constructed of ledge stone removed from a nearby block destroyed in the fire. Part of the church's trim is of Indiana limestone. The crowning glory is its signed Tiffany window showing the ascension of Christ, a duplicate of one burned in the fire.

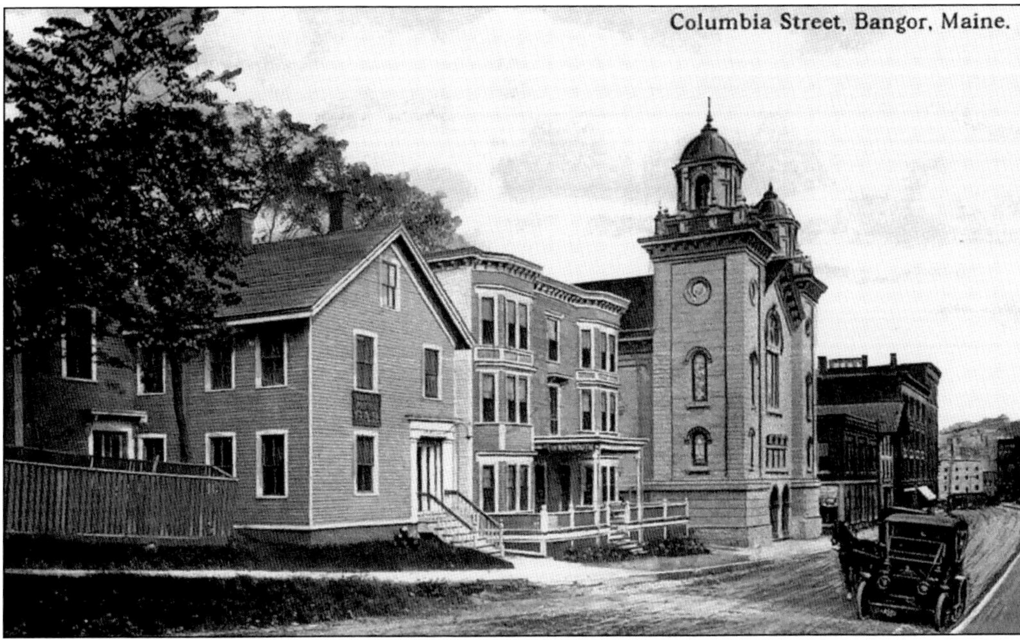

The words on the window at the front entrance of this church say Second Baptist, but for longer than anyone can remember it has been called Columbia Street Baptist, which is the name appearing in a modern sign stretching across the church's front. The first meeting to organize a Second Baptist Church in Bangor was held in 1845, when 27 people met on Broad Street. The congregation, long known for its outreach to seamen and laborers, grew rapidly, and in 1853, it moved up to Columbia Street. In 1902, Wilfred E. Mansur redesigned the building, adding the twin towers and enlarging the interior.

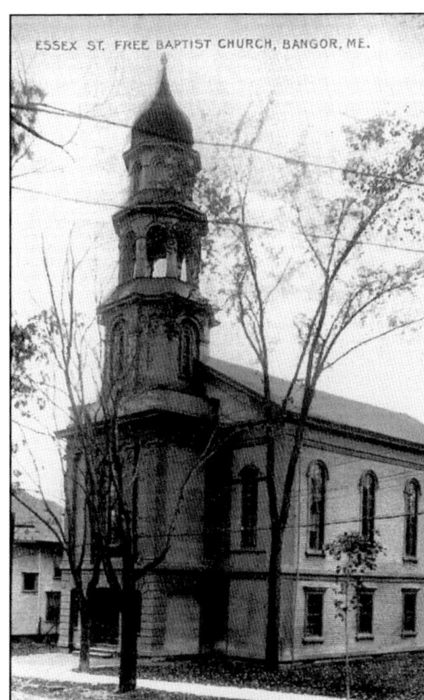

Who can forget seeing the old steeple of the Essex Street Baptist Church, now removed because of rot? It resembled a Russian onion dome, truly a unique sight in eastern Maine. The church was originally named Free Will Baptist, and like Grace Methodist and other area churches, it was designed by Harvey Graves. Dedicated on December 4, 1859, the new church was described in the local *Whig and Courier* as follows: "On the whole it is a substantial, convenient, and beautiful edifice, and has cost (including the lot, but aside from the furnishing) $10,500."

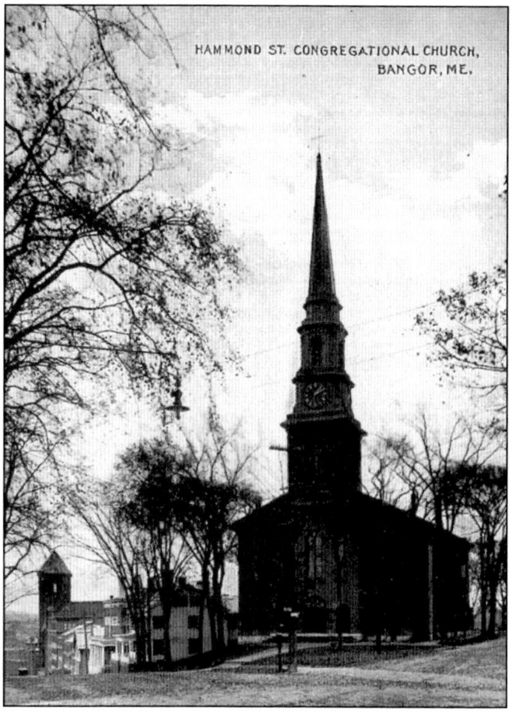

The Hammond Street Congregational Church near High Street was built by church members who were tired of trudging up the State Street hill to worship at the First Parish Church, now All Souls. There were others issues such as crossing the Kenduskeag Stream to the east side in the early days. So, west side Congregationalists dedicated the walls of their own church in 1833, greatly remodeling it in 1853, when the single spire and clock were added. As with other Bangor churches, the main auditorium is reached by twin stairs on either side of the entrance hall.

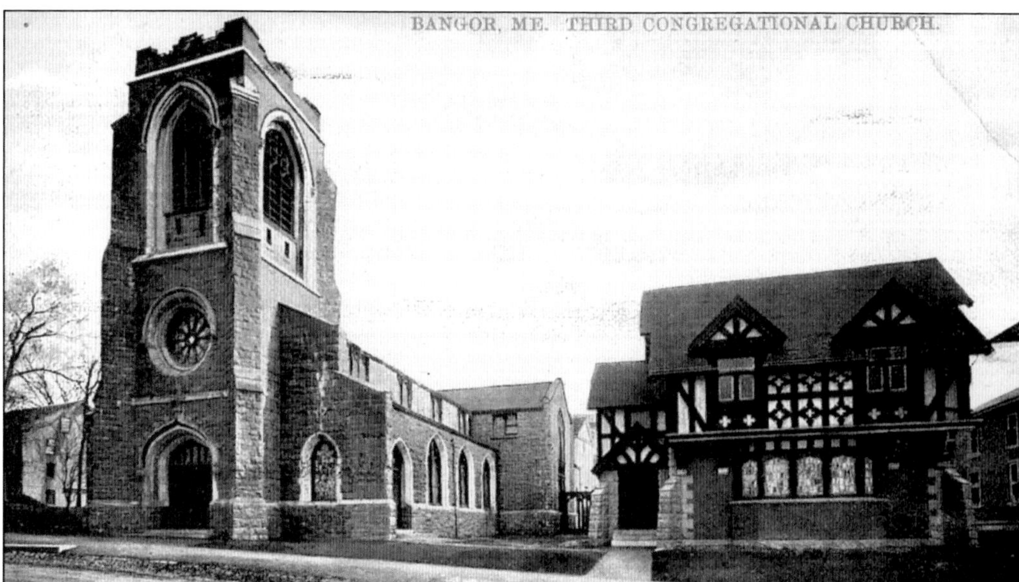

French Street lost three religious treasures in the great 1911 fire: St. John's Episcopal; this stately building, the Third Congregational Church; and the old English-style parish house next door. Today, historians refer to the church seen here as Central Congregational, apparently because of its location near downtown. Eleven memorial windows, two of them manufactured by Tiffany, graced the 1902 Gothic-style church. An earlier wooden church on the site was dismantled, during which time parishioners worshiped in the parish house that was already built. After its destruction in 1911, the church's pink granite was used to build part of All Souls Congregational Church on Broadway.

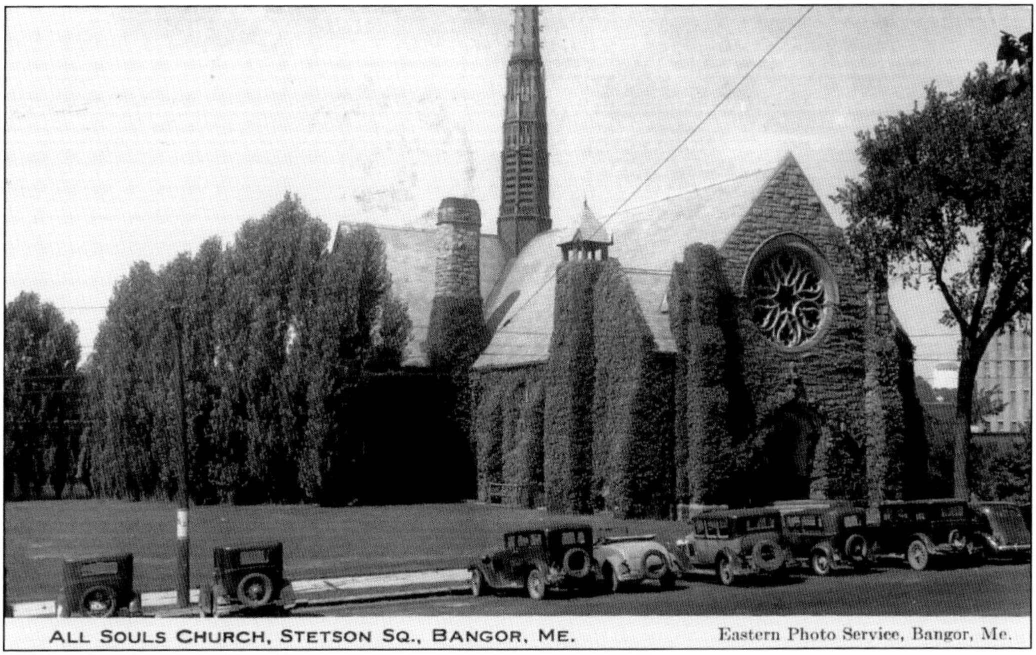

All Souls Congregational Church sits on the site of Bangor's first church, which was built facing French Street in 1822 by the First Congregational Society. The stones on its outer walls are two different shades. This was intended to symbolize the joining of the First Parish Society and the Third Parish, or Central Congregational Church, which burned in the 1911 fire and was located on French Street. Gothic Renaissance architect Ralph Adams Cram designed All Souls, and its beautiful stained-glass windows were created by the Connick Studios.

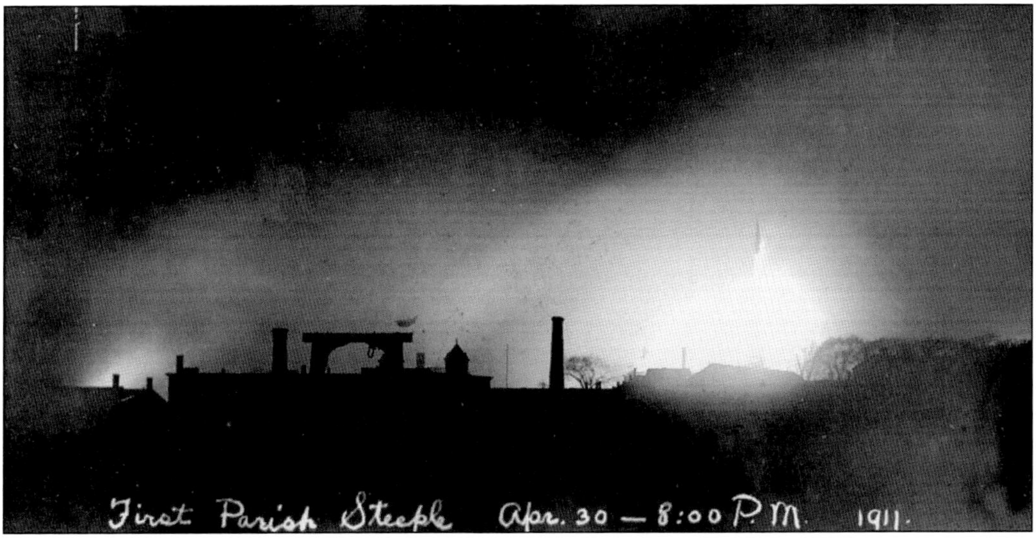

The burning of the First Parish Church at 8:00 p.m. on Sunday, April 30, 1911, may be the single most enduring image of the great Bangor fire. High atop the State Street hill the spire burned, visible for miles in all directions. The third Congregational church to occupy this site (the first was built in 1822) was an imposing building. A remodeled church, meant to keep up with other city church improvements, was dedicated in 1859. In 1897, Wilfred Mansur designed an adjacent parsonage, which also burned in 1911.

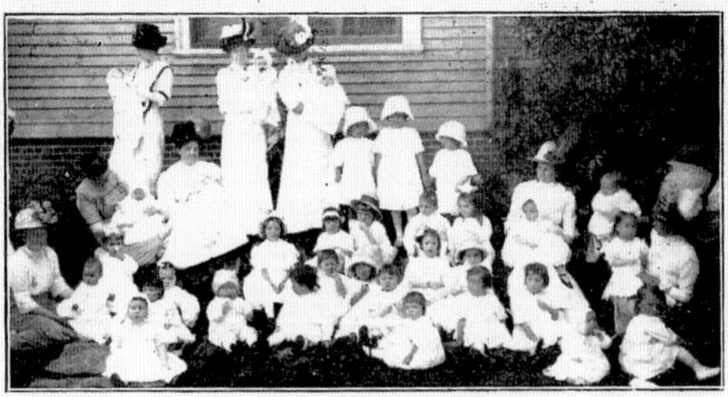

Cradle Roll Department of the Universalist Sunday-school, Bangor, Me.
Mrs. Olive A. Toothaker, Supt.

It is doubtful that many churches today have cradle roll departments, but in 1913, when this black-and-white card was postmarked, the Universalist Sunday school in Bangor certainly had one. The postcard's caption notes that Olive A. Toothaker was the Sunday school superintendent, an esteemed position for anyone, and usually a job for a mother selected from the church congregation. The city's Universalists have a long tradition of caring for the young. Church member Samuel Hersey left an endowment for the construction of the Hersey retreat at Sandy Point, where children enjoyed outings.

Church Vacation School

FREE

for All Children from 4 to 14 Yrs. of Age

Under the Direction of the

Churches of Bangor

at

First Baptist Church -- on Center Street
for Children from 4 to 8 Years Old

First Methodist Episcopal Church
on Pine Street
for Children from 9 to 14 Years Old

Grace Methodist Church -- on Union St.
for Children from 4 to 14 Years Old

June 27 to July 22 -- 9.00 to 11.30 a. m.
Daily Except Saturday

Songs, Bible Stories, Habit Talks, Handwork, Games
Dramatizing, Picnics
Offering Daily for Missions

A GOOD TIME FOR ALL! WELCOME, BOYS AND GIRLS!

Three Bangor churches joined forces in this undated church broadside, perhaps dating from the 1920s, to create a church vacation school. Even today, a sure sign of summer for churches is vacation Bible school, or VBS. The atmosphere is less formal than church school during the school year. Songs, Bibles stories, crafts, and picnics have long been favorites at these events. Does anyone know what a "habit talk" is? The phrase seems to have vanished from the language.

This Greek Revival building at 117 Court Street was the church of the Pentecostal Assembly in 1959, when this advertisement appeared in a city directory. Pastor Clifford A. Crabtree and his wife, assistant pastor Helen Crabtree, were pillars of the church. They appeared on television in the 1960s and oversaw the construction of a large new building, Glad Tidings Church, at 1033 Broadway. Pentecostal church historian Patricia Parkhurst Pickard has written that church members used to meet in modest quarters upstairs on Pickering Square and other downtown locales before moving to this former mansion on Court Street.

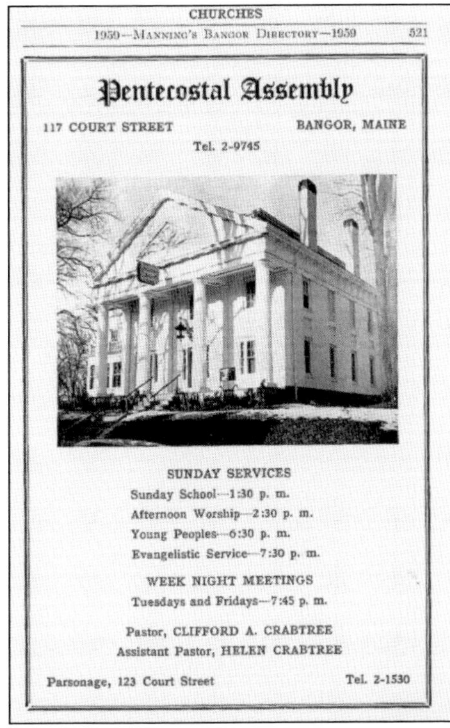

CHURCHES

1959—MANNING'S BANGOR DIRECTORY—1959 521

Pentecostal Assembly

117 COURT STREET BANGOR, MAINE

Tel. 2-9745

SUNDAY SERVICES

Sunday School—1:30 p. m.
Afternoon Worship—2:30 p. m.
Young Peoples—6:30 p. m.
Evangelistic Service—7:30 p. m.

WEEK NIGHT MEETINGS

Tuesdays and Fridays—7:45 p. m.

Pastor, CLIFFORD A. CRABTREE
Assistant Pastor, HELEN CRABTREE

Parsonage, 123 Court Street Tel. 2-1530

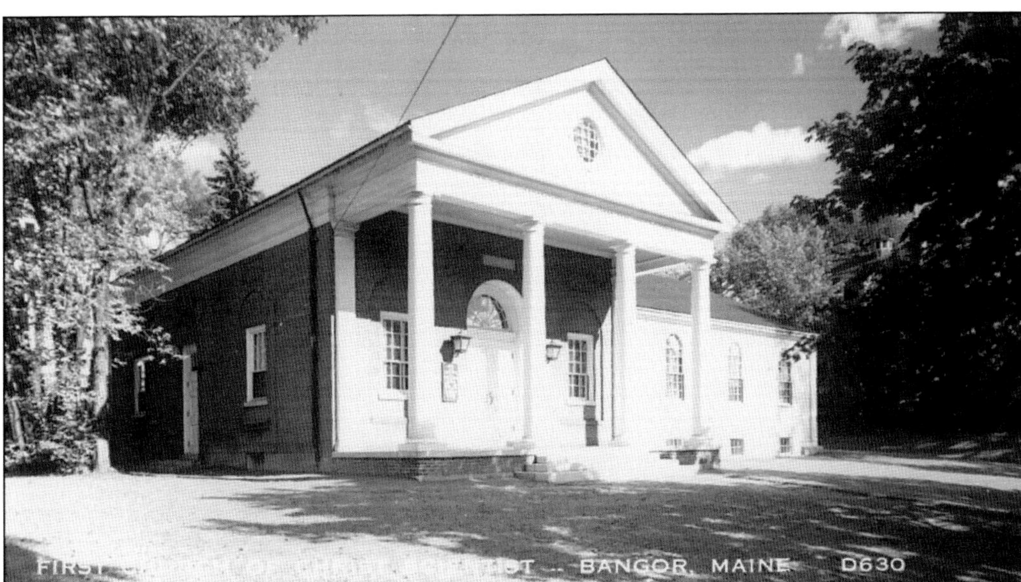

Members of the First Church of Christ, Scientist have long been a small but dedicated group. The 1916 Bangor directory listed the city's practicing Christian Scientists—all four of them. Later, Christian Scientists built this impressive church at 183 French Street. The 1944 directory lists Josiah L. Smith as first reader and Nettie Getchell as second reader. The Christian Scientists, who followed the teachings of Mary Baker Eddy, have sold this building and have a reading room at 118 Harlow Street. They also built a modern new church on outer Broadway. The 183 French Street building is now a synagogue owned by the Reformed Congregation Beth El.

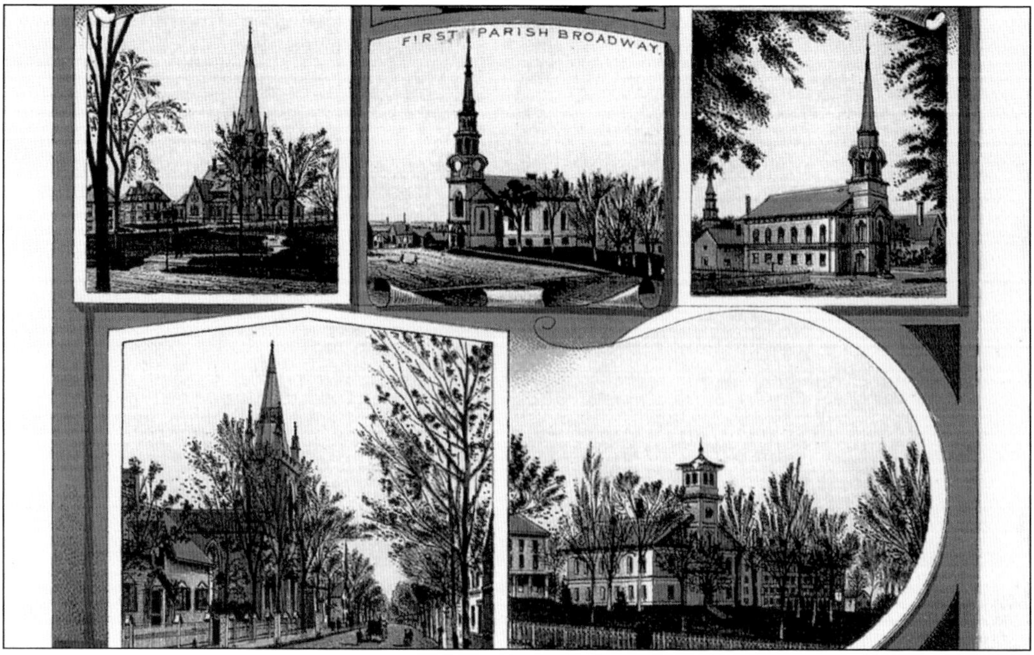

This collection of five Bangor churches, published shortly before the beginning of the 20th century, adds credence to the saying, "A city skyline truly is defined by the height of its steeples." Sadly, three of the churches shown here were destroyed by fire: St. Mary's Catholic Church (top left) in 1978; First Parish Congregational (top center); and St. John's Episcopal (bottom left) by the great fire of 1911. The remaining two still stand: Grace Methodist (top right) and the chapel of the Bangor Theological Seminary (bottom right).

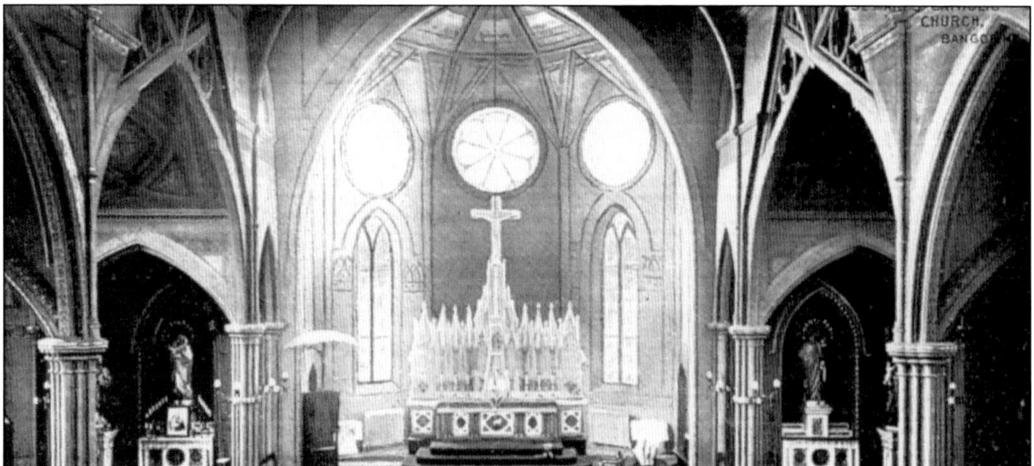

An interior view of St. Mary's Catholic Church on Cedar Street can only hint at the intricate workmanship that went into designing this house of worship. Dedicated in 1874, St. Mary's represented a separation from the city's east side Catholic church, St. John's. The church was built to serve Roman Catholics west of the Kenduskeag Stream. Architectural historian Deborah Thompson writes that the church was of a warmer design than St. John's, owing to a mixture of stone, wood, and brick. St. Mary's burned one cold Friday night in 1978, and a new church was later built on Ohio Street.

Ten

Touring Bangor's Outskirts

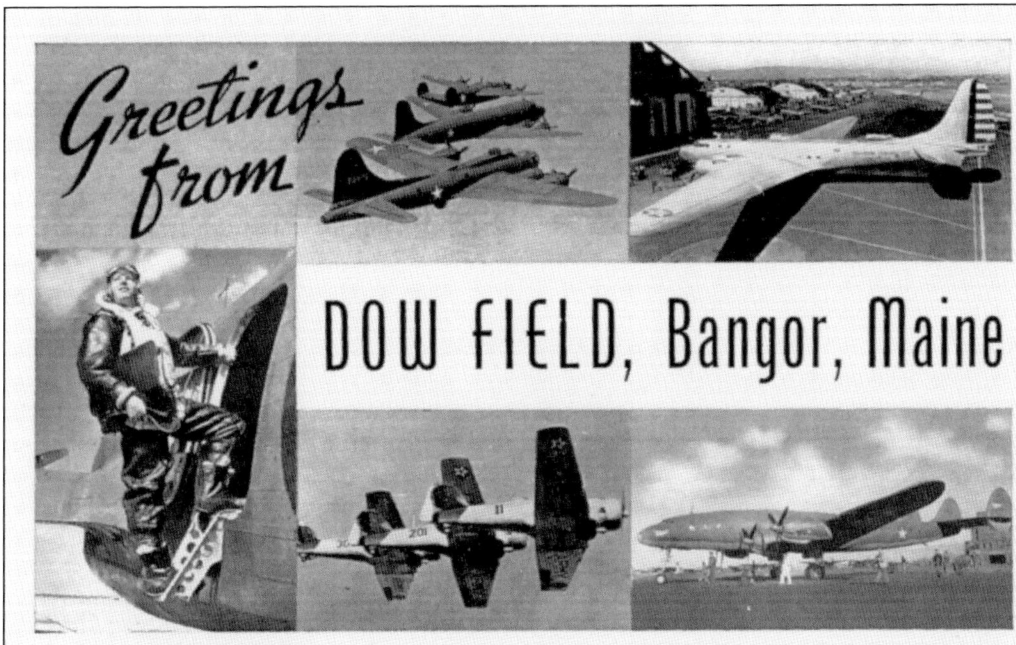

Dow Field put Bangor on the map during World War II and through the cold war era of the 1950s and 1960s. The U.S. Air Force base was built on the city's outskirts on a former hayfield once owned by Edward Godfrey. At one time, the influx of base personnel and their families swelled Bangor's population to 39,000, much larger than its present 33,000. The Bangor International Airport, which took over the closed base in 1968, makes full use of the base's two-mile runways, which are long enough to land the space shuttle on.

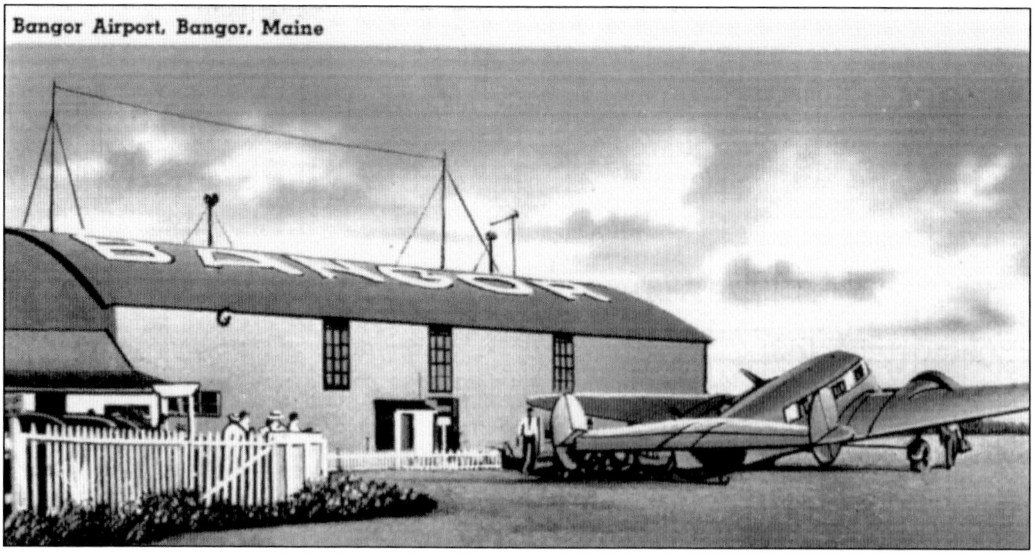

The Bangor Airport in the 1930s was a far cry from today's modern Bangor International Airport. Pilots bumped along a shorter runway located off Union Street and often landed their aircraft with the large "Bangor" rooftop lettering as their beacon. The airport, which traces its roots to the early 1920s, was host to a Lockheed Electra when this postcard view was taken. Amelia Earhart, who flew women and girls over Bangor from this airport in 1934, was flying an identical airplane when she and her navigator were lost in the Pacific Ocean on an around-the-world flight in 1937.

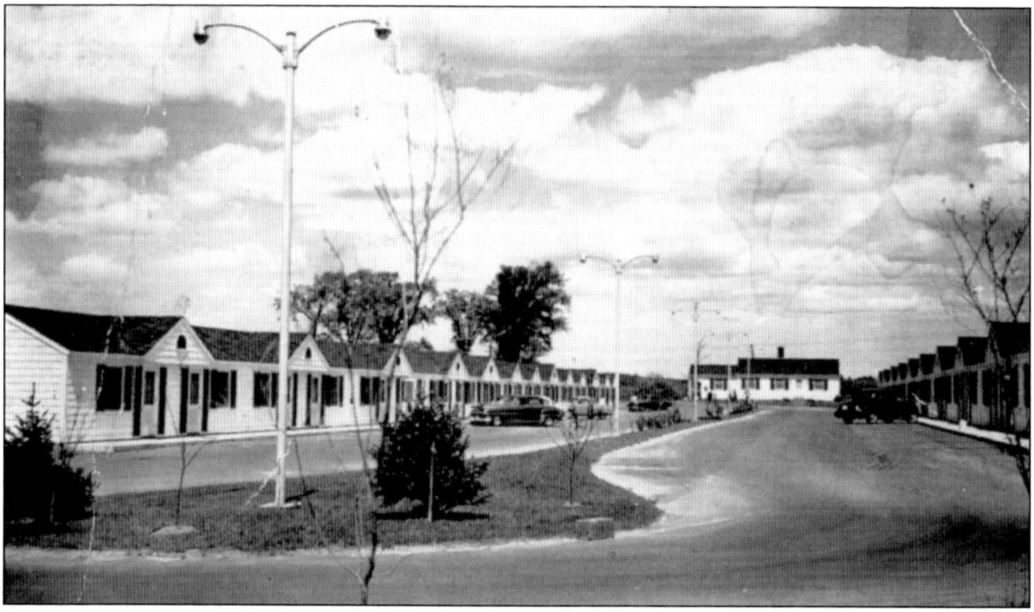

The 76-unit Queen City Motel was located at 1476 Hammond Street near the Pilots Grill restaurant. As Bangor built more motels closer to town on Odlin Road and to the north, on Hogan Road, the motel underwent several name changes and changes of ownership. It was once named the Scottish Inn and later the Ranger Inn. Older residents may still refer to outer Hammond Street as "the bulge" due to the wide curve of U.S. Route 2 that bypasses the extended runway of Dow Air Force Base.

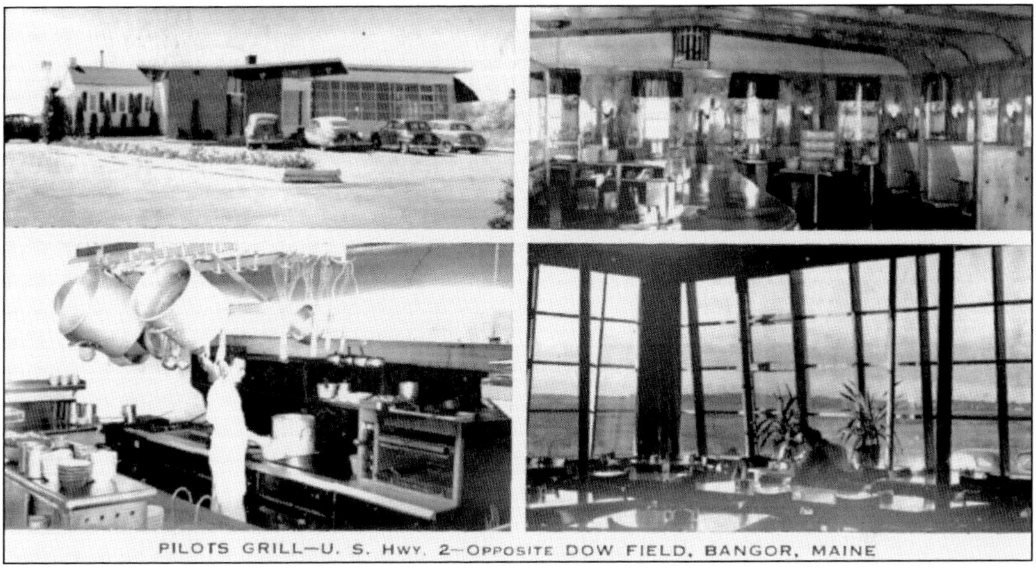

Who has not dined at the Pilots Grill sometime during its 63-year history? The back of this postcard boasts that "Maine's finest restaurant" served steaks, chicken, and seafood. Originally located near the Dow Air Force Base runway on Hammond Street, the restaurant was moved by the Zoidis family two miles farther out on U.S. Route 2 during base expansion. They expanded the landmark in its new location, serving the rich and famous along with regular patrons lured by its quality, but relaxed, atmosphere. Bill Zoidis and his daughter Paulette closed the institution on New Year's Eve 2003.

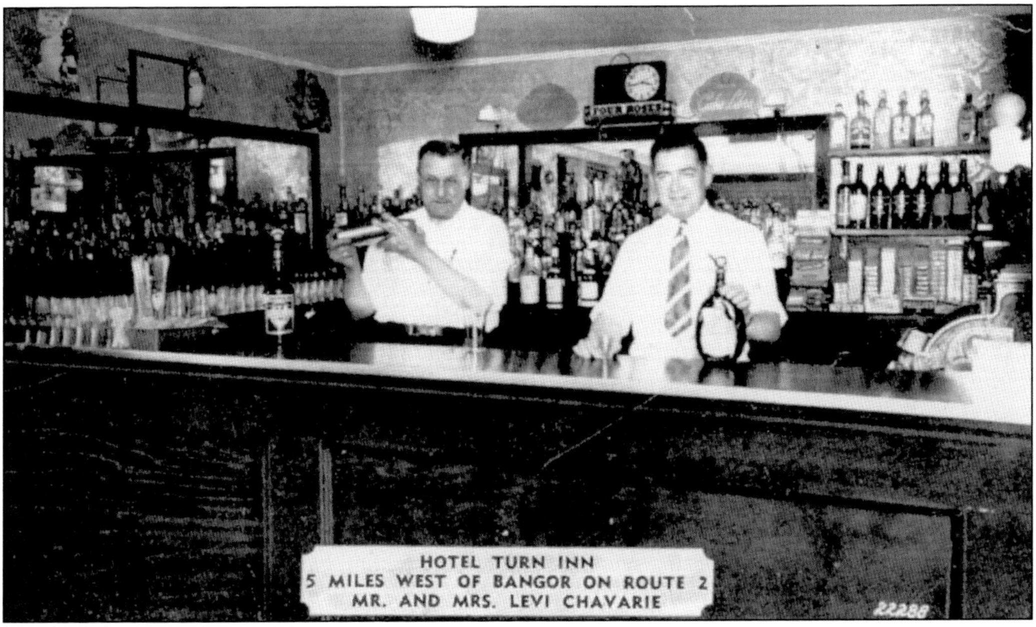

The Hotel Turn Inn, located five miles west of Bangor on U.S. Route 2 in Hermon, featured a cocktail lounge and dance floor popular with patrons who drove from miles around. Owner Levi Chavarie catered to U.S. Air Force personnel from Dow Field who returned every Saturday night. The Turn Inn's grand reopening on March 17, 1944, revealed a spruced-up private dining room and special cocktails mixed by Charles Burpee, formerly of the Poland Spring House.

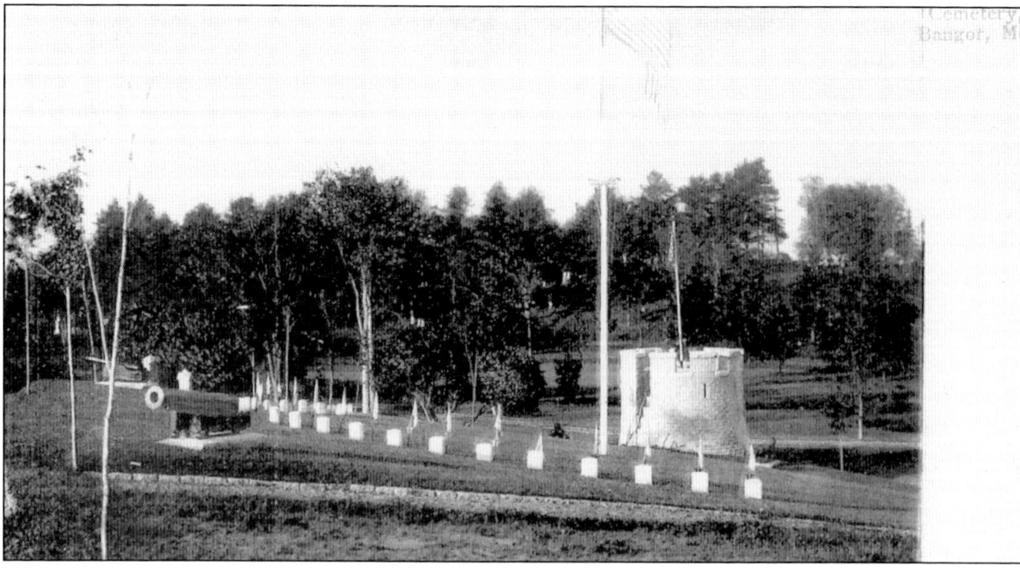

Since its dedication in 1836, the Mount Hope Cemetery has been a quiet retreat from the city's hustle and bustle. This postcard view, dating from *c.* 1908, pictures the Mount Hope Avenue side of the cemetery, which features a small stone fortress, cannon, and a ring of Civil War grave sites. Mount Hope has grown through the years to the point where all burial lots in the old cemetery section are full. Today, burials are in the city grounds and extended cemetery property across Mount Hope Avenue near the Veazie town line. The Maine Korean War Memorial is located near the scene pictured on this card.

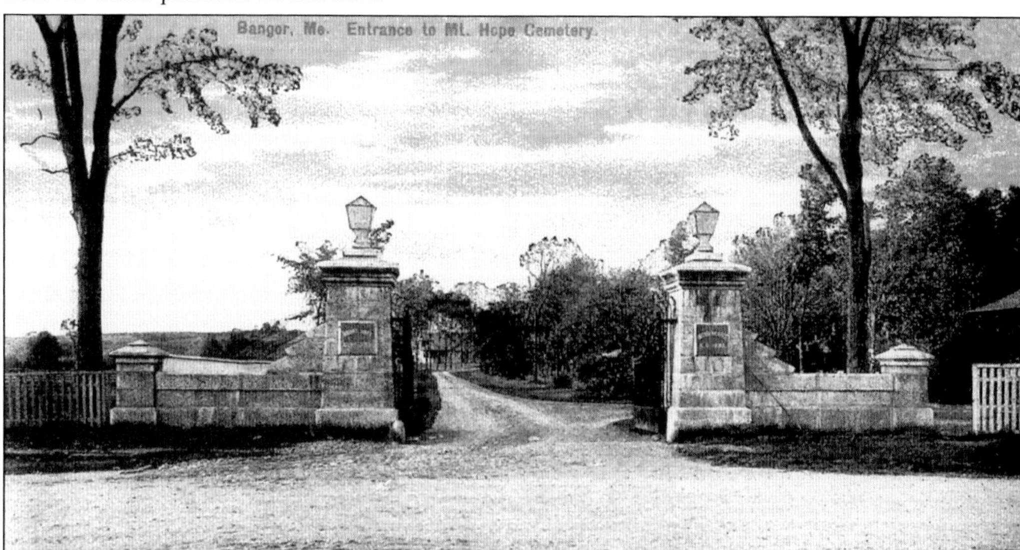

The imposing front gate of Bangor's principal burial place still greets visitors to Mount Hope, which is America's second landscaped cemetery. Mount Auburn Cemetery in Cambridge, Massachusetts, where famous poets, politicians, and theologians are interred, was the nation's first full landscaped cemetery. Designed by Charles G. Bryant, Mount Hope is the final resting place of Hannibal Hamlin, Abraham Lincoln's first vice president; Alfred Brady, a gangster who was gunned down by FBI agents in downtown Bangor; and many ordinary citizens. Trudy Scee's book *Mount Hope Cemetery: A Twentieth Century History* was published in 2001.

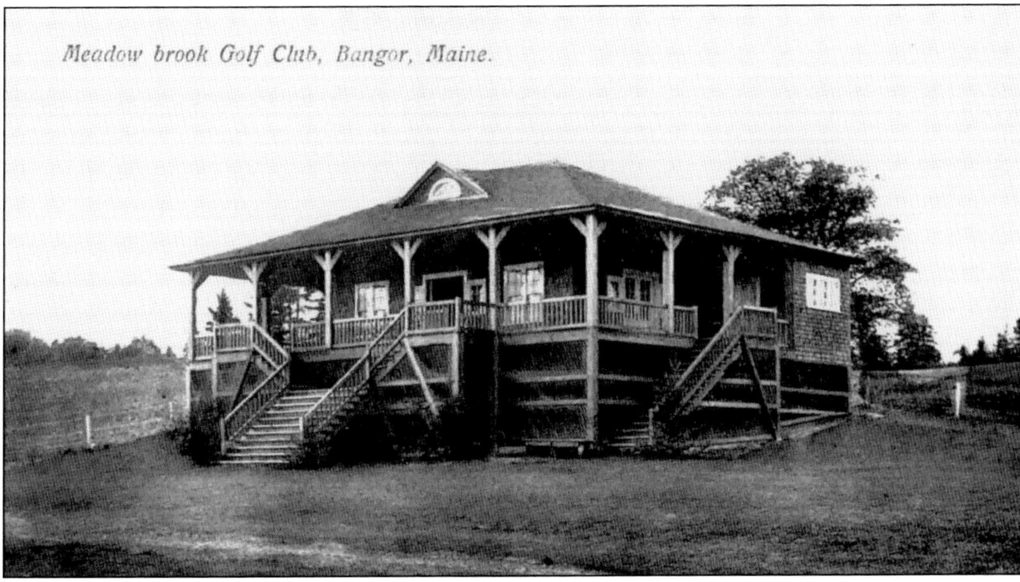

The Meadowbrook Road, a residential neighborhood located off outer State Street on U.S. Route 2, is all that is left to remind people of a long-ago favorite called the Meadow Brook Golf Club. Dating from the 1930s, the course, located between the end of Meadowbrook Road and Mount Hope Avenue, was popular with local golfers in the days before motorized golf carts and fancy equipment. The spacious wooden clubhouse was razed many years ago.

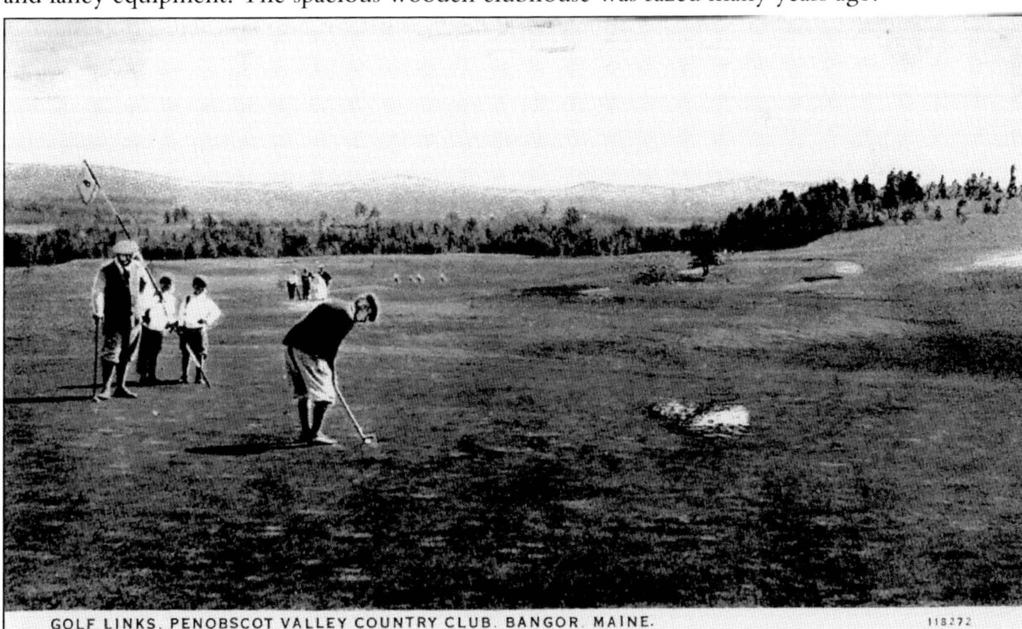

Many golfers have long preferred the well-manicured links and breathtaking mountain views of the Penobscot Valley Country Club in Orono (not in Bangor, as this postcard's title proclaims). Bangor doctors, lawyers, and businessmen have long frequented the club, along with the everyday enthusiast. This card, postmarked in 1928, shows the baggy "plus four" attire of the time and, no doubt, a rougher course that is more representative of today's courses in Scotland, where the sport was born.

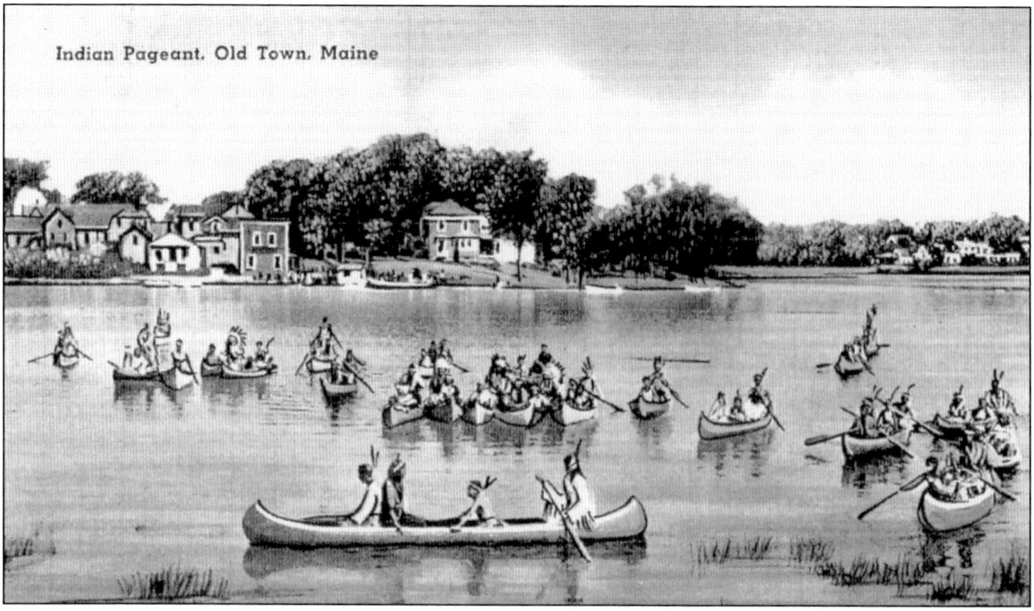

No book of Bangor photographs would be complete without mention of the region's Native American heritage. Twelve miles upriver from Bangor is Indian Island, an island settlement of the Indian nation once accessible only by water. This 1940s view captures an Indian pageant at which the Penobscots dressed in their regalia and paddled colored canoes in the Penobscot River. A modern bridge now links Old Town to the island.

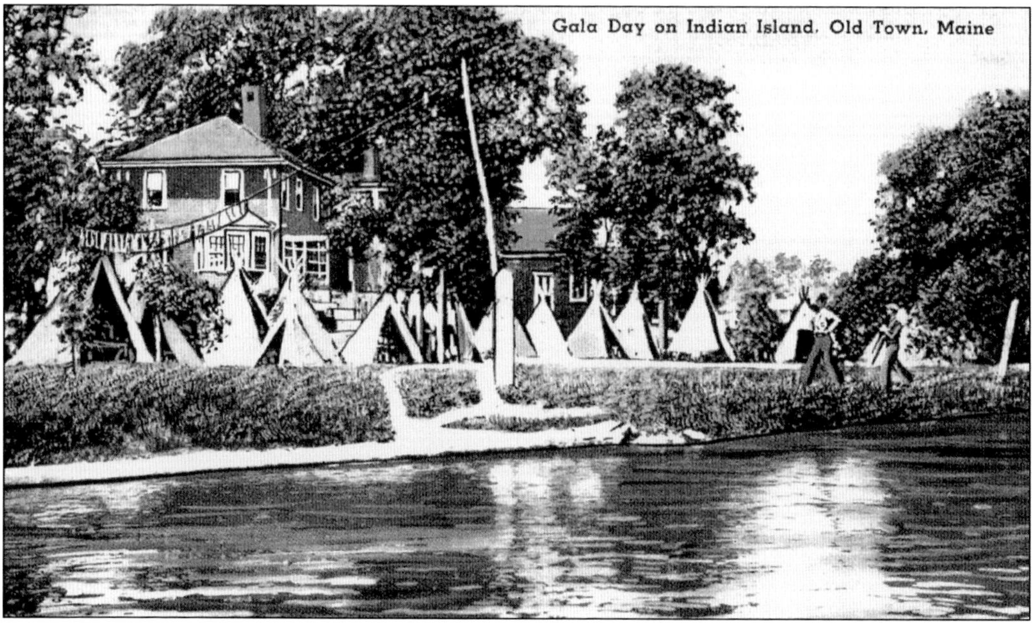

Gala Day on Indian Island attracted many visitors each summer. Members of the Penobscot nation would paddle people the short distance from the mainland to the island. Native entertainers would perform Indian dances, serve food, and sell lovely beaded souvenirs and baskets. Molly Molasses, a native-born Penobscot, was a well-known figure in Bangor during the mid-19th century.

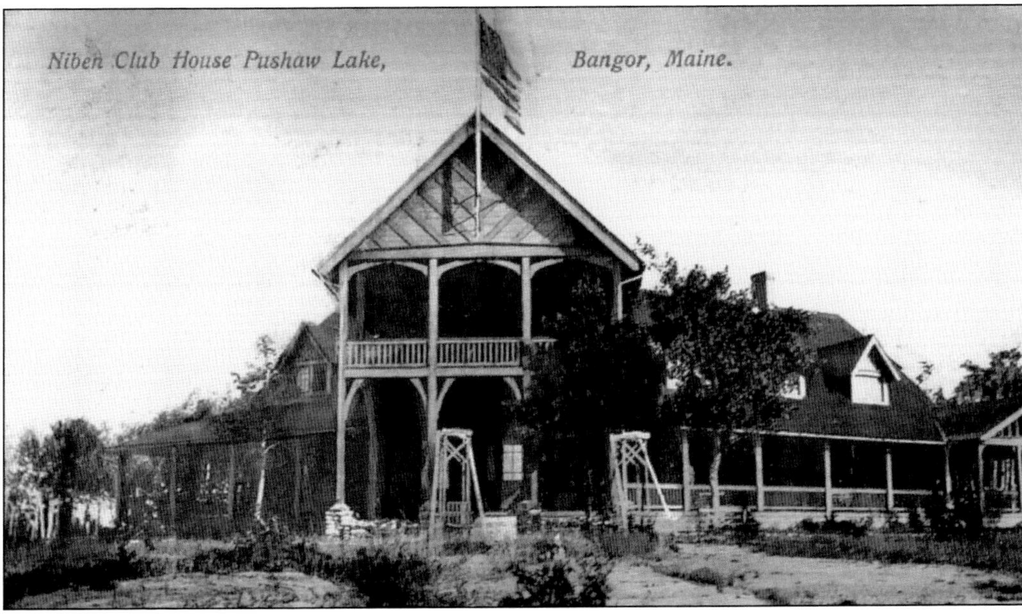

Many of Bangor's upper class liked to ride their bicycles or walk the 10 miles out to the Niben Club, a Victorian-era clubhouse located on the south end of Pushaw Lake. The final stretch of the trail was a wooden-plank pathway that crossed Forest Avenue and led directly to the picturesque playhouse. The pathway, which originated in Bangor, was on the bed of the old Veazie Railroad, which ran from Bangor to Milford in the 19th century. Contrary to this card's white lie, the clubhouse was located in Orono, not Bangor. The Niben, which opened in 1897, was later destroyed by fire.

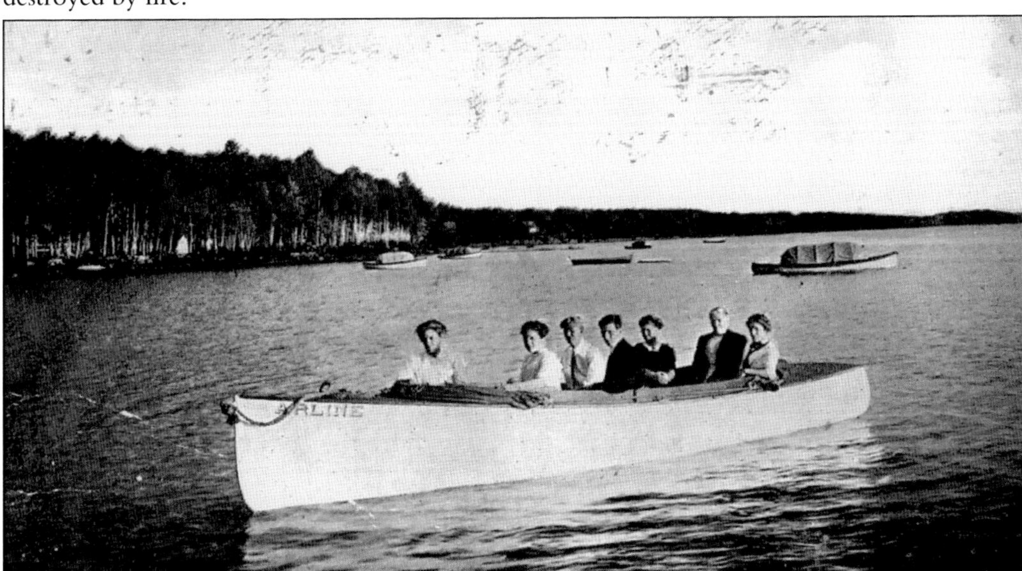

This boatload of seven adults was photographed on the Old Town side of Pushaw Lake, or Pushaw Pond. The lake is bordered by four towns: Glenburn, Orono, Old Town, and Hudson. Today, it is favored by yearlong residents desiring the easy commute to Bangor and other communities who have expanded and winterized once seasonal cottages. Some of the large lake's landings include Lucky's, Double AA, and Gould's.

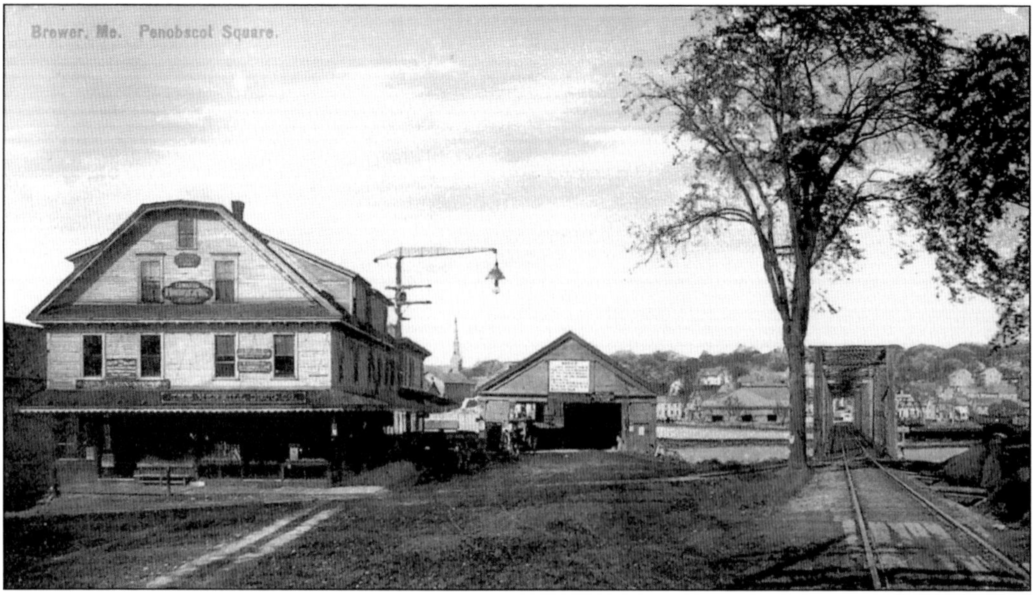

Bangor's twin city of Brewer, located directly across the Penobscot River, has long been a loyal friend and admirer of its big brother. In this card showing Penobscot Square, postmarked 1912, are the old covered vehicular bridge and the iron railroad bridge (right). On the left is a large business block razed in 1997 during construction of the third link to Bangor, the Penobscot Bridge.

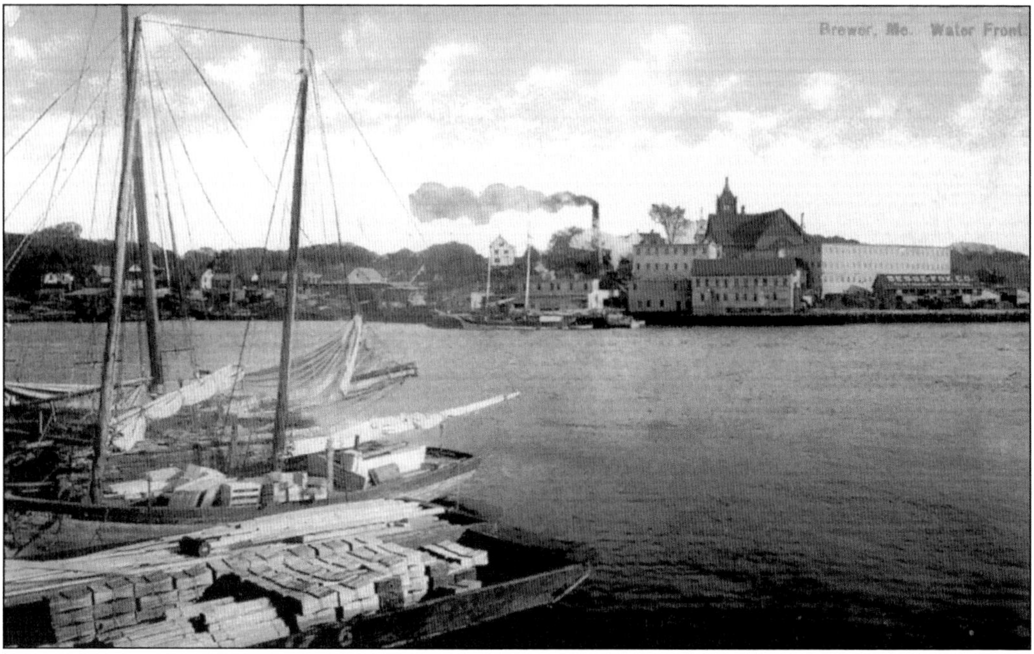

In 1911, this was the view that Bangoreans had when they gazed across the Penobscot. Crowning the scene is the First Congregational Church, beneath which are the Smith planing mill and sailing vessels tied up along the docks. The twin cities of Bangor and Brewer each share about eight miles of valuable river frontage. Bangor was settled by Jacob Buswell in 1769, and Brewer was settled by John Brewer in 1771.

Eleven

Moonlight Serenade

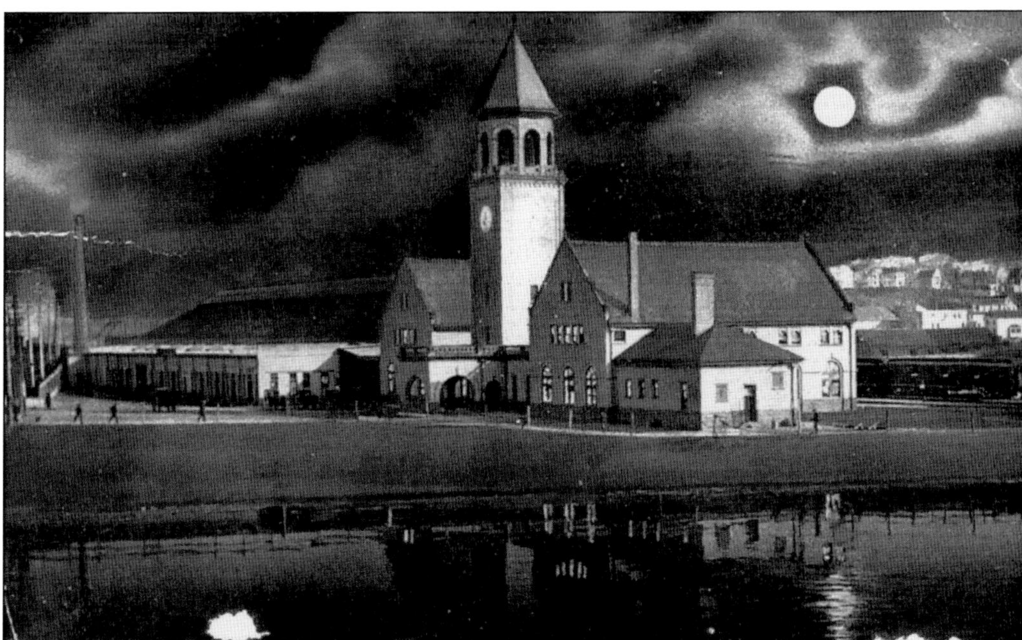

Few scenes in Bangor's past were lovelier than the Union Station bathed in moonlight. Although the moon glow in this postcard is probably a studio fabrication, the overall effect is still stunning. Architectural historian Deborah Thompson writes that the design of the railroad terminal's bell tower was meant to complement the steeple of the First Congregational Church built a decade earlier across the river in Brewer. To see both illuminated at night was one of the joys of living in Greater Bangor.

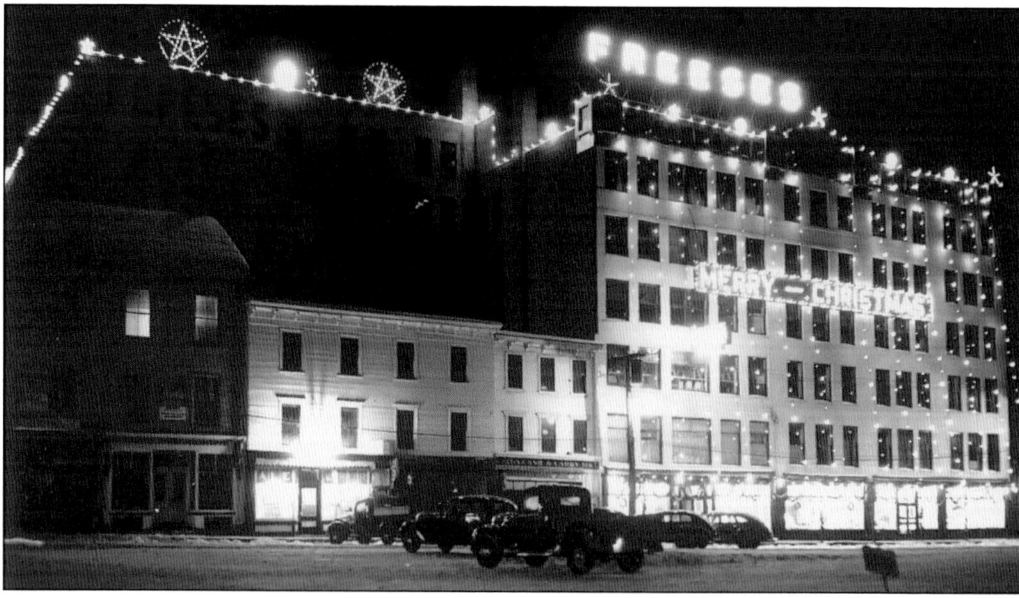

A downtown Christmas centerpiece for decades was the holiday decoration of Freese's Department Store. This view, taken from Pickering Square in the 1940s, shows the lighted stars high atop the roof alongside the Freese's sign that beckoned shoppers from far and wide. Even more elaborate decorations dazzled shoppers at the store's Main Street entrance. WABI television broadcast live from Freese's during the holiday season, opening the show with the store's pulsating lights while Leroy Anderson's "Sleigh Ride" played in the background. (BDN.)

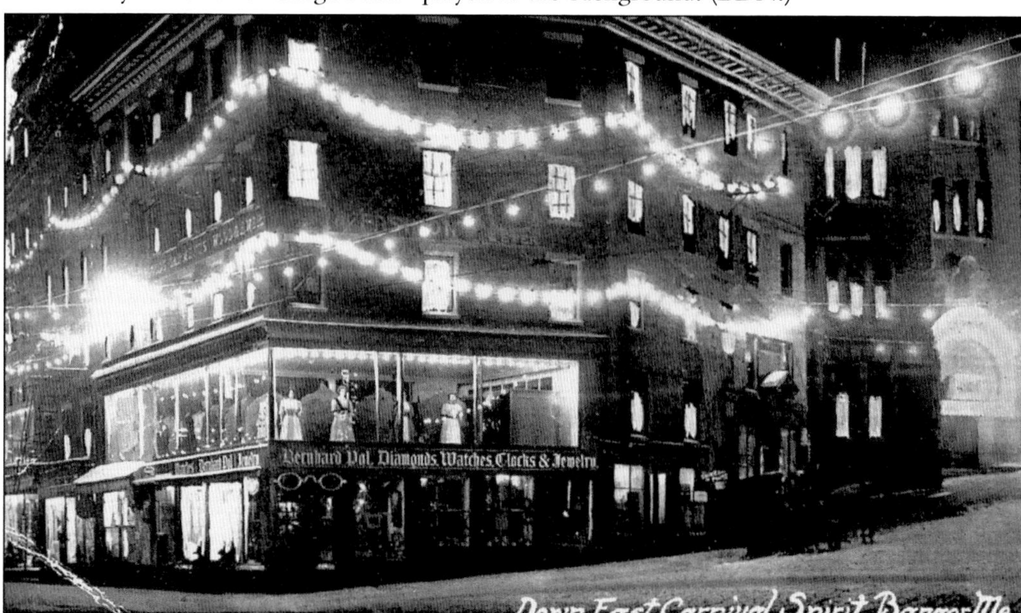

Downtown shoppers got the spirit each year during the city's Down East Carnival week. Nearly every building was wrapped in colored lights to attract residents and visitors by the thousands. This postcard, dating from 1914, was taken at the intersection of Hammond and Main Streets, known as Pol's Corner. Merchant Bernhard Pol, who sold diamonds, watches, clocks, jewelry, silverware, and optical goods at 5 Main Street, strung lights across the outside of his store.

This linen-style postcard (named so because of the texture of its surface) pictures a scene still familiar in downtown today. The view of the telephone building at night could have been taken today if not for the vintage cars in the foreground that date the view to around the early 1940s. Also, today's Verizon company building has communication towers and dishes that would have been alien to Bangor residents in the prewar era. The Art Deco landmark on Park Street was built in 1931.

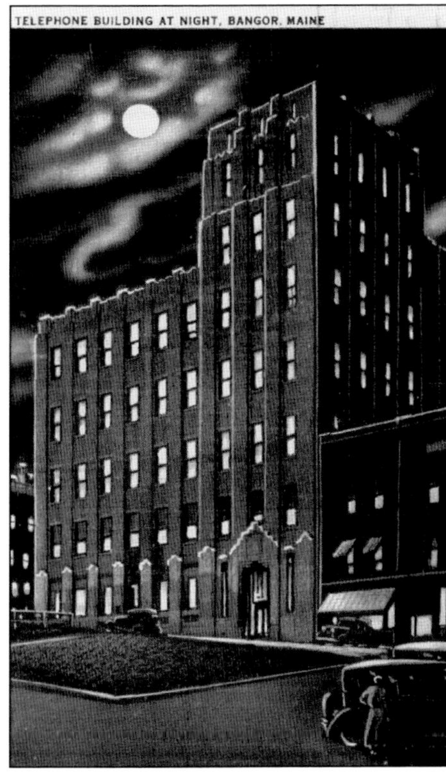

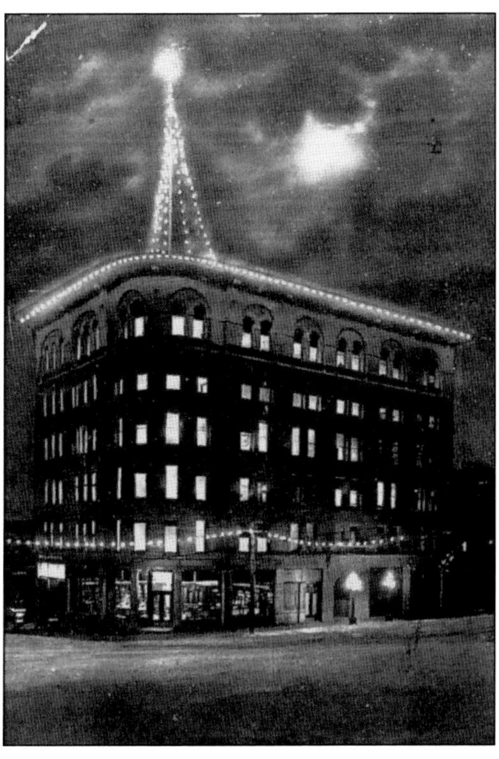

Bangor's Graham Building was also lit up during Down East Carnival week, as seen in this postcard. Built by and named for the family who owned the Bangor Railway and Electric Company (later renamed the Bangor Hydro Electric Company), this block was brand new by the time the postcard was mailed on October 4, 1912. The six-story building replaced a smaller Graham Building on Central Street that was destroyed in the 1911 fire. Passengers caught trolleys from a first-floor waiting room here, which was later home to the post office pharmacy and much later Bookmarc's bookstore and cafe.

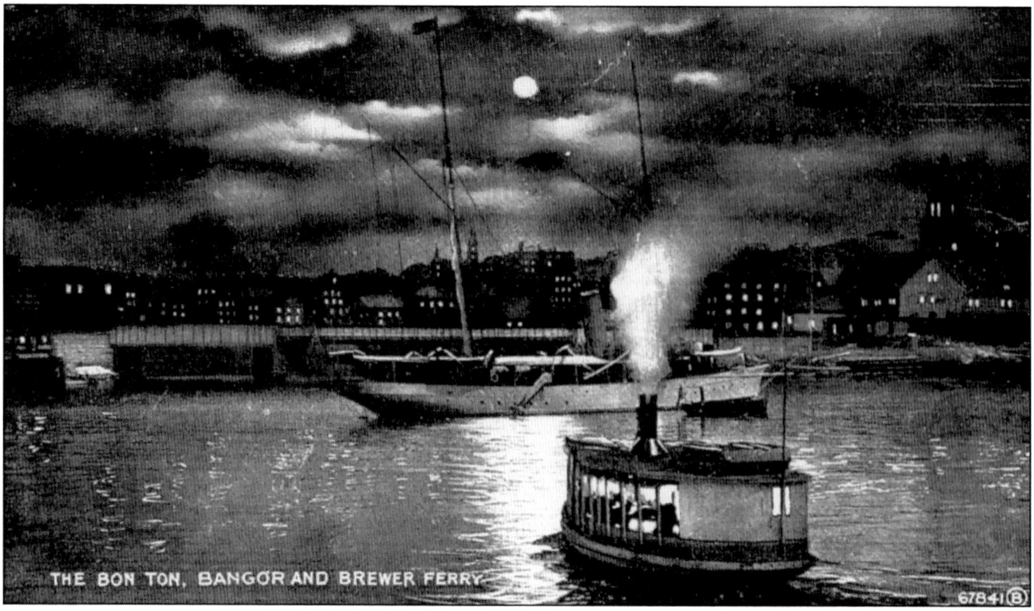

The tiny *Bon Ton* ferry boats carried passengers from Wilson Street in Brewer to Union Street in downtown Bangor in the years prior to the construction of the Joshua Chamberlain Bridge in 1959. On Saturday nights, the boats made a late run to accommodate shoppers and moviegoers who might have watched a film at the opera house on Main Street. Workers at the Eastern Fine Paper Company in South Brewer were loyal passengers on the *Bon Ton,* which saved a lot of walking over to Brewer's Penobscot Square through the long bridge to Bangor.

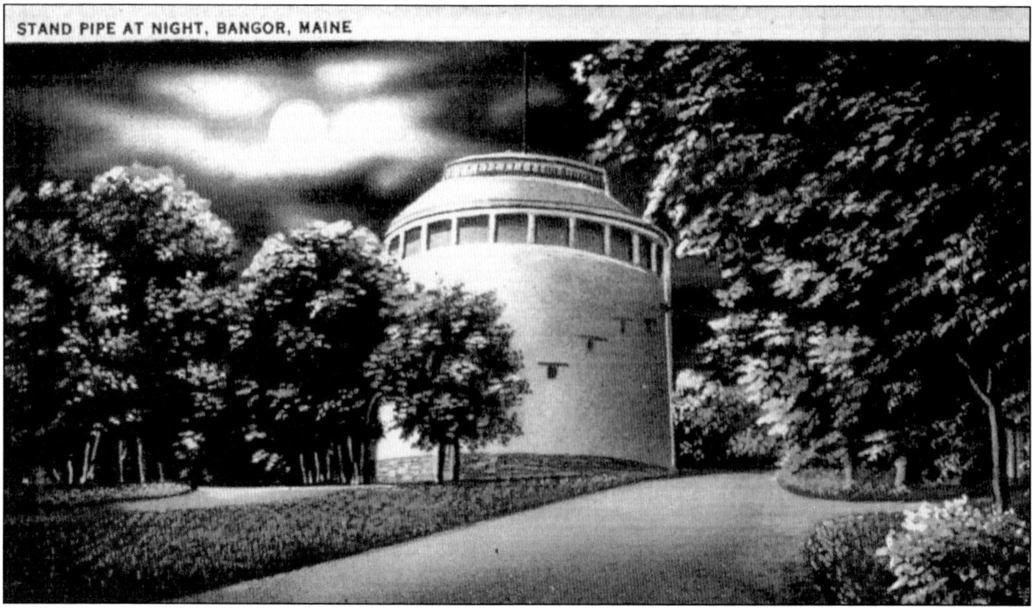

This linen-style postcard shows a scene that never seems to change. The city's standpipe takes on a magical quality after dark, especially when its crown is lit with a circle of lights. In the 1980s, a local city councilor proposed replacing the white lights with colored ones, but traditionalists would not hear of it. City residents protested in letters to the editor and city council appearances. The lights have stayed white ever since.

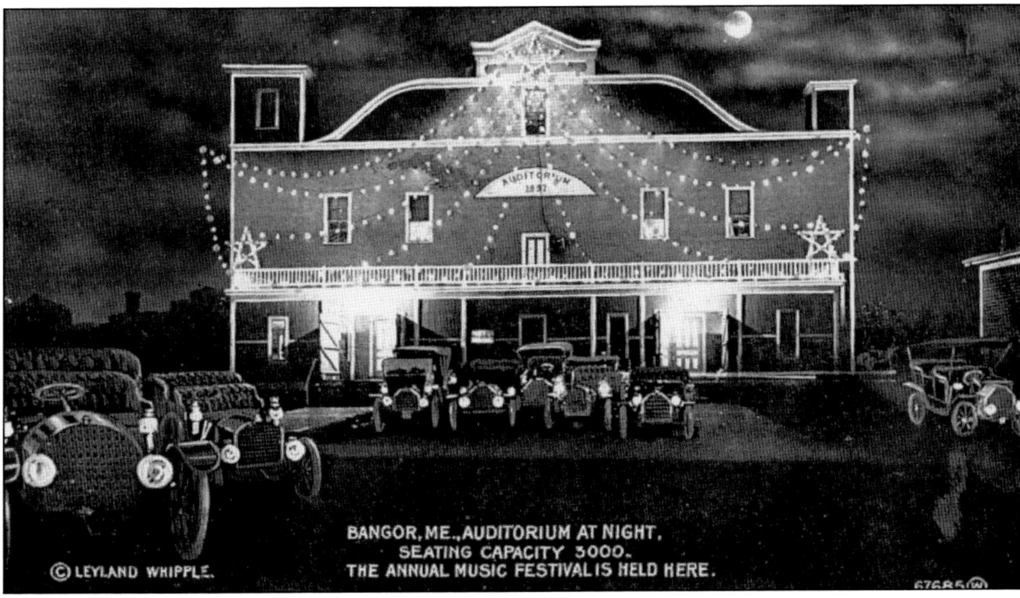

Every year during the annual Maine Music Festival, workers would transform the old Bangor Auditorium on Main Street into a showplace complete with lighted stars and dazzling colored lights. The old wooden building was barnlike but was popular with operatic singers and orchestras who found the acoustics close to perfect. This 1913 scene, taken by Leyland Whipple, pictures old automobiles and a moon that were probably painted onto the scene for full effect.

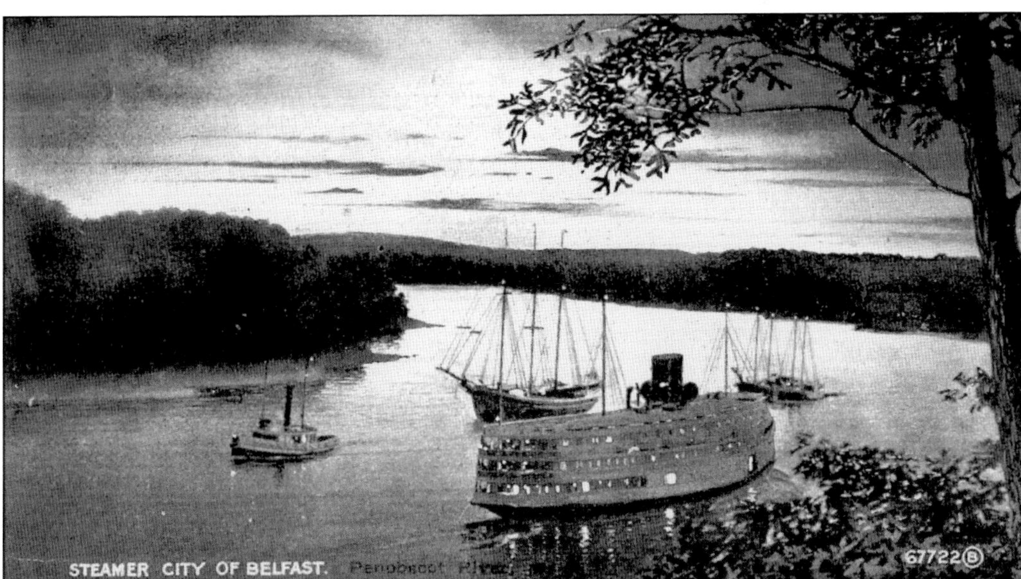

Most people living today did not have the privilege of seeing the steamer *City of Belfast* gliding up and down the Penobscot River after dark. One of three of the so-called Boston steamers, the *City of Belfast* made frequent stops along the river, including those in Rockland, Northport, and Belfast, before making its final stop in Bangor. Note the tugboat and sailing vessels in the background.

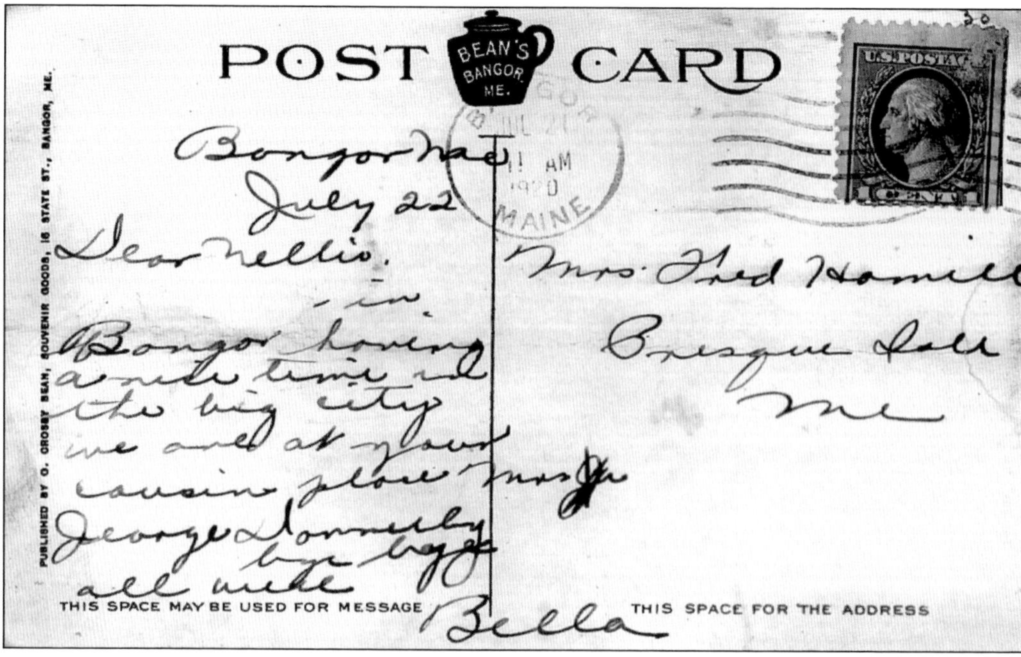

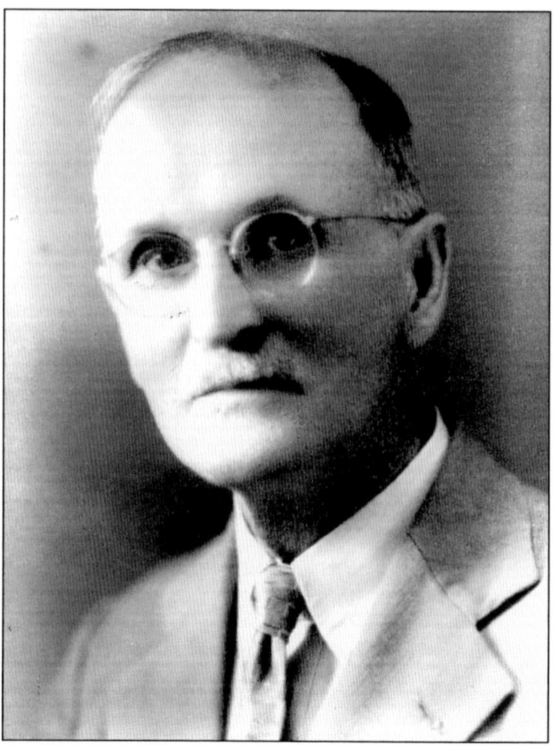

O. Crosby Bean was a Scottish immigrant who operated a book and souvenir shop in downtown Bangor. Many of the postcards reproduced in this book were published for Bean and bear his distinctive logo, a little black bean pot, on their reverse sides. This portrait was kindly loaned for publication by his granddaughter, Nancy Lord.

Suggested Reading

Nonfiction Histories and Trade Books

Bangor and Vicinity Illustrated. Compiled and published by Edward Mitchell Blanding, 1899.

Bangor, Maine, Voices from the Past: Bangor the First Hundred Years, 1834-1978. Juniper Press, 1978.

Cobb, Margo. *If the Walls Could Talk.* Bangor-Brewer YWCA, 1999.

Goldstein, Judith. *Crossing Lines: Histories of Jews and Gentiles in Three Communities.* William Morrow & Company, 1991.

Headlines in History: One Hundred Years of Front Page News. Bangor Daily News, 1999.

Heseltine, Charles D. *Bangor Street Railway.* Connecticut Valley Chapter of National Railway Historical Society, 1976.

History of Penobscot County, with Illustrations and Biographical Sketches, 1882. Cleveland, Ohio: Williams, Chase & Company.

Holbrook, Stewart H. *Holy Old Mackinaw: A Natural History of the American Lumberjack.* Macmillan, 1939.

Lunt, Dean. *Here for Generations: The Story of a Maine Bank and Its City.* Islandport Press, 2002.

Mundy, James H., and Earle G. Shettleworth Jr. *The Flight of the Grand Eagle.* Maine Historic Preservation Commission, 1977.

Mundy, James H. *Hard Times, Hard Men: Maine and the Irish.* Harp Publications, 1990.

Mundy, James H. *Second to None.* Harp Publications, 1992.

Richardson, John. *Steamboat Lore of the Penobscot,* 1938, 1991.

Scee, Trudy Irene. *The Inmates and the Asylum: The Bangor Children's Home 1835–2002.* The Hilltop School, 2002.

———. *Mount Hope Cemetery: A Twentieth Century History.* Mount Hope Cemetery Corporation, 2001.

The Story of Bangor: A Brief History of Maine's Queen City. Bookmarc's Publishing, 1999.

Thompson, Deborah. *Bangor, Maine, 1769 to 1914: An Architectural History.* University of Maine Press, 1988.

Vickery, James B., ed. *An Illustrated History of the City of Bangor, Maine,* 1969, 1976.

———. *The Journals of John Edwards Godfrey,* 1985, three volumes.

Wasson, George S. *Sailing Days on the Penobscot,* 1932.

Zelz, Abigail Ewing, and Marilyn Zoidis. *Woodsmen and Whigs: Historic Images of Bangor, Maine.* The Donning Company Publishers, 1991.

Novels Set Partly, or Entirely, in Bangor

Hamlin, Adreana. *Pink Chimneys: A Novel of Nineteenth Century Maine.* Tilbury House Publishers, 1987.

King, Stephen. *The Dead Zone*. Viking Press, 1979.

———. *It.* Viking Press, 1986.

Kline, Christina Baker. *Desire Lines.* William Morrow and Company, 1999.

Patterson, Gardner. *Bangor.* Thompson Printing Company, 2003.

Wasson, Mildred. *The Big House.* Houghton Mifflin Company, 1926.

Williams, Ben Ames. *The Strange Woman.* Houghton Mifflin Company, 1941.

Index